'Paddington Pollaky

PRIVATE DETECTIVE

'Paddington' Pollaky

PRIVATE DETECTIVE

The Mysterious Life and Times of the Real Sherlock Holmes

BRYAN KESSELMAN

The History Press

For Anne-Marie

Cover image: *Pollaky* by Faustin Betbeder 1874 Courtesy of The Ohio State University Billy Ireland Cartoon Library & Museum

Every effort has been made to secure rights to items in copyright. Any omissions notified to the author or publisher will be credited in any future editions.

First published 2015

The History Press
The Mill, Brimscombe Port
Stroud, Gloucestershire, GL5 2QG
www.thehistorypress.co.uk

British Library Cataloguing in Publication Data.
A catalogue record for this book is available from the British Library.

ISBN 978 0 7509 5974 2

Typesetting and origination by The History Press
Printed in Great Britain

Contents

Introduction

Some time ago I was driving my car on the way home from a singing engagement, singing the Colonel's song from Gilbert and Sullivan's *Patience* to myself. This involves a long list of people of the type to make up a 'heavy dragoon', and includes the name 'Paddington Pollaky'. I couldn't remember who he was – I had known once. I decided to check at the earliest opportunity. Who would have guessed that this would lead me to write an opera about him as well as this book?

My initial researches led me to look at the 'Agony Column' of *The Times*. Here was subject matter for musicalisation. Why not write an opera about the mysterious people who advertised there? What if Paddington Pollaky, who was one of them, was an important character in the piece? What if he were the main character? I began to work out a plot. This involved a certain amount of research into his life. I gathered a huge amount of facts, some of which had not been examined much before, and certainly not placed in juxtaposition with each other. It seemed that a biography was inevitable. There were frustrations as well as successes, and you will read about some of them in the following pages. I have tried to find original sources for everything, and not to rely only upon rumour and tradition. Where there is doubt, I have indicated it.

An investigation into Pollaky and his life must necessarily be hampered by the fact that he destroyed all his case records. Nevertheless, plenty of material exists, buried away in newspaper and court reports, and hidden in archives in various cities. Among these are a number of documents, which, if not of huge historical import, lend a new colour to certain famous events of the past.

He was a fascinating character. Described variously as Detective, Private Investigator, and Adventurer, he was also an Alien Hunter (aliens of the foreign kind), and evidently something of a busybody, but one who seems genuinely to have had the best interests of others at heart. He himself often felt frustrated at the stubbornness of some of those around him – but more of that in its place.

W.S. Gilbert mentions Pollaky in three of his dramatic pieces – *No Cards*, *An Old Score*, and most famously, *Patience*. Even Charles Dickens and Lewis Carroll wrote about him. You can read about these references in Chapter 12 and in the Appendices.

My voyage of discovery has taken me to a number of archives in London; involved numerous emails and letters to archives and copyright holders in England, America, Germany, and Slovakia; and involved a trip to Bratislava in an attempt to uncover any little detail of Pollaky's early life which might remain in his birthplace.

I have quoted letters, newspaper articles, and reports at length, preferring to let Pollaky and those who wrote about him speak for themselves, but I have added commentary as guidance to these passages when necessary. Many of the items can be read as stand-alone short stories, worthy of dipping into, although I hope that the reader will make an effort to get to know this unusual man by following his story in its entirety. The book almost follows a chronological order, but inevitably if one wishes to follow the threads of a life in a connected way, some concessions have to be made. Being naturally averse to endnotes, and in particular to wretched jargon (e.g. *ibid.* and *loc. cit.*), I have included information that might be put there in the body of the text. There is, however, a comprehensive bibliography at the end. All transcriptions of handwritten letters were made by me (except for that of Lewis Carroll). I have not indicated pagination in those letters, nor have I kept the original number of words per line.

But firstly to Mystery Number One – who was Ignatius Paul Pollaky?

In 1909 George Routledge & Sons published a book by James Redding

Ware called *Passing English of the Victorian Era*. The following definition appears on page 185:

> O Pollaky ! (*Peoples'*, 1870). Exclamation of protest against too urgent enquiries. From an independent, self-constituted, foreign detective, who resided on Paddington Green, and became famous for his mysterious and varied advertisements, which invariably ended with his name (accent on the second syllable), and his address.

This definition by no means tells the whole story, but it's a start. 'Peoples' 1870' refers to the origin of the expression (a slang word of the man in the street), and the year it came into use. We learn that 'Pollaky' should not be pronounced as **Poll**aky (as in the song from *Patience*) but Poll**ak**y, with the stress on the second syllable. Ware is wrong on one count, though: Pollaky did not invariably finish his advertisements with his address (and, who knows, may not always have used his name either).

Bryan Kesselman, 2015

In Hungary

Pressburg, Hungary, 1838. Summer – late afternoon. School over, a 10-year-old boy and two friends climb in and around the castle ruins that look out over the Danube, its high walls dominating the view of the city from the other side of the river. Their chatter is all nonsense, of course, to everyone but themselves; and their shrieks of laughter as they imitate their teacher who talks through his nose and is often angry because the class doesn't pay attention in these hot days, echo around the castle walls. Then, suddenly, a woman's voice calls, 'Ignatz, come at once, your father wants you to carry his violin.'

'Coming,' he calls.

'Just look at your clothes! Go and change at once, don't let your father see you like that.'

And so on. Is this a possible scene from the boyhood of Ignatius Paul Pollaky? So few details exist of his early life in Hungary, that I have made this up. All that follows, however, is fact. In this chapter, I have detailed a little of the detective work I attempted in my efforts to uncover previously unknown facts.

In 1914, Ignatius Paul Pollaky applied (for the second time) to become a British Citizen. He told Detective Superintendent Charles Forward of the Brighton Police that he was born in Pressburg (Pozsony), Hungary, on the 19 February 1828.

His father was Joseph Francis Pollaky, a Common Councillor according to his 1861 Marriage Certificate, or a Private Correspondent and Musician according to his 1914 naturalisation papers as recorded by Detective Superintendent Forward.

Had Joseph Pollaky been accorded the honorary title *Regierungsrath*? This title nominally denotes a government official, but in countries ruled by Austria, as Hungary was at that time, it was a title awarded for meritorious services which might equate with 'common councillor'. Ignatius's mother was Minna Pollaky; both parents were Hungarian subjects. Pressburg is now called Bratislava, and is the capital city of Slovakia. It has had a number of names over the years, often with alternative spellings: Posonium, Pisonium, Posony, Pozsony, Presburg, Preßburg, Pressporek and Poson are examples. The name Bratislava has been in use since 1919, the year after Pollaky's death. As you will read later, in 1863 he went back to Pressburg during an investigation, and would surely have visited his parents if they were still alive.

According to the announcement of Pollaky's 1861 marriage his father's middle name was François, and the Pollaky family address in Pressburg was Old Castle Hill. The castle is on a hill, but there is and was no street name that exactly translates in that way. Of course, it is possible that he simply meant that they lived on the side of the hill upon which the old castle stands. From 1811, after a disastrous fire destroyed it, until 1957, when restoration work began, the castle was in ruins, a shell, and that is how young Ignatius would have known it. One might imagine him, as suggested above, wandering around the ruin, and gazing out over the Danube to the land that lay south of the river and beyond.

The spelling of these names follows English conventions, and it is more likely that father and son were in reality Josef Franz and Ignatz or Ignaz Pál Polák(y). The surname Pollaky is fairly uncommon, so much so that it is tempting to make use of all sorts of scraps of information, even if they lead nowhere. What, for example, should be made of a letter written from Vienna (in German) in 1868 by a married lady called Julie Pollaky to Sir George Airy, Astronomer Royal in England, in which she asks for any information he might have about her brother? Her brother, August Weiss, bears little connection to this investigation, nor does she – but her husband is possibly a member of the Pollaky clan. (In the event, Airy replied, in English, that he knew nothing of the lady's brother – and there the matter rests, we don't know why Julie Pollaky thought that he *should* know anything.) Of more interest, perhaps, though still as mysterious, is a notice printed in Budapest (also in German) in November 1885 announcing the death of one Fanny Modern, whose maiden name was Pollak [*sic*]. Among the mourners listed are Ignatz Pollaky, brother, and Marie Pollaky (relationship not listed).

Finding information about Pollaky's early life proved extremely difficult. Were the Pollaky family in Pressburg comfortably off? What was their religion? Polak, Pollak, Pollack etc. are often (but not necessarily) names of Jewish families. On the other hand there are baptismal records in Slovakia from the eighteenth and nineteenth centuries showing a small number of Pollakys who were Roman Catholic. The surname implies that a male ancestor was from Poland. He was married twice after he arrived in England, both times in a (Church of England) church ceremony, and all his children were baptised. What did his family and friends call him? – Ignatz, Ignatius, Paul, or perhaps Náci (which is a shortened version of Ignatius). The last is pronounced *na:tsi*, which now has other connotations but did not then.

First theory: since I found no records of an Ignatius Pollaky (or variation of that name) born in 1828, or in the years either side, in Bratislava, Slovakia, or any part of what was Hungary or Austria, I contacted a genealogist based in Slovakia who suggested the following was a possible match: on 1 May 1829 a child was baptised at the (Roman Catholic) Blumentál church in Pressburg under the name Franciscus Polák. His father was also called Franciscus Polák and his mother Maria Polák (née Woszinger). All first names were written in Latin, and so it seems likely that Franciscus Polák was in reality Franz. It seemed quite possible that Minna (Pollaky's mother's name) might be a diminutive of Maria. Could it not be that the child was baptised with his father's name though he might grow up known by another?

But I did not feel satisfied with identifying this Franciscus Polák with Ignatius Paul Pollaky, and so as not to leave a stone unturned, I decided that it was necessary to make a visit to Bratislava, the one-time Pressburg, the city (now in Slovakia) in which Pollaky claimed to have been born. A brief record of my visit follows, leaving out most details that are not relevant to my researches. My discoveries, or lack of them, will become clear. One thing is certain, though: I walked in places where the subject of this book walked as a child and young man, and saw buildings that he must have seen.

Sunday, 6 April 2014

The plane landed at Vienna Airport at 10.30 a.m. The bus to Bratislava took only one hour. There was no border control as we entered Slovakia.

In the afternoon I walked to Bratislava Castle. Entry was free, but it cost 2 euros for permission to take photos inside. The castle has been beautifully restored from the dreadful ruin it was, with white plastered walls inside and out. But the place is incredibly sterile as a result. The souvenir shop had nothing to recommend, but the old books – calendars and almanacs – displayed on the top floor of the castle museum were interesting.

Monday, 7 April

I left the hotel and began to walk towards the Slovenský Národný Archív, Drotárska Cesta (Slovak National Archives) – a long walk. I eventually managed to board a 207 bus which took me most of the rest of the way. The remainder was then uphill and downhill: a hot sun and a cool breeze.

I arrived at the archive building at 9.30 a.m. They found a young lady who spoke English quite well. With her and two Slovak speakers we were able to establish that they would have no information relevant to my researches there. They thought at first I was after records from *19*28 and were surprised when they found they were 100 years out. But they were able to direct me to two more archives in Bratislava. By 10.30 a.m., when I left, the sun was stronger and the breeze weaker. I returned to the city centre. The Old Town is very pretty, though there is too much graffiti.

At noon I arrived at the second archive: Štátny Archív, Križkova 5 (State Archives). The two young men I met there were also very helpful. They spoke little English, but managed to tell me that it was now lunchtime and that their colleagues were now all out. They recommended the third archive as recommended by the previous one. But they took my email address and a photocopy of a page in a Bratislava guidebook I had found in the hotel which mentioned Pollaky.

Tuesday, 8 April

I took a taxi to the Archiv Hlavného Mesta SR Bratislavy (Bratislava City Archives), Markova 1. The lady I met there spoke Slovak and German. We used the latter to communicate with, and that proved most satisfactory. She knew nothing of the name Pollaky, only Polák and Polágh, and found a copy, in Slovak, of the reply to an email I had sent to the archive which translates as follows:

> In respect of information about a family named Pollaky, who allegedly lived in Bratislava around the year 1828 we inform you that in Bratislava there is no such name. At that time they lived several families named Polak Pollak Polagh etc. (but not the name Pollaky). We have no directories or census of inhabitants for the given year in our archive. If you wish to consult the archival documents, the archive reading room of the Bratislava City is open to the public from Monday to Thursday.

And this despite the fact that I knew the name Pollaky had existed. I filled in a form on the subject of my researches, which she kept. She then brought me a huge old tome with births of children in the Blumentál Church area entitled *Rodný Index Nové Mesto Blumentál 1770–1888*. (I had mentioned finding details of Poláks mentioned in records of that area.) I read there of births with no other details except years. Could one of these be Ignatius – Josephus Polák born 1827, or Franciscus Polák born 1830? They seemed vaguely possible.

She then brought me a print-out from the Mormon Family Search website which listed the baptism of an Ignatius Polák on 31 July 1819 – Father: Josephus Polák, Mother: Marina Vincek.

I pointed out that 1819 was nine years too early, had this been the man I was after he would have been ninety-nine when he died – just about possible, I supposed. Had he therefore lied about his age to make himself appear younger than he really was? I wouldn't put it past him; vanity might be the explanation. My helper then suggested that the Ignatius Polák listed might have died as a child, but that the parents had another son later to whom they gave the same name. Such things are known to have happened, but there are no records to confirm this.

This family lived in Malacky, some twenty-two miles north of Bratislava (Pressburg), but close enough for someone to claim that they came from the more impressive place; after all, my grandfather was born in the little village of Przedecz in Poland, but often claimed he was from Warsaw. It was also possible that the family had moved from Malacky to Pressburg before the next son was born, or, if Ignatius Paul Pollaky had been born in 1819 in Malacky, and baptised there in the Kuchyňa church, they might have moved to Pressburg when he was still an infant.

After lunch I visited the Bratislava Museum of City History. I learned there that the Jewish Quarter (now largely demolished) was below the castle area, and this would have been on the side of the hill. This is relevant if one considers the possibility that Pollaky may have been Jewish by birth. There are no Jewish Pollakys listed anywhere, but there were Jewish families called Pollak living in Bratislava, as I discovered by contacting people listed on JewishGen website who were researching that name in that area, though I found no likely Jewish connection at that time.

⌐⊃

Second theory: Ignatius Paul Pollaky may have been born Ignatz Pál Polák in 1828, and baptised with the name Ignatius; the younger brother of the then deceased Ignatius Polák baptised in 1819 in Malacky, born there or in Pressburg if his family had moved there by the time of his birth. Josephus Polák and Marina Vincek (the name perhaps shortened to Minna) would then be his parents. It is perhaps too much of a leap of faith to believe that Fanny Modern née Pollak whose death in Budapest was mourned in 1885 was his sister, and that her given name corresponds to the middle name of their father, and that Marie Pollaky, the other mourner, was their elderly mother.

On my return from Bratislava, I continued online looking through the many records and scans of documents on the Family Research website of all the variations of the Pollaky name which might exist. I tried Polak, Polaki, Polaky, Pollak, Pollaki, Pollaky and several others. All had hits, sometimes the same family varied spelling between one record and another, but I still had to conclude that if what Pollaky said about his family is true, there are currently no records to be found which make an exact match. Looking at this second theory harder, I discovered that the Ignatius Polák baptised in 1819 had two older brothers, Josephus, baptised 1814, and Paulus, baptised 1817. This means that if Fanny Modern was their sister, and Marie Pollaky was their mother, the mother would have been quite old in 1885 when she was listed as a mourner. Moreover, I could find no trace of a daughter being born to that family. We must be careful; there were three other Ignatius Poláks, one born 1822 and the others in 1824, though none of them have parents with the correct names. (There is also an Ignatium Polaky born in 1783, and an Ignatius Polaki who became a father in 1794, both far too early to be of interest.) Third theory: he might still be connected to mother (Marie) and sister (Fanny) but not to the Polák family.

Breakthrough

And suddenly, without warning, came the breakthrough I had been looking for. The *Toni and Gustav Stolper Collection 1866–1990* held by the Leo Baeck Institute, New York, a huge document, several hundred pages long, contains the following passage:

> Translation from a MEMO written by Anna Jerusalem
> The Family of Professor Dr. Max Kassowitz 1842–1913
> The name of KASSOWITZ first appears in a register of Jewish families at Pressburg of 1736 ...
> The father of Max's mother Katharina, nee Pollak, 1821–1878, named Ben Joseph Schames* and was caretaker of the Congregation. He was an intelligent, enlightened popular man whom his grandson Max lovingly remembered. When Max left Pressburg for the University of Vienna, his grandfather asked him to promise never to let himself be baptised.
> A brother of Mother Katharina ... Ignaz Polaky who compromised himself politically [aged] 19 1848, went as a fugitive to England, where he founded a Private Detective Agency; he acquired a high reputation with the Police, was knighted and awarded numerous distinctions; he was twice married to Christian Englishwomen, preserved great affection for his relatives on the Continent whom he frequently visited in later years.

There it was! Ignatius (Ignaz) Pollaky was the son of a Synagogue sexton and he had a sister called Katharina. So it seems that his family had lived on the (old) castle hill in Pressburg in the Jewish Quarter which no longer exists. As far as the rest of the paragraph goes, this book will show if the other statements are accurate in later chapters. Pollaky himself inflated his father's importance in his declarations, but it is interesting to note the description of the elder Pollaky as

---

* The word 'Schames' is not a surname; it means that Joseph was the caretaker or sexton.

intelligent, enlightened and popular. The original German as well as the English translation is included in the Stolper papers. Toni Stolper and Anna Jerusalem were both daughters of Max Kassowitz, and therefore Pollaky's great nieces.

It seems likely that Pollaky had been involved in the dramatic events which took place in Hungary in the late 1840s, and that his activities had come to the attention of the authorities, causing him to try his luck elsewhere.

Hungary at that time had not been an independent country for many years. From the mid-sixteenth century, it had been variously divided between the Ottoman and Habsburg empires. By 1718, the Habsburg Empire had fully wrested control of it for themselves.

The Habsburgs, with their capital in Vienna, spoke German, hence the common use at the time of the German name Pressburg for Pollaky's home city, rather than its Hungarian name, Pozsony. Like other countries and states ruled by Austria, Hungary was straining under the leash for independence.

On 15 March 1848 the Hungarian Revolution began. This was not the first time the Hungarians had fought for independence from Austria. From 1703 to 1711 Rákóczi Ferenc (Francis II Rákóczi) had led an unsuccessful struggle for Hungarian independence.

On 13 April 1848 the Hungarian Declaration of Independence was presented to the Hungarian National Assembly, and passed unanimously two days later. Naturally, the Austrian rulers were not going to accept this, and there were a number of insurrections throughout Hungary as a result. By July 1849 the revolution had been quashed by the Austrian army (with help from Russia). Hungary finally gained autonomy, though not full independence, from Austria in 1867.

There were anti-Jewish pogroms in Pressburg that took place in April 1848, and this also may have influenced Pollaky's need to leave Hungary. There had been several losses of life. Some of the younger Jewish intellectuals were committed to the revolution, and after the pogroms, the Jews were ordered to leave Pressburg.

It seems clear that Pollaky had made his position there untenable, due to his support for the Hungarian revolution, and that he had fled. He made his way first to Italy.

At that time, the northern states of Italy were also trying to free themselves from Austrian rule. In early July 1849, Italian patriot Piero Cironi (1819–62), had been arrested by the Florence police for his involvement in these affairs, and on 12 July 1849 Cironi wrote of his imprisonment. The previous morning he had been joined by a young Hungarian from Pressburg, Ignaz Pollaky, who had been arrested in Livorno when on the point of embarking for Genoa. Cironi who wished for amicable conversation with a like-minded person, felt that it was unfortunate that Pollaky spoke Italian badly, but wrote that they had conversed in French instead.

Pollaky was not held for long – a few weeks later he arrived in England.

2 Arrival in England

Pollaky arrived in London on 20 September 1849 on a day that was fresh and fine, with a west wind. The ship docked at Gravesend, Kent. The written records of entry on the relevant page in the records of Alien Arrivals in England are all in different hands, which implies that the individual passengers signed their own names there. His name is written as *Pollaky Ignatz* (Professor) – in Hungarian style the surname appears first.

There are, however, a number of conflicting records as to when Ignatius Pollaky first arrived in England. On 15 February 1846, a native of Austria called Pollacky (with the extra 'c') arrived in Dover from Ostend, Belgium on the *Princess Alice*. This individual then disappears from records. This is almost certainly not our man, unless he had made an earlier visit as a lone teenager to England. Pollaky was somewhat approximate when asked when he had arrived in England, whether because of faulty memory, or because he would write down whatever year was most convenient is hard to say.

On his application for British nationality made in 1914, he wrote that he arrived in 1851, whereas according to his earlier application for British nationality made in 1862, he arrived in 1852, although in a letter of 31 July 1862 to Sir Richard Mayne, Chief Commissioner of the Metropolitan Police, he writes, 'during 12 years of residence in London & England I never was tried or convicted on a charge of felony or misdemeanour'. That would place his arrival in 1850.

Later, however, in the same letter he writes:

> Mr Hodgson in the year 1858 wrote a letter to the Austrian Ambassador in London stating that during my residence in London (10 years) my conduct was always very good and that I during that period was instrumental to bring repeatedly Criminals (Foreigners) to justice (This letter is still on Record on the Books of the City Police.)

(Charles George Hodgson 1812–68 was Superintendent of the London City Police Force, the Austrian Ambassador at that time was Hungarian-born Count Rudolf Apponyi.)

Hodgson's letter would place Pollaky's residence in London from 1848. From it we can surmise that during the 1850s Pollaky was working at bringing foreign criminals to justice. However, that letter, if it was on record at the time, is certainly not available to examine now.

There is little information as to his activities or to his place of residence until some way into the 1850s. He does not seem to be recorded on the 1851 census, but that may only mean that he was out of the country at the time, and, given his itinerant way of life at that time, perhaps this should not be surprising. The census was not by any means foolproof, and an interesting example comes from 1851 in which one Hungarian resident (born 1829) of Bermondsey, London is listed as, 'A Person refusing to give name'.

Pollaky evidently spoke, read and wrote a number of languages well. The best idea of his spoken English comes from an interview given in 1877, discussed in detail in Chapter 11. His characterful use of written English in his letters does include a few spelling mistakes, but what native writer does not suffer from occasional lapses? Examples of his characteristic use of English and his handwriting include: always using 'th' after numbers to indicate the date – 1th, 2th, 3th, 4th, 21th etc., frequently heading private letters, written in English, not *Private & Confidential*, but *Private & Confidentielle*, and almost always writing the letter 'K' as a capital letter – even in the middle of a word. As well as English and Hungarian, he is known to have spoken German, French, Spanish, and Italian, and he may have been familiar with Polish and Greek as well. On 7 January 1861 *The Times* reported that he acted as court interpreter for a Greek man, Staveis Kollaky (the similarity between surnames is a coincidence), who had been charged with stealing 180 yards of silk; on 23 March 1871 he acted as interpreter for one Liebitz Goldberg, who spoke Polish. (On both these occasions, Pollaky had been present on other business; his presence in the vicinity of the trials had been fortuitous.) It may be that he was able to interpret both Greek and Polish though perhaps these two gentlemen spoke other languages that he understood. We have already heard of Piero Cironi's opinion of Pollaky's Italian, others also would cast doubt on his language abilities, but his own self-confidence seems to have carried him through.

Something of the humbug, particularly in his early days when he was trying to make himself seem more important and effective as an investigator than he really was, as well as his being, perhaps, a bit of a busybody, combine in his letters with great energy. When he felt deeply about things, or became agitated, his handwriting became faster, stronger, less legible and had a greater number of errors. He does, however, manage to come over through his letters, as well as through newspaper reports about him as genuine and as having his heart in the right place – likeable, though sometimes extremely frustrated by the apparent resistance of officialdom to credit him with that genuineness. He tried very hard to ingratiate himself with Sir Richard Mayne (1796–1868), Chief Commissioner of the Metropolitan Police, but failed at every turn. From the coldness of Sir Richard's responses to Pollaky, it is clear that he had very little patience with private investigators at the best of times. Both Sir Richard Mayne and Ignatius Pollaky are buried in Kensal Green Cemetery. (Pollaky in Plot 17308, Sq.68, Row 2.)

From the 1860s his newspaper advertisements and several letters he wrote included statements that he specialised in intelligence on foreigners living in Britain. Later still he would recommend registration of all foreigners upon arrival in Britain, with the further recommendation that they should officially contact their countries of origin before applying for British nationality. The latter suggestion was not met with universal approval. (See Chapter 13.)

3 'Inspector Bucket', Lord Lytton, Lord Derby, Lord Palmerston, the Road House Murder and Whicher

One of the major figures in Pollaky's life was Charles Frederick Field, whose father, John, may have been the publican of the 'Earl of Howard's Head' in Chelsea. Field was probably born in 1803, the fourth of seven children to John and Margaret Field.

In 1829, when the Metropolitan Police Force was created, Charles Frederick Field joined as a sergeant. He was promoted to inspector in 1833, and after an active career became Chief of the Detective Division in 1846. The new police force was headed by joint commissioners Charles Rowan and Richard Mayne.

Five foot ten and inclined to be stout, Field married Jane Chambers in 1841. He is described on the marriage certificate as 'Inspector of Police' residing in Limehouse, East London. His father, John Field, was described somewhat laconically, as 'dead'. Charles Field reputedly became the model for Inspector Bucket in Charles Dickens's *Bleak House* which began serialisation in 1852. Dickens, in a letter to *The Times* on 18 September 1853, denied it. That we know a fair amount about this colourful character is, nevertheless, due in no short measure to his writings.

Dickens wrote about Field on a number of occasions. Firstly as Inspector Wield in his piece *A Detective Police Party* published in 1850, then, again as Wield, shortly after in *Three Detective Anecdotes*. Dickens himself, in a letter of 14 September 1850 to his colleague William Henry Wills, associated the cleverly disguised name, 'Wield' with Field. In 1851 he wrote another short piece entitled *On Duty With Inspector Field*. All these appeared in *Household Words*, Dickens's own magazine.

In 1851 Dickens had engaged Field to provide security at a performance of a comedy by Lord Lytton, a friend of Dickens. The play, *Not So Bad As We Seem*, was to be performed by Dickens's amateur theatrical company (with Dickens himself in the cast), and Lytton who had acrimoniously separated from his wife was afraid that she would interrupt the performance. Dickens and Field were on friendly terms; Dickens occasionally accompanied Field when the latter was on duty. More information about this appears in Chapter 12. Dickens wrote in a letter dated 18 April 1862 to his friend, author George Walter

Thornbury (1828–1976), that Field had been a Bow Street Runner, but there is no evidence to support this.

In December 1852, Field retired from the police force and opened a Private Inquiry Bureau at 20 Devereux Court. This building, built in 1676, had previously been the Grecian Coffee House where patrons had included Oliver Goldsmith the novelist, and Sir Isaac Newton and other members of the Royal Society. In about 1842, the coffee house had ceased business, and the premises was divided into 'chambers'. Known as Eldon Chambers, a number of professional people kept offices there.

After his departure from the police force, the press often continued to refer to Field in their reports as *Inspector* Field – a fact that got him into trouble as the police believed him to be giving the impression that he was still associated with them.

Field was by no means the first to advertise his services as a private investigator. As early as the days of Queen Anne, who reigned between 1702 and 1714, one John Bonner was reputed to have published the following:

> This is to give notice that those who have sustained any loss at Sturbridge fair last, by Pick Pockets or Shop lifts: If they please to apply themselves to John Bonner in Shorts Gardens, they may receive information and assistance therein; also Ladies and others who lose their Watches at Churches, and other Assemblies, may be served by him as aforesaid, to his utmost power, if desired by the right Owner, he being paid for his Labour and Expences [sic]. (*Social Life in the Reign of Queen Anne* by John Ashton, 1882.)

Reference to Bonner's advertisement can also be found in *Anecdotes of the Manners and Customs of London During the Eighteenth Century* by James Peller Malcolm (1810), where it is explained in different terms: 'John Bonner of Short's Gardens had the bare-faced effrontery, in 1703, to offer his assistance, by necromancy, to those who had lost any thing at Sturbridge Fair, at Churches or other assemblies, "he being paid for his labour and expenses".' This kind of criticism, justified or not, would mark the attitude of many towards private investigators. Pollaky in particular suffered owing to that aura of exotic mysteriousness which hung around him, arousing suspicion and dislike.

One-time Bow Street Runner and first Chief Constable of Northampton, Henry Goddard, had been known to accept work in a private capacity possibly as early as the 1830s, and continued to do so until the mid-1860s. Much of Goddard's private work came from the Forrester brothers, John and Daniel, who ran a detective agency from within the Mansion House building. They had been employed by the City of London Corporation, John Forrester from 1817, and Daniel from 1821, but they were not connected with the City of London Police which was formed in 1832.

In 1862 one of Pollaky's early advertisements for his new inquiry office appeared in *The Times* directly above one placed jointly by the Forrester brothers and Goddard. The Forresters were by that time no longer at the Mansion House. Was it purely coincidence that Pollaky's first business address was so close to that recently vacated by them? They were the most successful and the best known private investigators of their time. Had Pollaky hoped that some of their success might come his way if he used an address associated with them?

The Times – Wednesday, 7 May 1862
A VIS aus ETRANGERS. – Les feuilles publiques ont à plusieurs reprises signalé l'existence à Londres d'associations d'escrocs, dont le but special parait être de victimes le commerce et l'industrie. – Bureau de Renseignements, Mr Pollaky, P.G. [*sic*] Inquiry-office, 14 George-street, Mansion-house.

INQUIRIES. – Messrs. FORRESTER and GODDARD, late principal officers at the Mansion-house, city of London and the public office, Bow-street, undertake important and CONFIDENTIAL INQUIRIES for the nobility, gentry, solicitors, bankers, insurance companies and others in England or abroad. Offices No. 8 Dane's-inn. Strand.

Pollaky often advertised in languages other than English. A loose translation of the above is: 'Warning to Foreigners. – Public papers have repeatedly reported the existence in London of associations of crooks, whose particular purpose seems to be victims of trade and industry. – Intelligence Bureau, Mr Pollaky, P.G. Inquiry-office, 14 George-street, Mansion-house.

Pollaky's Work for Field

It may have been from as early as 1853 that Ignatius Paul Pollaky began working for Field's Inquiry Bureau. He continued to do so until 1861. Though it is impossible to be precise as to when his employment there began, by looking at the advertisements which Field placed in *The Times*, it is possible to see a progression, which taken in conjunction with various news reports allows glimpses into Pollaky's development. During that time it seems that he worked on his own behalf as well.

Little trace of Pollaky's early activities in England have been found, and that only from what he himself later wrote. What though, might one make of the following anonymous advertisement from 1852? Just the sort of skills he might have advertised at that time, though there is no way of finding the identity of the individual who actually placed it.

The Times – 1 April 1852
A Continental POLYGLOT PROFESSOR, translator and interpreter of
10 modern languages – English, French, German, Dutch, Spanish, Italian,
Swedish, Danish, Portuguese, and Russian – celebrated by his divers polyglotic
publications, recently settled in London, is desirous of obtaining PUPILS to
teach, documents and books to translate, new works to arrange, counting-
houses and schools to attend, private classes to form, a permanent situation; or a
partner, able to advance £500 cash, to set up a general translating, interpreting,
and consulting office for all nations. [...] At 36 Northumberland-street,
Charing-cross.

Field had a number of assistants, they are rarely identified by name. The following
is typical:

Hull Packet and East Riding Times – Friday, 30 June 1854
CAPTURE OF A RUNAWAY BANKRUPT [...] Mr. Inspector Field [...]
forthwith despatched his assistant to America.

In 1856 Field's advertisements might offer rewards for lost items: £200 for
a missing parcel, lost on a journey between Calais and Dover, containing
precious stones, £25 for a lady's dressing case left in a railway carriage – both
advertised on 18 December – 'Information to be given to Mr C.F. Field, late
Chief Inspector of the Detective Police of the Metropolis, Eldon-chambers,
Devereux-court, Temple', the first of these proudly declared. On 25 March the
following year he advertised to, 'RENDER his SERVICES to any candidate
at the forthcoming elections'. He sometimes advertised that he had agents in
America, and that he would send a specially appointed officer to the continent
on the first day of each month.

But from 2 March 1859, a change can be seen in both style and form. That day
he placed two advertisements in *The Times* one above the other. The second was
fairly standard fare; the first was in French. There can be little doubt that it was
written by Pollaky. He was, after all, the language expert there.

The Times – Wednesday 2 March 1859
BUREAU de RENSEIGNEMENTS PARTICULIERS. – Affaires
Continentales. – Le public est informé qu'un agent spécial de cet établissement
partira de Londres pour le continent le 1er de chaque mois [...]

Pollaky's name soon began to be placed before the public in newspaper reports,
though not yet in advertisements. The following is one of the earliest examples.

Falkirk Herald – Thursday, 2 February 1860
THE MISSING MR GEORGES HIRSCH
During these last 14 days, information has been received in London from Paris that a Mr Georges Hirsch who had lately come from South America, had mysteriously disappeared, and a reward of £100 has been offered for intelligence as to his whereabouts. The opinion on the Continent was that he had been murdered in England, or that another Waterloo Bridge tragedy had been enacted. The case was placed in the hands of Mr Polaky [*sic*], the foreign superintendent of Field's Private Inquiry Office, who, from his inquiries set at rest the idea that Mr Hirsch has been foully used. It appears that, on the 31st of July, 1859, Mr Hirsch wrote a letter to Messrs Rimmel, the eminent perfumers of 96 Strand, purporting to be signed by Marchand and Mathey, of Rio Janeiro, intimating that the house could dispose of a large quantity of Messrs Rimmel's various goods; that, on or about the 12th day of December last, Mr Hirsch called on Messrs Rimmel, and selected perfumery to the amount of £240; and that, after he had so selected the goods, he prevailed on the above gentlemen to discount £700 value in bills which Hirsch had brought with him; that, on or about the 14th December, Hirsch proceeded to different parts of the country, adopting the English name of Stevens, and taking with him various small Bank of England notes, having previously changed the large ones – amounting to £550, and endorsed them in his new name. Mr Pollaky traced Hirsch to several towns in England where he had been purchasing goods, and to the hotels where he had been living in London and Liverpool under his assumed name. What could have induced Mr Georges Hirsch to have acted in the manner described will no doubt have hereafter to be explained. It is almost needless to say Mr Hirsch never paid Mr Rimmel for the goods, nor did he return to this gentleman after he had obtained discount of the bills. The Home Office was set to work to cause inquiries to be made about the missing Mr Hirsch but a telegraphic message from Mr Field to Paris soon put out of the question further trouble on the part of the Government.

Two weeks later, Pollaky's name was again mentioned in a newspaper report. Five of the crew of the ship *John Sugars* were charged with conspiracy to injure the captain, and to charge him with the loss of the ship. Three of them were eventually found guilty, and sentenced to imprisonment.

Morning Chronicle – Friday, 17 February 1860
THE ALLEGED WILFUL SINKING OF A MERCHANT SHIP
Yesterday morning the inquiry instituted by the Board of Trade for the purpose of investigating the circumstances connected with the wilful sinking of the barque *John Sugars* was resumed at the Greenwich Police-court before Mr Traill the presiding magistrate.

Mr Cumberland attended for the Board of Trade, and Mr Digby Seymour, MP, for the defence. Mr Ignatius Pollaky, from the Mansion-house, acted as interpreter; and Mr Henderson, from Lloyd's Shipping Insurance-office was present to watch the proceedings.

The mention of Pollaky being from the 'Mansion-house' is something of a puzzle, although in October 1861 he wrote a letter to Henry Sanford on Mansion House-headed writing paper. He would over a year later, open his own office in George Street, Mansion House (now Mansion House Place). The following report gives him his usual title, though it does misspell the name of the ship.

Lloyd's Weekly London Newspaper – Friday, 11 March 1860
THE RECENT ALLEGED WILFUL SINKING OF A SHIP AT SEA
The extraordinary contradictory evidence set forth in the official inquiry at the Greenwich police-court, respecting the alleged wilful scuttling and abandoning of the barque *John Lugars* [*sic*] (Captain Hewett), has led the owners of that vessel to indict five of the crew (upon whose statement the inquiry was instituted by the Board of Trade) for perjury and conspiracy. Four out of the five being Prussians, Mr Pollaky, superintendent of the foreign department of the Private Inquiry Office, Devereux-court, Temple, having interpreted the evidence during the inquiry, was retained for the identification of the men; and a true bill having been returned by the grand jury at the past Old Bailey sessions, a warrant, signed by Mr Gurney and Alderman Hale, was placed in the hands of Inspector Hamilton and Sergeant Webb, of the city detective force, and they, in company with Mr Pollaky, went in search of the men, and succeeded eventually in arresting them in Ratcliffe highway.

Further information about Pollaky can be found in the Old Bailey trial transcript. The initial inquiry had taken place in Greenwich before Police Magistrate James Traill. Pollaky had acted as interpreter for the German-speaking crew members. When he then appeared as a witness at the trial at the Old Bailey in May 1860, after firstly stating that he had acted as interpreter and that he had, 'interpreted well and truly', he was then briefly cross-examined by Mr Sergeant Ballentine who was acting for the defence, and then by Mr Digby Seymour who was now acting for the prosecution.

Mr Sergeant Ballentine: What else are you besides an interpreter?
Pollaky: I am superintendent of a private inquiry-office in the Temple – I am not a servant of Mr Field's; I am in connexion with him – I have never been engaged as interpreter in any nautical inquiry before – I am not connected with nautical matters.

Mr Seymour: Were you employed by the Board of Trade?

Pollaky: Yes; I saw another interpreter there to check me.

From which can be seen that Pollaky was fully entitled to act independently from Field.

The advertisements in *The Times* evolved during the period 1859 to 1861, and on 21 May 1860, Field's office placed one which included the phrase, 'The foreign Superintendent of this establishment will this week proceed to Paris, Belgium, and Germany'. It is surely only a small step to the view that he had often been the agent sent on European missions. The advertisement placed on 30 June 1860 offers the information that, 'The foreign superintendent, who is conversant with the French, German, Italian, Spanish, Turkish, and other languages, is in daily attendance, between the hours of 2 and 4 p.m.' – information not only on Pollaky's working hours, but also of his amazing facility with languages, mentioning Turkish among his polyglot skills. Pollaky's importance to the company was evidently growing, and that passage now appeared regularly, but his name was not yet mentioned in the advertisements. And then the following advertisement appeared:

The Times – Thursday, 6 September 1860
IF Mr MORITZ FRIED, late of Vienna, will be good enough to CALL on Mr Pollaky, 20 Devereux-court, Temple, he will HEAR of SOMETHING to his ADVANTAGE.

And Pollaky's name suddenly springs up in one of Field's advertisements.

Finally, Field must have allowed his name to be mentioned, like a reporter being given a by-line for the first time, and he is credited as an important member of the team. In the future advertisements would read not, 'The foreign superintendent is in attendance between the hours of 2 and 4 p.m.' but 'Ignatius Pollaky, superintendent Foreign Department, in attendance between the hours of 2 and 4 p.m.'. Pollaky's presence must have been deemed enough of an asset to Field's company to make it worthwhile for his name to be featured in this way. Probably Pollaky himself had a hand in ensuring that his name was given this prominence, he was, after all, a pushy young fellow with high ambitions.

The Road House Murder

In 1860 the infamous Road House murder took place. This is described (with a small mention of Pollaky) in Kate Summerscale's book *The Suspicions of Mr Whicher*. In 1861, a year after the murder, J. W. Stapleton published a book called

The Great Crime of 1860, in which he also discussed the matter in some detail. There are a number of references in Appendix IV of that book to Pollaky being present at one of the official examinations into the case in November 1860, although the reason for his presence mystified everyone. It is noted that the 'proceedings were being closely watched by Mr Pollaky, who appeared to take notes of any expressions made by Mr. Saunders' (the examining magistrate).

Jonathan Whicher, the police inspector in charge of the investigation, joined the Metropolitan Police Force as a police constable in 1840 and became an inspector in 1856. Charles Dickens, writing his story *Detective Police*, the same piece in which he disguises Field's name as Wield, described Whicher, then a sergeant, 'Sergeant Witchem, shorter and thicker-set and marked with small-pox, has something of a reserved and thoughtful air, as if he were engaged in deep arithmetical calculations.' It is possible that Dickens's friend and occasional collaborator Wilkie Collins based the character Sergeant Cuff in his 1868 novel *The Moonstone* on Whicher, who in 1893 would be described as, 'the Prince of Detectives' by ex-Chief Inspector Timothy Cavenagh in his memoirs. (The same phrase would be used to describe Pollaky a few years later.) Whicher must have resented Pollaky's presence hanging over his investigation, and he figures again in Pollaky's story in a not too favourable light. Later in *The Great Crime of 1860*: 'Mr. Saunders did not meet Mr Pollaky at Bath, but they were seen in conversation on the Bradford railway station on Saturday.' And again: 'The mysterious Mr Pollaky was there, and took notes of several parts of the proceedings.'

The Times had reported on Pollaky's presence at the time, and its reporter was as puzzled by it then as Stapleton was when he wrote his book, stating on 9 November that, 'Among the persons present to-day the reporter recognised Mr J. Pollaky, [...] but the nature of his visit did not transpire.' On 12 November, the reporter hazarded a guess about Pollaky's mission, stating that it was, 'believed to have no reference to the tracing the murderer [*sic*], but rather to collect information in reference to the extraordinary proceedings which have taken place during the past week', – a statement which really leaves us very little the wiser.

The fact of Pollaky's presence, and he was already well known enough to be featured in Stapleton's book, puzzled many, and must have annoyed not a few. It would certainly not have been pleasant to Inspector Whicher, who was having enough problems trying to solve this infamous case (while at the same time dealing with the demands of public, press, and Sir Richard Mayne), without having the interfering presence of this mysterious Hungarian watching the proceedings. Pollaky must have been there for a reason, but that reason remains a mystery.

Pollaky's name continued to appear:

The Times – Thursday, 3 January 1861

C. – Milan. – The documents have been returned to the Federal authorities, as I understood from his Excellency, by mutual consent, in June last, the MATTER is, therefore, de facto SETTLED. – POLLAKY. Superintendent, Private Inquiry-office, No. 20, Devereux-court, Temple, 2d January, 1861.

On 6 October 1860 Field had advertised in *The Times* for information regarding a certain Ernest Brown who had embezzled various sums of money. Ernest Brown or Brewer, the name varies depending on which report one reads, tried very hard to evade capture, but, as the following item shows, had a hard time of it. Field assigned Pollaky to the case.

The following news item was published in Australia but had previously appeared in a number of English newspapers in one form or another. An exciting case of tracking down and following a criminal, it shows a tenacious Pollaky at work in late 1860 and early 1861. The report is quoted in full. Sergeant Spittle, who also appears later in this book, takes the role that would be assumed twelve years later by Inspector Fix in Jules Verne's *Around the World in Eighty Days*:

Sydney Morning Herald – Friday, 10 May 1861
THE DETECTIVE SYSTEM

The detective police have, within the last few days, obtained a clue likely to lead to the apprehension of a criminal who, in September last, absconded from his employer's service, after having embezzled over £10,000, a considerable portion of which he is believed to have had in his possession at the time he left this country. The person referred to was a man named Ernest Brewer [Brown], who had been for twenty years in the service of a firm of foreign merchants, carrying on business in Throgmorton-street, and in whom the greatest confidence was reposed. It would seem that he took advantage of his position, and, by falsifying the books and other means, obtained possession of a very large sum of money.

He absconded about the 20th of September, at which time one of the principals of the firm was on the Continent; but he was expected home, and the culprit, possibly anticipating that a discovery would take place, resolved upon flight, having previously taken the most extraordinary precautions to prevent being detected.

As it was supposed that the culprit would endeavour to make his way to the continent, the matter was placed in the hands of Mr Pollaky, the superintendent of the foreign department in Inspector Field's detective establishment, but for several weeks he was thrown off the scent. At length, he ascertained that Brewer had gone to Ireland, and thither he started, but was just a week too late; the culprit had left. It was, however, ascertained that he had gone to Liverpool, and it was for some time supposed that he had gone to America, as on the very day that he was at Liverpool one of the Cunard steamers went thence to New York. This opinion was materially strengthened by the fact that very shortly afterwards a number of the Bank of England notes which Brewer was known to have had in his possession at the time he absconded were paid into the Bank of England through different American Bankers.

There is no doubt, however, that this proceeding was merely a dodge on the part of the culprit to deceive those who were in pursuit of him, and put them on a false scent; and that by some means or other he contrived to transmit the bank notes to America, in order to have them exchanged and returned to this country. The ruse, clever as it was, however, did not prove successful, and the pursuit continued, but the culprit resorted to so many clever contrivances, that, although he had one or two narrow escapes, it was found impossible to capture him.

At length he found that this country was becoming too hot for him, and on the 10th of December he applied, in the dress of a common labourer, to the captain of a sailing vessel called the *Lady of the Lake*, then lying at Gravesend, bound for South Africa, and eventually engaged a berth in the steerage under an assumed name, and sailed in due course, no doubt fondly imagining that he had at last succeeded in distancing his pursuers.

He was, however, again mistaken, for the *Lady of the Lake* had only left a short time when Mr Pollaky was again upon his track, and having ascertained that there was no further doubt that the person who had gone as a steerage passenger in the *Lady of the Lake* was the same individual for whom he had been so long in search, he lost no time in procuring a warrant for his apprehension, which was placed in the hands of serjeant [sic] Spittle, city detective police, for execution. The necessary inquiries to ascertain whether the passenger was the right party, of course, occupied some time, but the officer was despatched by the very first vessel proceeding to Port Natal, which was the *Celt*, a screw steamer, that left Plymouth direct for South Africa, a few days since. As the *Celt* is a steamer, and the *Lady of the Lake* a sailing vessel, it is not at all improbable, notwithstanding that the latter had so much start, that the *Celt* may arrive first at her place of destination; and should this not prove to be the case, and the culprit should by any means suspect that he is pursued, it is by no means improbable that he will make another bolt, and the journey of sergeant Spittle may be extended to Australia, the most likely place the fugitive will resort to. – *Bell's Weekly Messenger*, February 16.

Pollaky's star was in the ascendent. However, day to day work continued; on 25 May 1861 he placed an advertisement on behalf of Field for information regarding the identification of a victim of a 'MYSTERIOUS MURDER' which had taken place the previous March, when 'the BODY of a FEMALE was discovered under a heap of stones, in a declivity of the Rheinecker Berges, between Brohl and Niederbreisig-on-the-Rhein'. Asking for information to be sent to Field, the advertisement is signed, 'J. [*sic*] Pollaky, Superintendent of the Foreign Department.' He now felt it important that his name appeared everywhere he could possibly get it. (The initial 'J' sometimes appears in reports and advertisements before his name instead of I.)

Pollaky and Lord Lytton

During his employment in Field's office, Pollaky felt somewhat limited in his opportunities, and on occasion tried to strike out on his own: with mixed success at first, but with ever-growing confidence in his abilities. He must have felt the need to test himself to see whether or not there was a future in this new kind of work. Perhaps knowing of Field's previous connection with Lord Lytton, he decided to try his luck in that direction himself.

Hertfordshire Archives holds within its collection two documents: correspondence between Pollaky and Lord Lytton from 1858. It is evident that he is communicating on his own behalf – the letters have nothing to do with Field. Given Field's past work it would be strange if he had no knowledge of these letters, and yet he is not mentioned, even in passing.

Edward Bulwer Lytton (Lord Lytton) was a prolific novelist, poet and playwright whose works included the play mentioned on page 21, and also novels: *The Last Days of Pompeii* and *Paul Clifford* – whence comes the infamous opening line, 'It was a dark and stormy night [...]'. Lytton was born in 1803, and in 1831 was elected Member of Parliament for St Ives, Cornwall, and remained an MP until 1841. In 1852 he became a member once more, this time for Hertfordshire. In 1858 he became Secretary of State for the Colonies under Prime Minister Lord Derby. It is at this point that Pollaky enters the scene – albeit briefly.

On 29 November 1858, Pollaky wrote the first of his letters to Lord Lytton. Not for the last time, he seems intent on exaggerating his own abilities and importance to a high-ranking political figure. His letters were sent from No. 20 Devonshire Place, Edgware Road, West London, where he may have been living with his first wife, Julia.

He writes to Lord Lytton requesting a private interview as he says he has a confidential communication to make, 'of the Greatest importance, the delicate nature of which does not permit me to put it in writing'.

On the reverse side of this first letter, Lord Lytton's secretary has written a copy of the response sent to Pollaky, agreeing to an interview at a quarter to two the following afternoon. We must assume that this meeting took place.

The following month (actual date is unknown), Pollaky wrote the second of his letters. This is more specific as to the reason for these communications, and, bearing in mind Lord Lytton's position as Secretary of State for the Colonies and

Pollaky's (self-proclaimed) expertise as an investigator into foreigners, it makes some sense. Pollaky requests Lord Lytton provide him 'with the means to proceed to the Ionian Islands, and "especially" to Syra' (Pollaky's emphasis) so that he may be able to obtain the evidence that he had mentioned in his interview with Lord Lytton of the conspiracy there. He also asks Lord Lytton to ask Lord Derby (the Prime Minister), 'if I have not many months ago informed him of the existence of such a Conspiracy'. A record of Pollaky's communication with Lord Derby does not seem to exist, although Lord Lytton had been investigating problems in the Ionian Islands, and Lord Derby had received communications from a 'confidential agent' that year. Those communications, though, seem to have been in connection with voting intentions of Irish members, and nothing to do with Pollaky. In the event, it was Gladstone, the future Prime Minister, who was sent to the Ionian Islands to investigate the complicated happenings connected with the British Protectorate there.

Two questions are immediately raised. Firstly, what was the information that Pollaky said that he had, and, secondly, had Pollaky indeed been in communication with Lord Derby? It seems likely that he did have something to communicate – though perhaps of limited importance, since he felt it necessary to justify himself in the second letter. He may very well have written to Lord Derby at some time, but his communication may have been ignored or not deemed to have been of any significance. Pollaky, as mentioned earlier, seems continually to have tried to make himself appear to be impressive in order to raise his status.

Further confirmation that Pollaky was acting independently from Field can be seen by examining the address the letters were sent from. Since they were not sent from Field's office, it seems likely that he had kept them secret from his employer, and it may be that his later departure from Field may not have been met with much resistance if Field had become aware of incidents of this sort. And yet he continued to work with Field for some time after the letters to Lord Lytton, and later stated on record that he held him in high regard.

There is one other possibility. It may be that at the time of this correspondence Pollaky had not yet started working for Field. There are two gaping holes that have yet to be filled: firstly, what did Pollaky do before he arrived in England, and secondly, what did he do for the first nine years or so after he arrived?

Pollaky's Mission to Bucharest and Egypt, and Lord Palmerston

In Pollaky's letter to Sir Richard Mayne of 31 July 1862 (mentioned in the previous chapter) he refers to work undertaken by himself in 1854. Although the letter was written some eight years later, from an historical point of view, it is possible that Pollaky was involved in a mission of some kind that year. If so, it would be the earliest date currently known for his work. The letter is entitled by Pollaky, 'Memorial to Sir Richard Mayne Chief Commissioner of the Metropolitan Police K.C.B. ect ect [*sic*]'. It forms part of Pollaky's long and unsuccessful campaign to achieve British Nationality. (A memorial is a formal letter to a government body.)

Pollaky writes the following on page two:

> in the year 1854 I was employed by Lord Palmerston and by the directors of the East India Cy. in a Confidential Mission to Bucharest & Egypt for which services the Sum of nearly Five hundred pounds of public money was paid to me. … That after my return to England Lord Palmerston continued to receive my visits.

On 4 August 1862 Pollaky wrote to Horatio Waddington, Permanent Under-Secretary of State for the Home Office, with regard to his Naturalisation application:

> Lord Palmerston has employed me in Secret Mission and that I for such services received 400 to 500£ of which a Record will be found.

Pollaky states that the money was paid on the direction of Lord Palmerston by Ross D. Mangles, Chairman of the East India Company.

Finally, on 19 March 1863, Inspector Detective Frederick Williamson wrote a brief report to Sir Richard Mayne:

> I beg to report that the attached anonymous letter sent to Lord Palmerston, has been compared with the handwriting of I.P. Pollaky, by Mr Hamar an Inspector of Fraud at the Post-office, who is of opinion that they were not written by the same individual. The handwriting of the anonymous letter is not known.

The anonymous letter referred to has not been identified, nevertheless, the fact that it was deemed necessary to compare the handwriting with that of Pollaky is suggestive. Was there some communication in 1854 between Pollaky and the office of Lord Palmerston who at the time was Home Secretary? (He became Prime Minister the following year.) March 1854 saw the start of the Crimean War. In July Bucharest was in danger of being captured by the Turkish Army. Egypt was at that time part of the Turkish/Ottoman Empire. So dates begin to match with Pollaky's assertions. What is just as interesting is his claim that Lord Palmerston continued to receive his visits, implying that he had visited him both before and after on a number of occasions. If Pollaky indeed mixed in these circles his desire to work on his own behalf becomes easy to understand, as does his later frustration at his treatment by the Home Office with regard to the refusal to grant him British Nationality.

The Palmerston Papers are held in the archives of Southampton University. A search of these quickly revealed that in 1859 Pollaky indeed wrote two letters to Lord Palmerston. The first was written ten days before Palmerston became Prime Minister, and the second five months later. Pollaky's chatty letter of November 1859 does imply a familiarity with Palmerston and it may be that the latter felt it necessary to drop this informal relationship after he became Prime Minister in June that year; Pollaky certainly hints of the likelihood of Palmerston not wishing to continue corresponding with him near the end of the letter. This second letter in particular refers to matters appertaining to the Unification of Italy. Pollaky, it would seem, had been engaged by the *Morning Post* to act as Special Correspondent in Zurich during some important negotiations there. The editor, Algernon Borthwick, certainly had a special correspondent in Zurich at that time. Of course, since these correspondents were usually anonymous, it is impossible to confirm that Pollaky was their man in Zurich, but there seems little reason to doubt that he was. Furthermore, in October that year, Pollaky was described on his first wife's death certificate as a 'Newspaper Correspondent'.

Pollaky's Letters to Lord Palmerston

Hartley Library, University of Southampton – Palmerston Papers MS 62 Broadlands Archive PP/MPC/1575–6 – I. Pollaky to Palmerston 1859

PP/MPC/1575
Berne, 2th June 859

Private & Confidentielle!

Your Lordship –
In ten or twelve days I will be able to give You the exact contents of the so called written engagements between Russia and France – Your Lordship can see 'on the seal of the Enclosed letter' dtto [sic] Warschaw [sic] 20th last, that the Source is first class and admits of no doubt, should your Lordship however not recognise it – I will aquaint [sic] Your [sic] personally from whom it comes –
    The letters A & S. means [sic] Austria & Siebenburgen, (Transilvany) –
    Here also England looses [sic] every day more an[d] more ground – what a change – 3 years ago Mr Gordon was generally loved here – and the French Ambassador a mere puppy – now quite the reverse[,] Mr Harris nobody likes, and Jurgot is everything[.] Harris's appointment for Berne is a great mistake, and will not be without consequence in the Present Crisis
    I have the honnour [sic] to remain Your Lordships
    Most Ob Servant
    I.P.

The enclosed letter Your Lordship will Kindly return when I come to London

PP/MPC/1576
London 14th November. 59.

Private !

My Lord!

I once related to You the fact of my entering Giberaltar [*sic*] at 10 o'clock at night, in spite of the strictest ordres [*sic*] of the Comandant [*sic*] de Place – I will now tell You; what you Know to be true; that I went to Zurich as the special Correspondent of the Morning Post and that 'I prevailed' on Mr Borthwick to Keep the whole matter from You until the reception of my first letter from Zurich – when according to our prearranged plan he (B) would go 'to Your Lordship' saying 'that he received information by a Gentleman who was introduced to him by a friend' naming to You at the same time my name, and see what effect it would have upon Your Lordship, when asKed if he Could place reliance upon information derived from me – This was our plans [*sic*]. Your Lordship will best Know if Mr B. acted accordingly, as related above –

I said to Mr. B at our 1th interview that 'Your Lordship Knew me well' but that I have reasons to believe if asKed Your opinion, You would certainly object to my going, and that it would be far better to Keep it from You until my first letter from Zurich has reached the M.P. [*Morning Post*]

Now, My Lord which of the 2 exploits as related above was the more difficult? both were equally successfull [*sic*].

To bring Mr B. (who to say the truth) looked upon Your Lordship as a Demi-God, and upon eache [*sic*] word from You, as an oracle – to bring Mr. B., I say to act with me in concert this piece of inocent [*sic*] intrigue with me a perfect stranger whom he Knew than only since two hours – You [*sic*] Lordship will allow that this is a feat not inferior to my entering Giberaltar [*sic*] in spite of the utmost vigilance exercised at that place.

Now to the facts, which if desired, I can evidence by – proofs

Private!

on the 18th July I wrote a letter to Mr B. – demanding a private interview – on the 19th I received his answer, asKing me to see him on the 20th at 5 o'clock in the afternoon – I was of course punctual he begun by saying – "that he could only give me a few minutes hearing, which did not prevent me to set heartily at worK – to explain to him the important benefits for the M.P. in sending me to Zurich as its Special Corr. saying that I have the honnour [*sic*] to be Known by Y.L. [Your Lordship]

The first sKirmishes were anything but success on my part – and I thought allready [*sic*] of covering my retreat when all of a sudden I found out his weaK point, I ralied [sic] – opened fire from all my batteries, and after one hour and 50 minutes hard fighting, I saw myself accepted as 'our Special Correspondent' of a paper considered by the whole world as Your L[iberal] organ. The next day 21th the final arrangements were all settled during my taKing tea with Mr. B. who gave me a Cheque upon Messrs Twining & Co. for £60. I left on the 22th for Zurich

It remains only for me now the 2 reasons to explain for adressing [sic] You this –

Eight days after the 1th Conference I wrote to Mr. BorthwicK as follows 'The reinstalation [sic] of the Italian fugitif [sic] Prince has been agreed and determined upon by the 2 Emperors, and that a private written agreemente [sic] exists between them, to that effect – etc –' – of course th[is] was in contradiction to every line written in the M. Post and Mr. B. 'went on to write his leaders' exactly in the opposite direction – of course he has taken Y. Lds. opinion on this my letter as he told me, that he does so every day upon every important subject.

Now, My Lord, am I right in my informations[?] There is no denying facts the Emperors letter admits no other interpretation.

I served Mr. BorthwicK well but he is not a very great politician and is perhaps bound by other ties, but he did not treat me handsomely; and if I did not bring an action against him it was for fear of having Your Lordships name mixed in this Affair either direct or indirectly —

Mr B. looked upon my information which was most positive as a canard, as there was no other paper, even the "Times" who did not write to the contrary to what I said – as to the payment to Austria Your Lordship will remember that I was the first who told You so –

Your Lordship Knows what I said about the next summer – You will see in time if I am right as I was right about last Mai [sic] – You may smile But only then Your Lordship will Know to appreciate my services and until then I will not trouble Your Lordship again.

Please to read the first leader of the "Times" of this day, and say if I did not word for word specify the position of Austria after the Zurich Treaty, as it now stands –

Your most Obd
Servant
IP
Monday

(On a separate piece of paper is written: 'Mr Pollaky about his going to Zurich for the Morning Post.')

The Times of that day had a long leader about this matter as Pollaky indicated. The *Morning Post* was, in fact a Tory paper, but it did seem to favour the Liberal Palmerston in the 1850s, and the fact that Pollaky knew this shows how aware he was of political matters.

It seemed vital to make a trip to Southampton University to look at the Palmerston Papers in the Hartley Library, and see if there were any other references to Pollaky. There were none with his name, but two other items were most suggestive.

Pollaky may have remembered the year incorrectly, as there seems to be no trace of communication with Palmerston or Ross Mangles from 1854. However, on 10 October 1857, Mangles wrote a letter to Palmerston (catalogued as PP/ GC/SM/47 enc 1), detailing some dealings with 'our friend' who he had seen the previous evening. 'Our friend' had evidently brought him some information, but Mangles was not certain that it was accurate. 'Our friend' had been in communication with an agent in Jassy, Romania, and gave information that the Berbers had bought many rifles to arm the 'Faqueers'. Mangles, hedging his bets, doubted this intelligence, but stated that it might at the same time be quite true. He concluded his letter with a request that Palmerston should advise how much 'our friend ought to be paid for his services', feeling that Palmerston would know better what the amount should be.

This letter to Palmerston is held together with another (PP/GC/SM/47). The second letter is from Robert Vernon Smith, Liberal Member of Parliament. He gives further details of Mangles' dealings with this mysterious anonymous person. Mangles had written (says Vernon Smith) to all the Governors of the East India Company about 'our "Secret" friend', and they had given him £70. They had the 'impression that the man did not know all the languages which he professed to know'. He had told them that while at Jassy he had tried to open all the drawers in the room of his contact there, while that person was out of the room, 'but found unfortunately that none of his keys would fit them!'

While the individual concerned is not mentioned by name, it seems not inconceivable that it was Pollaky himself who was 'Our Friend'. It places him in Romania, if not Bucharest, and the reference to his claim that he spoke a number of languages certainly sounds like Pollaky. Furthermore, the reference to the Berbers sounds like the Egyptian connection as mentioned by Pollaky. The year 1857 was a troubled one for the East India Company, perhaps marking the beginning of the end of colonialism. It was the year that saw the beginning of the Indian Mutiny, and the year that Palmerston proposed placing the government of India under the British Crown, thus removing rule from the East India Company.

Brief Biographies of those Involved in these Affairs

Henry John Temple, 3rd Viscount Palmerston (1784–1865), first became Prime Minister at the age of 71. He served two terms, 1855–58, and 1859–65. In October 1857 he announced that the East India Company's government of India would be ended, and introduced a bill transferring administration of India to the Crown the following year. Letters to his wife often began, 'My dearest Emily', but were signed more formally, 'Palmerston'. He died at the age of 81 while he was still Prime Minister.

Ross Donnelly Mangles (1801–77) was Member of Parliament for Guildford from 1841 to 1857. In that year he became Chairman of the East India Company, a position whose incumbent changed annually. He seems though to have been connected with the company before that, having written an article as early as 1830 entitled *A brief vindication of the Honourable East India Company's government of Bengal, from the attacks of Messrs. Rickards & Crawfurd*.

The East India Company (founded in 1600 to trade with India and other parts of Asia and originally called the 'Governor and Company of Merchants of London trading with the East Indies') to all intents and purposes ruled India from 1757 using its own private armies to exercise control. The company had managed the mail route from Suez, Egypt to Bombay, however, in 1852 one of its ships had got into difficulties and the mail it was carrying was lost. In 1854, they discontinued that service. The company continued its activities for another fifteen years after Palmerston's Government of India Act of 1858 and was finally wound up in 1873.

Adolphus Frederick Williamson (1831–89), nicknamed 'Dolly', was, by the time he was 19, a police constable in the Metropolitan Police. At 29, he was a police sergeant, and by 1862, the year of his marriage, he was Inspector of Detective Police. He was promoted to Superintendent in 1869 and made Head of the Detective Department at Scotland Yard. By 1881 he was Chief Superintendent, and eventually became Chief Constable of the Criminal Investigation Department (CID), reporting directly to the Chief Commissioner of Police. He was in office during the period of the Whitechapel Murders of 1888.

Williamson died in 1889, aged 57. Arthur Griffiths, writing of him in 1901 (in *Mysteries of Police and Crime*), gave the following description: 'Few but the initiated recognised the redoubtable detective in this quiet, unpretending, middle-aged man, who walked leisurely along Whitehall, balancing a hat that was a little large for him loosely on his head, and often with a sprig of a leaf or flower between his lips.' An enthusiastic gardener, he was well known for growing flowers.

Williamson's name reappears a few times in these pages. His obituary in the *Standard* of 12 December 1889, ended by regretting the low pay of the police, and implied that it was more profitable for a detective officer to become a private investigator.

Horatio Waddington (1799–1867) became Permanent Under-Secretary to the Home Office in 1840 and resigned his post shortly before his death owing to ill health. In 1815 aged 16, he published a poem called *Wallace*, and in 1819 translated a scene from Shakespeare's *Coriolanus* into Latin. In 1860, after the murder at Road had been discovered, it was Waddington who, by the direction of the Home Secretary Sir G.C. Lewis, wrote to Sir Richard Mayne requesting that 'an intelligent officer of the Metropolitan Police' should be sent to investigate, resulting in Whicher being sent to Road.

Waddington gave evidence to the Select Committee on Transportation to Australia in 1856, saying that transportation was, 'a bad punishment in itself, failing to deter criminals at home, or reform them abroad'. He sat on the Royal Commission on Capital Punishment in 1864–66, which produced its conclusions in a report of over 700 pages. He contributed much to the discussion, including the following remarks: 'There is another argument against Capital Punishment which has great weight with many people, namely, the possibility of executing an innocent man. Have you ever considered whether the possibility of that is of such weight as to have any effect upon your opinion? – I cannot say that it is impossible.'

It may seem that Waddington was against capital punishment, however, he then went on to say, 'It is commonly said that it is better that nine guilty persons should get off, than that one innocent person should suffer. That is true perhaps, but it is not true to say that it is better that 999 guilty persons should get off, than that one innocent person should suffer.' Many would now disagree with this last statement. Waddington too makes further appearances later in this book.

The conclusion of the Commission was that capital punishment should be retained for cases of murder and used at the discretion of the judge.

Private investigators were considered to be conducting a very shady sort of business. It is hardly surprising that most people were suspicious of anyone asking for personal information about themselves or their neighbours. Furthermore, the official police resented both interference in their work and the implication that by the very existence of private investigators, the police's own competence was called into question. On 3 March 1864, *Hansard*, the official report of proceedings of the House of Commons and the House of Lords, included a report on a debate which took place in the House of Commons in which concern was expressed about the activities of private investigators. John Roebuck MP had received a letter from Captain Bicknell, the Chief Constable of Lincolnshire, complaining of the number of letters the Lincolnshire police were receiving from private inquiry offices regarding the character, respectability and wealth of a number of people. Bicknell's letter went on to point out that these inquiries, of which most people were completely unaware could injure the prospects of the subjects, and that their names might be listed by the inquiring companies in their 'register of persons deemed unworthy of credit'.

Marriage One

4

On 20 May 1856 Ignatius Paul Pollaky married Julia Susanne Devonald at St James Church, Paddington and rented furnished rooms at 20 Devonshire Place, a street which contained a number of lodging houses. Julia was the daughter of Erasmus Lloyd Devonald, a surgeon of 71 Great Titchfield Street and 6 Howley Place, London, and Anne Devonald née Nicholas. Anne Devonald was 55 when her daughter married, but Julia's father had died in 1852 aged 58. The houses were only two miles apart. The residence at 6 Howley Place was a large one, in a smart road.

Erasmus Devonald and Anne Nicholas were married in 1817. He was from Moylgrove, 5 miles west of Cardigan, Wales. They had ten children, six of whom survived infancy. Julia, the youngest, was born in 1831. Devonald, whose practice was based at the Titchfield Road address, had been described in the Medical Directory as 'in practice prior to 1815'. As he was born in 1794, that would mean he began practice aged 20. He contributed articles to medical journals and books including *The Physical and Moral Condition of the Children and Young Persons Employed in Mines and Manufactories* published in 1843.

His views on conditions of employment and the health of the young extended to girls involved in millinery and dress-making:

> Mr Devonald, surgeon, Great Titchfield Street, states that he has known several who have married, and whom he has attended for years: 'Their health and strength are gone; they are completely disorganised; has known numbers of young healthy women who in this way have been reduced to a permanent state of debility. Many of them die, especially from consumption. Many of them, after their health has been ruined, are compelled to give up the business.'

Devonald also contibuted to *The London Medical and Surgical Journal* of 1833, in which he wrote a long article entitled 'Observations on the Pathology and Treatment of Cholera'. Headed 'Mr Devonald's Successful Treatment of Cholera', he recommends his own method in glowing terms, writing that he has had several cases under his care, and that he has developed a treatment, 'the result of which has been so successful that I feel myself duty bound to publish it'. After mentioning, 'the fatal effect of stimulating medicines', and the symptoms of the disease, he continues describing his cure. The system, he writes, 'cannot be relieved in the first instance by the mouth, owing to the irritation of the stomach'.

He continues with an alternative:

> Let us try further to assist nature, by replacing if possible, part of the lost nourishment; to effect this, inject about half a pint of beef tea, made with all spices, up the rectum, as often as the bowels are open; you will not only find part of the beef tea absorbed, but the evacuations will gradually decrease, and after several repetitions entirely stopped; the pulse you will find also gradually rise; after this desirable object is effected, I usually have recourse to calomel to restore the secretions, followed by castor oil.

He goes on to describe some particular cases where he has used this treatment, the patients being, 'restored to [...] former health'.

This was not the first time this treatment had been suggested. On 13 October 1832, F. Kelly, a surgeon of Liverpool had a letter published in *The Lancet* detailing his own use of this method.

As late as 8 October 1853 *The Lancet* had an article recommending this method of treatment. Indeed this seems on the whole to have been recommended in medical journals throughout the rest of the nineteenth century. In 1880, John Harvey Kellogg, inventor (with his brother Will Keith Kellogg) of Corn Flakes, advocated the use of this method in his book *The Home Hand-Book of Domestic Hygiene and Rational Medicine (Vol. 2)*, not for cholera specifically, but for gastritis.

Julia Devonald was 25 when she married Pollaky. He was 28 and is described on their marriage certificate, most unhelpfully, as a 'Gentleman'. By the time of their marriage, the Devonald family seem to have given up the Great Titchfield address, and were all living at 6 Howley Place, Paddington. She, though pale, weak, and the baby of the family, was at 25 independent-minded, and may have resisted any attempts by her family to give up thoughts of marriage with a foreigner who had no prospects. They may have found him odd. She probably found him fascinating.

Not being one to idle about, Pollaky was soon busy and may even have briefly visited America later that year.

The Pollaky's were not to be married for long, as on 3 October 1859, Julia died. Cause of death was diagnosed as phthisis (consumption, or in modern terms tuberculosis). She died at 6 Howley Place, her parental home. Her eldest sibling

Jane Augusta was recorded on the death certificate as being present. There is no record of where her husband was at the time. Was he away, and she staying with her mother and sisters – she had returned to her family, perhaps, for the comfort and support they could give her while her husband was at work.

Julia is described on her death certificate as, 'Wife of Ignatius Pollaky, Newspaper Correspondent'. Pollaky's work as a newspaper correspondent is discussed in Chapter 12.

Pollaky Alone

5

After Julia's death, Pollaky, bereft, continued with his work, corresponding with Palmerston a month later. He found other living quarters; the rooms he shared with his late wife had become unbearable to him. He was an energetic and passionate man, and Julia had been the love of his life, until fragile and ill she had been snatched from him to a place from which there is no return. And so, the 1861 census, taken 7 April, finds him living at 10 Devonshire Place, only a few doors away, where he is described as a lodger; presumably he was now renting a single room. Many of the inhabitants of Devonshire Place were professional or trades people and included a schoolmaster, clerks, a builder, and a harrier. William Bromley at No. 22 was an 'Historical Painter'.

Pollaky was now thirty-two. The others at 10 Devonshire Place were his landlady, Elizabeth Hughes, a widow, fifty-two or fifty-four years old, her daughter Mary Ann, twenty and unmarried, and Sarah Gregory, servant, twenty-one. Mary Ann is described on the census as a Governess, her mother as a Lodge House Keeper.

In 1841 Elizabeth and Francis Hughes (Mary Ann's parents) had been living at 36 Stafford Place, Westminster with their baby daughter who had been born early that year. But, despite the census record, they were, in fact, only married on 2 September 1842 when their daughter was about 19 months old. Elizabeth had at first assumed Francis's surname for propriety's sake. By 1843, they had moved to Devonshire Place. Francis Hughes died in April 1843 at the age of 37, and is described on his burial record as a 'Gentleman'. In his will, made shortly before his death, he refers to his wife as, 'Elizabeth Sells now living with me', and to Mary Ann as, 'my daughter by the said Elizabeth Sells'. He left his estate in trust for his daughter and her children should she have any, stipulating that no control could be given to any husband she might have in the future, while making provision for her mother to live in the house and enjoy any rent she might receive, as long as she remained, 'sole and unmarried'. In the 1851 census, Elizabeth is listed as a 'Lodging House Keeper' with a servant and a lodger who was a banker's clerk. That census indicates that she had been a widow for the past eight years.

One imagines that life for the newly widowed Pollaky was fairly lonely, but business was brisk, and he was earning well. There were other compensations, particularly in the comforting form of his landlady's daughter, Mary Ann, and on 2 June 1861 they were married at the church of St Mary Magdalene in Richmond, Surrey where she may have been living that year – for although she appears on the census with her mother at Devonshire Place, this does not mean that she lived there all the time. She had been a governess, possibly in Richmond. Pollaky's address on the marriage register is recorded as Devereux Court, Temple – he was staying in Field's premises at No. 20. The wedding was announced in *The Times*:

The Times –Tuesday, 4 June 1861
MARRIAGES [...]
POLLAKY – HUGHES. – On the 2d inst., at the parish church, St Mary's Richmond, Surrey, by the Rev. William Bashall, Ignatius Paul Pollaky, of 20 Devereux-court, Temple, son of Joseph Francois Pollaky, of Old Castle Hill, in Pressburg, Hungary, to Mary Ann Colombe Hughes, only daughter of the late Francis Hughes, of Maida-hill.
(Mary Ann's third name 'Colombe' appears only in this announcement.)

How did his new mother-in-law feel about her daughter's marriage to this unusual man? A widower, 33 years old, with an exotic accent, smartly turned out perhaps, a hard worker, but foreign nonetheless. His change of address from Devonshire Place to Devereux Court must have been for one of three reasons.

1. He wanted a different address from Mary Ann for the sake of propriety – unlikely since she gave her address on the marriage certificate as Richmond.
2. It was more convenient for him to be living at or near his place of work – possible.
3. He had had a falling out with his soon-to-be mother-in-law, who may have objected to his marrying her daughter.

This is surely the most likely explanation. Had Mary Ann, perhaps, also felt the need to move out of her mother's house because her life had been made unbearable by her mother's objections and nagging?

Pollaky had been single for one year and eight months when he remarried. Was it a love match? The marriage lasted until his death almost 57 years later.

By 1862, the new Mr and Mrs Pollaky were living at 18 Maida Hill; Pollaky had in January that year set up his own Inquiry Office at 14 George Street, Mansion House. In the meantime, he was engaged on a number of projects, of which, perhaps, the most fascinating is his involvement in the American Civil War.

Confederate Correspondence

Between 12 to 14 April 1861, soldiers of the Confederate States of America attacked and captured Fort Sumter, South Carolina, which had been controlled by the Union Army. This was an attempt to force Abraham Lincoln, newly inaugurated President of the United States and his government to accept the secession of the Southern States. The Confederacy would soon consist of eleven states, all in favour of slavery, whereas Lincoln had already expressed his intention to abolish it. So began the American Civil War.

The Union established a naval blockade, damaging the economy of the South which found it essential to procure ships capable of breaking the blockade, and supplies for the ships to carry to beleaguered Southern forces. The Confederacy, under its leader Jefferson Davis, sent representatives to Europe, and particularly to England, for the purpose of raising funds and obtaining supplies and vessels, as well as attempting to gain recognition by European governments. They failed completely in the last, despite their own confidence that Europe was so reliant on the cotton produced by the Southern States, that recognition would be a comparatively easy matter. Indeed, there was great sympathy in England for the Confederacy, though not for slavery. Naturally, the Union States were not going to stand by and let their opponents do what they wanted without knowledge of exactly what they were up to.

Henry Shelton Sanford (1823–91) was born in Connecticut, the son of a successful brass tacks manufacturer. After his education in America, he studied at Heidelberg University, and in 1847 became Secretary to the American Legation in St Petersburg. Over the next two years he held the same position, but in different cities – firstly in Frankfurt, and then in Paris. In 1861 Sanford was appointed as US Minister to Belgium by President Lincoln, and it was then that he first made contact with Ignatius Pollaky. Sanford consulted Freeman Harlow Morse, US Consul in London, on the matter. Morse wrote of Pollaky in a letter to Sanford saying, 'there may be some risk in dealing with him, but it is a "risky business" anyway & I think we better engage him at once.' This letter is quoted in full below.

In June 1861, Pollaky was hired by Morse on Sanford's behalf to carry out surveillance of Confederate activities in Great Britain: to detect, track down, observe and report on all movements of Confederate agents in the British Isles, with particular reference to their attempts to raise money and acquire arms and ships to aid them in their war for the independence of the Southern States. He organised an efficient network of agents to carry out this task, and began to make his reports to Sanford.

Using methods including the bribing of postmen, Pollaky and his men were able to gain information on the intentions of the Confederates. He had a number of successes in tracking down armaments and other supplies, including ships intended for the Southern States, but found himself hampered, not only by lack of funds (he had problems paying for his men's work, as he himself was not paid regularly by his employers), but also by the clumsy spying of a 'rival' team of agents set up by Morse and US Ambassador Francis Adams.

The long and involved correspondence that Pollaky had with Sanford over the next few months would be remembered by the former as being deeply frustrating. Pollaky's name was bandied about by those in authority in the United States with whom Sanford communicated, as if he was not carrying out his work as he should have been. In January 1862, Benjamin Moran, Assistant Secretary to the US Legation in London wrote of Pollaky in his journal (Vol. 2 p. 96) as, 'a German Jew [...] who is acting as a detective, and whom S[anford] was so silly as to employ'. It seems that Pollaky had presented Moran with a bill for work done for Sanford and Morse, though this amount, said to be £100, is not mentioned in the Pollaky–Sanford correspondence, where Pollaky seems instead to deem it fairly important that he be paid £15 expenses owing him. The comment written by Moran is, in any case, factually wrong. Pollaky was not German, and Sanford seems to have got better service from him than he paid for.

Pollaky's letters were very much a one-sided affair. He frequently complained that they were unanswered, and that his investigation was under-resourced and under-funded. And it seems that these complaints were justified. Not for the first or last time he was being treated with a kind of scorn that may have arisen out of prejudice against a foreigner who appeared somewhat exotic in his manner.

And yet, despite all commentary in books since written about the attempts by the Northern States to track Confederate movements in Brtain and Europe, mostly dismissive of Pollaky's role, his letters show that he was carrying out an investigation under difficult circumstances to the best of his abilities and with successful and useful results.

The Sanford Museum in Sanford, Florida has in their collection three folders of letters (HSS Box 139 Folders 12, 13 and 14) involving Pollaky. Almost all of the documents in 13 and 14 are from Pollaky to Sanford. He made some spelling mistakes but these are due to his not being a native English speaker, combined with the necessity of having to write hastily. In fact, Pollaky's command of written English is very good on the whole. As with his letters to the British authorities regarding his naturalisation a year or so later, his increased agitation at his perceived mistreatment can be seen in his handwriting as he evidently wrote at ever increasing speed. Folder 12 contains two letters from Morse to Sanford which both discuss Pollaky. Scans of the letters were generously supplied by the Sanford Museum, Florida. Letters from the Sanford Papers are indicated here with the letters HSS followed by the box and folder numbers, and then the scan number as supplied where one exists.

Folder 14 follows chronological order, but folder 13 does not – most of the letters there are undated, or only partially dated. Where it has been possible to find approximate dates, a suggested correct order has been restored.

Another source lies at the University of Rochester, which holds the William Henry Seward Papers in the Rare Books, Special Collections and Preservation Department of the Rush Rhees Library and contain a number of letters regarding Pollaky's activities. These letters are identified in the following pages with the letters WHSP followed by the date. Seward was President Lincoln's Secretary of State. The significance of these letters will become apparent.

This is not the place to discuss the history of the American Civil War in detail. However, the letters do shed a fresh light on activities of Confederate agents in England in 1861–62. In particular they seem to show that all parties in the matter were inexperienced amateurs at their game, with the possible exception of Pollaky, who seems to have received very little reward out of the business. Some letters are very difficult to read being very faint, damaged or torn, or in many cases with very untidy handwriting. The underlinings, capitalisations and misspellings are all in the originals.

From these selections, one can see the methods used by an investigator of the period, as well as something of the personalities of the writer, those he was spying on, and the recipients of the letters. That Sanford himself does not particularly shine forth in a favourable light possibly indicates a lack of personal management skills as well as his possession of a single-minded purpose which expected service for its own reward.

The weather for the most part was fine during those months of surveillance, and this made it easier for Pollaky and his agents to remain out of doors for the purposes of spying, but also made it harder to stay undetected by the objects of their watchfulness. This caused them some problems, as we shall see.

Some of the Names Referred to in the Confederate Correspondence

Adams, Francis	US Ambassador to England
Anderson, Maj. Edward Clifford	Oversaw Confederate Army purchases in England
Blakely, Capt. Theophilus Alexander	Irish-born owner and buyer for the Blakely Cannon Company, based in England
Bulloch, Capt. James Dunwoody	Purchasing agent for the Confederate Navy
Fraser, Trenholm & Co.	The Confederacy's European banker
Huse, Maj. Caleb	Confederate arms procurement agent
Isaac, Campbell & Co.	Army contractors
King, Thomas Butler	Commissioner for the Confederate State of Georgia in Europe
Mann, Dudley Ambrose	Confederate Commissioner
Mason, James	Confederate Commissioner to London
Morse, Freeman Harlow	US Consul in London
Moses Brothers	Merchants – Leadenhall Street, London
Slidell, John	Confederate Commissioner to Paris
Yancey, William Lowndes	Confederate Commissioner who spoke in favour of slavery in 1860

Pollaky consistently misspells three of these names: Bulloch as 'Bullock', Blakely as 'Blackley', and Yancey as 'Yancy'. These misspellings have not been commented on in the transcriptions. Others are indicated with [*sic*] in the usual way.

Letters Regarding Surveillance of the Confederates in London

HSS.139.12.   Morse to Sanford

The first letter, quoted in full, is from Morse to Sanford. It shows not only the fees expected by Pollaky for undertaking the surveillance required, but also that it was Morse who carried out the negotiations. Of special interest is the information that the job was offered in the first place to Charles Frederick Field who turned it down as he was worried about his police pension – with some justification as later events would show:

London June 29th 1861 [Saturday]

My Dear Sir

Field as I told you in a late [?] letter fears that he cannot enter upon work without endangering his pension &c. Mr Pollacky [sic], his associate has been absent from the city & returned within a day or two[.] Yesterday I had two interviews with him. He seems, if he will prove <u>true</u> just the man but declines to undertake to accomplish what I told him I wanted him to do unless we give him £100 – for say 30 or 40 days close work with such assistance as he may need[.] £25 – to be <u>advanced</u> & in 10 or 15 days 25 more & so on[.] This is to cover all his expense for the time he will work

He is unknown to me except from what you & Field have said & there may be some risk in dealing with him. But it is a 'risky business' any way & I think we better engage him at once. I told him that there was no doubt his terms would be acceded to & he better set about it at once. He has promised to look over the whole ground & lay his plans, get introduced to Huse &c but does not consider him self engaged only from day to day until we accept his terms & hand him his advance

Information recd last evening leads me to believe that the rebels are obtaining guns both from London & Birmingham[.] None have yet been shipped, & they have a steamer somewhere in these Northern seas & we must find her. I have sent a first rate man to look after the craft I hinted to you about.

I want to set Pollaky to find 1000 guns which came here from Birmingham last Thursday, said to be for Sweden & Norway but more likely for some wherelse [sic].

Mr Fields charge so far is £6.00.00 [pounds, shillings and pence] which I shall pay him when I next see him. Please write me by <u>return mail</u> & tell me how far I may be authorised to go with Mr Pollaky[.] I think it very important that we engage him fully so that he may be <u>wholly ours</u>, at once[.]

Very Truly Yours

F.H. Morse

HSS.139.12.   Morse to Sanford

In this letter to Sanford, written only two weeks later, Morse writes with impatience of Pollaky's progress to date:

London July 12th 1861 [Friday]

[…]

I had put Polaky [sic] on the track before the receipt of your telegram[.] He is still at work but not with astounding results. He has just reported his doings with Bullock, Huse & Cann [sic] promises good results, & says 'you will see' &c.

I have had to pay him thus far £56.00.00 & shall have to give him £50,– more soon.

I shall be pleased to see you here when you come over
Yours Truly
F.H. Morse

HSS.139.13.1.   Pollaky's own list

[Undated]

List of [Confederate] conspirators in London.

1	Capt Bullock	58 Jermyn St
2	Capt Blackley	Montpellier St Hyde Park
3	Capt [sic] Huse	58 Jermyn St
4	Lieut Hughes	Dtto
5	Capt Field	107, 108 Jermyn St
6	Major Anderson	58 Jermyn St & Hatchetts Hotel [Piccadilly, London]
7	Major Gore	Hatchetts Hotel
8	Mr Bingley	40 Albermarle St
9	Mrs Bingley	Dtto
10	Mr King	45 Albermarle St
11	Mr Yancy	15 Half Moon St
12	Capt Wallace	Liverpool
13	Capt Fairclough	Liverpool
14	Mr Mann & Son	40 Albermarle St
15	Junior	[ditto]
16	Mr Neil	[Address unreadable]
17	Isaac Campbell	Jersey St

Undated letters include information on 20,000 muskets in Hamburg bound for the States, Pollaky's work setting up his network of agents, and the whereabouts of some of the Confederate agents:

HSS.139.13.12.   Pollaky to Sanford

[Undated]

From 70 to 80 cannons (9 to 10 batteries) are on board and on the way to the Bahama [sic]. 3 Batteries (24 cannons) were stored in a warehouse on the river and are for the Bahama [sic]. All are cannons for light artillery, <u>new</u>, <u>six</u> and <u>twelve pounders</u>, some are plain trap cannons and some <u>rifled</u> <u>bronze</u> colored. They have all the name Bronn (where they were manufactured) on the ring of the thick end. The wooden work is painted <u>dark green</u>. Seats are brown (leather cloth).

Brought on board the Bahama Friday last: 242 pkgs. with muskets marked <u>N.E. Johns</u>. and 215 boxes muskets (new musket boxes) with no mark.

HSS.139.13.14. *Pollaky to Sanford*

Pollaky finding a lack of funds, found it necessary to start making conditions. Working without a proper contract of employment, he felt it necessary to write the final sentence:

[Undated – Possibly early August 1861; Sanford responded on 21 August.] According to the <u>very low estimate You</u> have of the Manns – <u>I gave them up</u> and did not watch them although I begun to hooK the Younger one. It appears now however that Mann Junior is a very active agent and that he is under direct guidance of <u>Mr Yancy</u>.

Have You as yet got any answer from Washington, because matters now assume a very great proportion and which can only be <u>effectually</u> met by a vast organisation to meet which our means are still inadequate – I shall also have to request You to give me <u>at least one weeks notice</u> in the case of your intention to discontinue the surveillance[.]

HSS.139.13.17. *Pollaky to Sanford*

Information about movements of Confederate agents. Pollaky states that he will now be too busy to send Sanford copies of his reports, and expects that Mr M. will forward them:

[Undated]

Sir!

The researches after the man Neil have only elicited that he has left his customary lodging & haunts[;] his landlady says he is gone to America[. I]f this is the case I hope Mr Morse has acted on my instruction, and given his full description as furnished to the Authority in U.S. – in which case his capture might be certain he is supposed to have Dispatches from Yancy & King.

You will surely not take it amiss if I tell You that after this week it will be utterly impossible for me to send You copies of Reports. As my time is fully taken up in discharge of my duties in Your service – (outdoors) Mr M … I doubt not will (if You desire him to do so) forward Your Originals & Copies.

HSS.139.13.18.   Pollaky to Sanford

[Undated]

A printed form with handwritten responses detailing the specifications of a particular (though unspecified) Iron Screw Steamer ship.

HSS.139.13.20.   Pollaky to Sanford

[Undated]

A report on the movements of various Confederate ships, and on armaments being taken on board to be carried to the Southern States. Pollaky regrets that he has had no communication from Sanford, and also says that he has had to relax slightly the watch on Bulloch's residence (58 Jermyn Street), as it has 'attracted the notice of the Parties'. He finishes with the usual request: 'Please let me have a line, so that I may know if you got my letters[.]'

HSS.139.14.1.   Pollaky to Sanford

A telegram from Pollaky, who was staying at the Old Ship in Brighton, to Sanford who was in Dover:

10th day of August 1861 [Saturday]
It is impossible to reach Dover before the leaving of the steamer. I only received your message five Pm. It will nevertheless be highly urgent that I see you before you leave as something fresh has turned up since yesterday if you remain in Dover I will come if properly advised.

WHSP   Sanford to Seward

Dover. Sunday, 12 August 1861
Private & Confidential

My Dear Seward:
I have stopped here on my way back from London (where I have been vainly seeking the means to secure thos[e] mentioned in my official), I met Pollaky, our head man in the secret serv[ice] & have gone over with him very fully the ground he has been on for the past six or seven weeks, and as I wish you to have some idea of the nature of his operations, I send you a general sketch, which he has just written at my request, of what he has been doing & what can be done. [Pollaky's 'sketch' is not present.]
[…]
My cordial greetings to you & Mrs Seward
Truly Yours H.S. Sanford

HSS.139.14.3. *Pollaky to Sanford*

'Brighton 16 August 61' [Friday]

Pollaky writes of an interview he had with Sanford. He had placed a watch on the premises of Candler's warehouse in Biliter Street, London, where guns and rifles were being packed, and stated his intention to return there the next day. He writes that Yancy seems happy with his treatment by the 'English Goverment' [*sic*], and that Mann has had an interview with the Spanish Ambassador.

HSS.139.14.4. *Pollaky to Sanford*

A letter sent by Pollaky from Field's office.

20 Devereux Court, Temple 18th August [1861 – Sunday]

[…]

Mann has had a long Conference with the Spanish Ambassador at Bedford Hotel, and the Coast of Spain ought simaliar [*sic*] to be watched.

Bullock receing [*sic*] daily letters from Scotland Liverpool New York letters arrive for him under the name of Barnett, Hatchetts Hotel.

WHSP *Sanford to Pollaky*

August 21 [1861 – Wednesday]

Dear Sir

Yours of 16th is at hand, having followed me in my absence from home – Please continue to write & <u>fully</u> to same address. The young <u>man</u> is of not much more account than his father – I would give attention mainly to the <u>practical</u> men – Your literary friend might be able to supply [unreadable] all political information of interest –

Yours &c H.S.

HSS.139.14.5 & 14.6. *Pollaky to Sanford*

Pollaky describes movements of the Confederates around England and Jersey. The CSS (confederates states ship) *Thomas Watson* was still in Liverpool waiting to load. Twenty-two cases of rifles were being moved to Manchester, and a further five cases shipped to Cuba:

London 26th August [Monday]

[…]

I enclose You a Report from my Literary Friend which will clearly show You our progress in that Quarter[.] I should recommend a more lavish expenditure and an additional staff of men[.] Doing the buisness [sic] as it is now done is both useless and wasting money – I beg You to relieve me from the Responsibility at Your earliest convenience as the improbability of giving satisfaction becomes daily more certain –

Was Pollaky being truly sincere when he asked to be relieved of his responsibility? If he was, his wish would be granted well before the end of the war.

Pollaky gives some information about Field in the following paragraph:

Mr M— also hangs back [...] for considerations easily understood – particularly if I tell You that Mr Field has been deprived of his pension by Order of the Secretary of State for meddling in international affairs – fiat justitiam. [Fiat justitiam: Let justice be done]

In 1861 Charles Frederick Field had his police pension stopped for four months. This was possibly due to his continued reference to himself as 'Inspector' Field, despite the fact that he was no longer employed by the police force. Why should this fact be worthy of mention in a letter to Sanford, since Field was by this time not involved, and why should Mr M— hang back because of Field? Sanford as US Consul must have felt the need to tread carefully with his enquiries if the Secretary of State was looking at what was going on, for the British position at that time was officially one of neutrality.

Pollaky continues: 'With the exception of my man in Liverpool whom I shall now soon recall unless I hear from you Speedily nothing is and can be done as we have no funds.' Towards the end of the letter he cannot help returning to this matter:

If You think fit I will continue my surveillance until You are in receipt of an answer from Washington, which will settle any further question – but You must remit funds and remain in constant direct Communication with me as Mr M— appears to be dans l'embaras [sic], what to do, even in the case that something good turns up. [Dans l'embarras: embarrassed.]

Finally, he writes that Sanford's presence 'for a few days only would be highly beneficial'.

HSS.139.14.7.Pollaky to Sanford

A description of the departure of the CSS *Thomas Watson* from England. She would be captured by the USS *Roanoke* off Charleston, South Carolina on 15 Oct 1861:

Monday, 26 8.30 p.m. [August]

In my last Report I stated that the Thomas Watson's Hatches had not been off from the time of her taking a bath alongside the Dock Quay. I knew from her appearance that she could not have room for much more cargo than what she already had aboard which was said to be a cargo of Salt − I ascertained today that she has not only Salt but a quantity of fire arms she has also a long gun covered over in her poop cabin in readiness to be run out in the quarter Deck for use when required, and also another brass gun under Hatches. I had scarcely ascertained this when I observed preparations being made to take her out of Dock and at high water this day, she was towed out into the River (quite unexpectedly as I heard the Dockmaster remark)

She had scarce cleared the Dock when she hoisted an immense Confederate Flag, and was towed up the River purposly [sic] to Display the Flag to the 'Northeners' [sic] she then returned down the River and altho' I ascertained that a Magazine boat was to meet her with a large quantity of powder, this did not occur this side of the 'Rock Light' which having rounded, I lost Sight of her, and have since heard that she received the powder and proceeded on her way to Charleston.

Description

The Thomas Watson is 367 Tons Shippers (Mess Fraser Trukholm [Trenholm] Co. Capt. Allen. She is ship rigged Hull black − Quarterdeck topsides white, with white painted nettings round poop Rails and taffrail lower masts bright, yards black figure head the bust of a man coat painted blue she has a large gilt eagle on stern and masts very taut.

HSS. 139. 14. 8.   Pollaky to Sanford

30 August '61 [Friday]

Sir !

The Princess Royal will not be ready for loading for another 8 or 10 days. Capt D. has returned from Glasgow to Liverpool, he visited yesterday the Glasgow Steamer 'Ostrich' in company with 3 other gentlemen and remained on board one hour and half.

Mr Morse got ill and is now laid up in bed[.] Your presence here is very urgent indeed −

HSS. 139. 14. 9.   Pollaky to Sanford

'10/Sept 61' [Tuesday]

Pollaky had received notice that Sanford would arrive in London, but since he himself had to leave and didn't want to miss him, he asked for details of date and time. He also reported that, 'Informations of the greatest moment have reached us concerning a wide spread Conspiracy in the State of <u>New York</u>.'

HSS.139.14.10.   *Pollaky to Sanford*

21 Sept 61 [Saturday]

Sir

Please hasten Your arrival here as much <u>as You possibly can</u> otherwise the interest of the U.S. Government might be greatly Compromised[.]

Was he being melodramatic? We know that he liked to be considered important, and that he needed to be seen to be providing vital intelligence. Was he just doing his job? Why did he not include his information with his letter? Was it truly so sensitive that he felt it could not be risked, or was it a ploy to make certain he was paid?

HSS.139.14.11.   *Pollaky to Sanford*

'Monday Sept 23rd 1861'

This letter, almost unreadable, so scrawled and faded is the handwriting, is a description of Pollaky on stake-out with a detailed timetable of his activities. It was sent from his new office address in George Street. Since this office didn't officially open until 1 January 1862, he was evidently already making preparations to remove himself from Field's office.

9 a.m. – he went on standby.

10 a.m. – a hansom cab arrived at 58 Jermyn Street. A tall dark man with a brush moustache got out. He and 'Captain B'. went to Campbells Army Contractors opposite.

11.50a.m. – they went back to number 58. and stayed there for five minutes.

Pollaky managed to speak to the cabman, who told him from where he had brought the first man. 'Captain B.' [Bulloch] then went away in another cab, but Pollaky could not follow as there was too much traffic. No conclusion is drawn from these movements, but it is significant that a few years later, Pollaky, tired of these types of activities, would employ others to do this tedious sort of work for him. The letter is signed 'Mephisto', one of the noms de plume Pollaky used in this correspondence.

He was working efficiently, so his subsequent treatment by Sanford and his associates seems a little unfair. He certainly thought so, but, of course, Sanford had to look after the bigger picture, and was not concerned with details. It nevertheless remains that Pollaky found it very hard to obtain payment for his services, and that his not unreasonable expectations were met with criticism by Sanford's associates who presumably felt that Pollaky should donate his time to the well-being of the United States of America gratis.

HSS.139.14.12. *Pollaky to Sanford*

Tuesday, 24 Sept '61

[…] The Surveillance is now established whole & everywhere[.]
The Postman will furnish daily the names of towns and dates of the letters which B. receives for which I promised 1£ per week.
This is of the greatest importance as You will perceive[.]

He notes that the *Thomas Watson* had been captured.

This suborning of the postman, for it was not legal for him to supply to Pollaky the information he wanted, shines only a small light on the methods involved in espionage. That the postman was corrupt, happy to receive his £1 a week does not excuse the corruptor. We can never truly know the lengths to which Pollaky was prepared to go in order to solve any of the cases with which he was involved. Instead, we have newspaper reports and the correspondence he sent to others to show us brief glimpses into his world.

HSS.139.14.13. *Pollaky to Sanford*

Sept '61

Messrs Isaac and Campbell the Army and Navy contractors 71 Jermyn Street have since 3 months been exclusively engaged to execute the ordrs [*sic*] for the South.

HSS.139.14.14. *Pollaky to Sanford*

Tuesday, 24 Sept '61
6.p.m.

Re Bullock [*sic*]

Arrived on duty at 8 o'clock this morning saw the Postman, who delivered a letter with the margate postmark, I gave him a half crown for the promises to keep me informed of the places from whence Capt B.'s letters arrive. at ½ past 10 p.m. B. came out and posted a letter in St. James's St. returned to 58 Jermyn St. Shortly afterwards a gentleman tall with black head and moustache drove up in a Cab 3560, entered remained up to ½ past 3 oc. B. went oposite [*sic*] to the Army & Navy Contractors Mess Campbell carrying a Sword in a black patent leather Case; remained there one hour and went afterwards to 15 Half moon St. where Yancy resides. Came out at 6 o'clock accompanied by Lt. Hughes B. returned to his residence, lighted his gas drew the blinds and did not come out again at 9 pm when I left – (Mephisto)

HSS. 139. 14. 15.   Pollaky to Sanford

Friday 27 Sept 1861

A brisk report detailing Bulloch's visit to Euston Square to ask after the arrival of cases of rifles that he was expecting.

HSS. 139. 14. 16.   Pollaky to Sanford

Pollaky had been asked to find a ship for Sanford, and had managed to find one.

Margate the 28 Sept 61 [Saturday]

According to Your intentions [...] I have looked out for you New Steamer suitable for the purpose for which You want them. [...] The Capt Mr H. is a man who will not stick at trifles. You understand as long as it pays well. He also expects to find the Crew trustworthy fellows, in fact he takes all the responsibility and will thro if necessary all life [sic] Stock overBoard –

Not certain of Sanford's commitment, he adds:

Be good enough to let me know if You intend to carry onto that Steamer [...] if so, I engage myself it shall go on properly an in a manner to give You satisfaction – I must give the Capt an answer within 8 days –

Captain H. does not come over as the nicest individual one could hope to meet, and what he meant by 'trustworthy fellows' when he described his crew, one can only imagine:

HSS. 139.14.17.   Pollaky to Sanford

Saturday, 28 Sept'61

Commenced watching at 7.40 a/m at 58 Jermyn St Piccadilly. Postman delivered 2 letters for Major Anderson one for Major Gore (all from Liverpool) Major Gore is as I learned only lately arrived in England. ½ past 9 Saw Gentl go to 58. White hat, mourning band on hat, light cape [...] and moustache also black beard, remained in about 10 minutes; went across to Messrs Isaacs & Campbells the Army & Navy Outfitters (I have not seen this man before). Major Anderson, Major Gore, Capt Blackley, Capt Huse & Lieut Hughes, went then all together to 15 Half Moon St and being joined by Yancy went to the Bath Hotel.

And so it continues – details of the watch being kept, but nothing of significance to report. Pollaky, undeterred by this, finishes with his intention of watching out for the ship *Princess Royal* and for Captain B. It is worth mentioning that Pollaky often refers to Captain B.; this could mean Bulloch or Blakely, but it is not always obvious from the context which man he was referring to.

HSS. 139.13.19. *Pollaky to Sanford*

'Sunday 29th, Monday 30th' [September 1861] A report about Bulloch. Pollaky had watched his place of residence in London for these two days and saw the arrivals of Major Anderson and Captain Blakely. The postman delivered a number of letters on the second day. Since Pollaky had managed to get the postman on his side he was able to ascertain that the letters were for Major Anderson, Captain Huse and Mr 'Weybrow', the last name, he thought, was Bulloch's newly adopted code name, however, the appearance in the next letter of a Mr Whybrow puts paid to that theory. The letters were from Paris, Liverpool and York.

All these gentlemen went out to perform their various tasks. Pollaky followed Bulloch who went to Isaacs & Campbells, the Army & Navy contractors, and stayed there for 30 minutes. The Confederates were now using Pickfords the removal firm to move military stores to railway stations so that they could get to the ships that would carry them to America.

Pollaky, declaring himself in this letter to be 'fully awake to the business', was supplying important information in his usual meticulous fashion, sincere in his desire to do the right thing and to be seen to be doing the right thing. From newspaper reports later in the same decade, and from his own actions, there is no doubt that he believed in the rights of the individual. In 1858, Abraham Lincoln had already spoken against slavery. What would be more natural than Pollaky supporting the Federal States of America in the struggle, albeit for payment. It is surely inconceivable that he would have agreed to support the Confederate side, knowing their support for slavery.

HSS. 139.14.18. *Pollaky to Sanford*

October 1th [sic] [Tuesday]

Re Bullock
Commenced duty 8a/m in the morning saw Postman deliver letters:

2 Capt Huse (Liverpool)

1 Mr. WhyBrow (York)

2 Major Anderson (Liverpool)

1 Mrs Brown in care of Major Anderson (Liverpool)

Capt Blackley & Huse went into Campbells Mr WhyBrow came out and went down James St.

Bullock & Lieut Hughes went afterwards into Campbells with a rifle covered with green baize and went back again with it to 58.

Porter came out in the afternoon hired 3 Cabs:

Hansom Cab 10324

4 Wheeler 11378

Dtto 1168

loaded the luggage – Blackley & Hughes went off[.] I followed them to the Euston Square Station and saw them label their luggage and start for Liverpool. I did not follow as my instructions are solely to follow Bullock – and simply watch the others – I returned to Jermyn St and remained there until 6 o'clock when relieved […]

Mephisto

This report continues on another sheet marked 'Confidentielle':

From information I received I determined to watch the Premises of Mss Campbell myself tonight – at ½ past 8 a van of Mss Pickford No 269 drove to the Warehouse and loaded 15 cases military stores. I suppose they contain parts of Rifles without the wooden parts, they are square boxes marked on the sides A.E.B on the top W_D they weighed very heavy – I followed the van to Vine St. Depot and assertained [sic] they are to go to Greenock in Scotland – This is all I could learn[.]

Pollaky speculates in this letter on the probable intention of the Confederates to ship the rifles from Greenock across the Atlantic Ocean. However, his information led him to conclude that at that time they would find it hard to get a ship. He ends his letter on a familiar tone:

I am still without a single line from You not knowing what may have become of my Rpts.

Major Edward C. Anderson kept a diary (now held at the Southern Historical Collection at the Louis Round Wilson Special Collections Library, University of

North Carolina). This includes an entry made in his most informative, articulate and amusing style. Dated early October 1861 (either 1st or 2nd – Anderson muddled the dates and days that week), although it does not refer to Pollaky, it does show the sort of pressure that the Confederates were being put under. He writes of how he was watched everywhere he went by private detectives. One in particular had followed him doggedly that day. At first the man was dressed 'in a neat suit of black clothes, dark hat, stand up collar, frock coat & heavy walking shoes', but later the same day, as Anderson bought a railway ticket, he noticed the same detective, who had 'completely metamorphosed himself'. He was now wearing a shiny white beaver hat, had turned down his shirt collar, and had glued onto his face, 'a jaunty little black mustache & goatee'. Anderson describes how he confronted the detective who was most discomfited at having been rumbled. Later that day he discovered that another detective had replaced the first, boarding the train to Liverpool which Anderson had taken while it stopped at Rugby. Anderson was able to name both men. The first was called Brett, and the second McGuire.

These were not Pollaky's detectives. Dublin-born private detective Matthew Maguire had been hired by Adams and Morse and this would later be approved by Thomas Haines Dudley, the Liverpool based US Consul who arrived in England in November 1861. Anderson, who evidently had a great sense of humour and allowed himself the luxury of a bit of teasing of the first detective, had this to say: 'Mr McGuire was an ugly, red headed villain whose faculties were by no means so acute as those of his metropolitan brother [Brett], and whose propensities for gazing innocently into the sky were remarkable. I used to stand near him on the pavement of the Hotel and admire his efforts to look unconcerned. Upon one occasion he followed me to Mr Crowders quarters and went fast asleep on the stoop.'

HSS.139.14.19. *Pollaky to Sanford*

'Liverpool 3th [*sic*] October '61' [Thursday]
This letter marked 'Strictly Private' has much that is hard to decipher owing to the condition of the document. Pollaky implies that Sanford is not telling him exactly what he wants him to do, despite their arrangement to the contrary. Nevertheless, he continues to receive information about the cases of rifles which are still in Greenock.

HSS.139.14.21. *Pollaky to Sanford*

A short report from one of Pollaky's agents. The information is about the origins of a number of letters received by some of the Confederates (from Yorkshire and Liverpool), and the movements of some of them during the day. The agent (G.Grub) was on watch from 8 a.m. until 5 p.m:

                                                    Oct 7, 1861 [Monday]
Saw Postman at 8 oclock. morning Deliver Letter at No 58 Jermyn St St James St. Piccadilly

Captain Huss [Huse]	1 Liverpool	1 York
Major Gore 2	" 1 ScarBrough [sic]	
"	1 Selby, Yorkshire	

Monday, 7th October 1861 arived [sic] at Jermyn St St James St. Piccadilly at 8 oclock morning saw Postman deliver Letters at 58 Jermyn St

Major Gore	2 Liverpool	Captain Huss
"	1 Selby	1 Selby
	1 Hull Yorkshire	1 Liverpool

Mr WhyBrow 2 Selby, 1 York, 1 Scarbrough [sic]

11 am Saw Major Gore and Mr WhyBrow go into park by Piccadilly: 12 saw Captn Huss go into 58 Jermyn St. Left at 12/30 for dinner returned at 2 oclock. remained till 5 pm. saw nothing of any account after 2 oclock − G.Grub −

HSS.139.13.3.   *Pollaky to Sanford*

                              'London Tuesday' [Possibly 9 October 1861]
Pollaky addresses Sanford as 'Dear Sanford', the only letter in which he does so. He wrote from London, but was about to carry out some investigations in Liverpool, where the *Princess Royal* was berthed. He asks Sanford to urge Morse to arrange for him to have 'the party political weight to back up my representation, & secure attention'. Pollaky signs the letter:

I am very hastily Yrs devotedly Vidocq I.

This is an in-joke – the real and famous French detective Eugène François Vidocq had died in 1857 (the 'I' is for Ignatius). There is a postscript:

a letter directed to the care of the Consul will reach me at Liverpool – dont emasculate your <u>dispatch</u>[.] P. told me he had heard that 20,000 guns were [sic] arrived being for shipment to America – at Hamburg[.]

HSS.139.13.4.   *Pollaky to Sanford*

                                    [Undated – Possibly October 1861]
Pollaky writes hurriedly as he is busy establishing his surveillance, and appointing his agents. The *Princess Royal* had unloaded her cargo.

HSS.139.14.22. X to Pollaky

'Liverpool 10th Oct' [1861 – Thursday]

A brief note untidily signed 'X' reporting the departure for the Southern States of a ship called the *Cheshire*. Who was X? We may never know.

HSS.139.14.23. Pollaky to Sanford

'10th Oct. 61' [Thursday]

Pollaky reports that he has placed a man to watch the premises of Moses Brothers in Leadenhall Street. He again complains that he has had no letters from Sanford (whose communication skills are evidently appalling) and hopes that Sanford has actually received his reports.

∽

In the meantime, Pollaky received a report from one of his agents, Ed Brennan, who had discovered that a fast steamer, the *Fingal*, was preparing to leave Greenock for America. The *Fingal*, which Bulloch had bought in September, was built in Glasgow by James and George Thompson in the Clyde Bank Iron Shipyard in 1861. After being loaded with the ordnance bought by Bulloch, it left Greenock on 10 October carrying supplies to the Confederate States. Brennan had written to Pollaky that day, and reported that he had not seen Bulloch or his friends, and doubted they had gone into the ship, 'unless they boarded her at dead of night'. He enclosed a sketch of the *Fingal*, mentioning that she carried a cargo worth several thousand pounds.

In fact, the *Fingal* travelled by a devious course to Holyhead where Bulloch boarded and took command on 15 October. His plan seems to have been to take her to America in British colours so as to evade any Union ships that might try to stop her. After an eventful voyage, which included a collision with a brig (the *Siccardi*), almost running out of water, an attempt by the US Consul in Bermuda to sabotage the mission while the *Fingal* was anchored there, as well as almost running aground, the *Fingal* arrived in Savannah on 14 November. It had successfully evaded the blockade that had been put in place by the Union forces. The cargo included a huge amount of weaponry, uniforms, and material for making more.

Bulloch wrote in his book *The Secret Service of the Confederate States in Europe or, How the Confederate Cruisers Were Equipped* (Volume 1, 1884) that, 'No single ship ever took into the Confederacy a cargo so entirely composed of military and naval supplies', and that his operations 'were greatly helped by the generous assistance of Messrs. Fraser, Trenholm and Co.' Of the difficulties he and his associates faced he wrote, 'It was necessary to act with caution and secrecy, because the impression had already got abroad that the Confederate Government was trying to fit out ships in England to cruise against American commerce, and during the whole period of the war all vessels taking arms on board, or cases supposed to contain arms or ammunition, were closely watched by agents and spies of the United States Consuls.' He remained with the *Fingal* until the middle of January 1862, and then returned to England, arriving in Liverpool on 3 March, to carry on with his work there. The 1891 English census lists Bulloch, who by that time had become a naturalised British subject, as a 'Retired Naval Officer'. His half-sister would become the mother of President Theodore Roosevelt.

Once in the Confederacy, the *Fingal* was converted into an ironclad vessel and renamed the CSS *Atlanta*. In 1863, the cumbersome and overweight *Atlanta* was captured by the USS *Weehawken*, and became part of the Union fleet.

HSS.139.14.24.   Pollaky to Sanford

'<u>Private</u> to Mr.S. "London 11th October 1861"' [Friday] This is a longer and more detailed report into the movements of the *Fingal* which had now departed British shores. Pollaky reports that he had given a full descriptive sketch of the ship to Morse who would be sending it to the United States. Bullock and other Confederate agents were busy inspecting and buying rifles; Pollaky now knew all the channels towards their ultimate destinations.

An important paragraph includes the information that the Confederates now knew they were being watched – 'Captain M. said that he cannot move a step without a detective on his heels' – and that their telegrams were being interfered with:

> This later assertion is not mere suposition [*sic*] of M … '<u>vous comprenez</u>' It is impossible my dear sir to watch a house unfortunately so situated like B. for 3½ months without attracting some notice in such a neighbourhood.
>
> You may rely on me – nothing will be left undone to secure success – I told You that I don't work in this matter for money but for an ultimate consideration – I assure You that the money I receive is in all insufficient for the work in hand; but I make it do the best I can.

Nevertheless, money, or the lack of it being forthcoming did trouble him, though it was like Pollaky to have nobler considerations in his mind – or at least to say that he did, which may amount to the same thing.

From this letter, we may gather that Sanford had communicated with Pollaky on the matter of Moses Brothers, as he writes, 'Your directions as to Moses Brothers are attended to.' Pollaky seems to have had an agent infiltrating the Confederate circle, as he mentions that his 'Literary Man' had been reporting on matters told him by Yancey.

My Literary Man is going slowly ahead in fact he has made no progress – as I believe only half I see and ¼ I hear I take his Reports as what they are worth trash. There is no evidence to prove their 'correctness nor do I see the immense importance of what Yancy may ungardedly [*sic*] say to him'.

We note Pollaky's characterful English: 'I take his Reports as what they are worth trash', and smile, but it does make one wonder about how he decided who to recruit.

HSS.139.13.11. Pollaky to Sanford

12th Saturday [October 1861]
Watched Moses Brothers premises 58–59 Leadenhall St. but nothing has arrived since Thursday worth noticing.

At this time in his career, Pollaky was actively engaged on the stake-outs himself, despite employing agents to work for him. This would change by 1875. Pollaky writes that Moses Brothers had been receiving rifles, and then sending them to Chatham, Kent. At 4 p.m. he added, 'We have now secured a clerk in the employ of Mrss Isaac & Campbells the Army & Navy Contractors.'

HSS.139.14.25. Pollaky to Sanford

'14 Oct. 61' [Monday]
Pollaky enclosed a copy of the official cargo list of the *Fingal*, writing, 'the source is <u>most reliable</u> and every Item is <u>correct and beyond a shadow of doubt</u>.'
The quantities were evidently huge and consisted of almost all of Bulloch's purchases made while in England. It also seemed that the Confederates were hoping to be recognised by the French government.

HSS.139.13.10. Pollaky to Sanford

Dated 'Oct 15, 1861' [Tuesday] by the Archivist.
Pollaky had that day received reports from his agents in Hartlepool, Stockton-on-Tees, and Scarborough, but they contained no useful information. He writes that, 'from Liverpool we hear of large quantities of blankets being stored up', and that rifles are, 'being manufactured in Glasgow for the South.' A number of Confederate agents were becoming very active. Pollaky enclosed a newspaper clipping with this letter, probably from the *Liverpool Times*:

RIFLED CANNON FOR THE STATES. – It is asserted that 'several shiploads' of Captain Blakely's rifled cannon have been recently shipped for the American States – North and South.

The 'several shiploads' must be an exaggeration, but if the American papers are to be believed, there can be little doubt that the Federal army, at last, is supplied with a number of the Blakely guns. It is just possible too, that the rifled cannon that formed a portion of the terrible cargo of the *Fingall* [*sic*], which cleared so mysteriously, the other day, at Greenock for 'Madeira and the west coast of Africa', were specimens of Captain Blakely's destructive weapon.

HSS.139.14.26.   *Thomson to Pollaky*

Another rare communication from one of Pollaky's agents, James I. Thomson, and addressed to Pollaky at Devereux Court. This letter is written in several directions with lines of text crossing over each other, and bears the mysterious inscription: 'Peruana = for Valparíaso' on the reverse.

15/10/61

London 19 George Street Euston Square. NW.

Tuesday evening October 15th 1861.

Sir I arrived at Leadenhall street at 12.45 pm today, leaving at 4.pm.

I paid the greatest attention [to] the premises of Moses Bros as also the wharehouses [*sic*] of Messrs. Candler & Sons, but nothing transpired to give me a clue of any kind.

Messrs. Candler & Sons are (I presume you are aware of the fact) 'beer merchants', but opposite to theirs are the premises of Messrs. Single & Jacobs, Bonded Carmen, who appear extensively Connected.

I attend again tomorrow at mid-day. My fee will be 4/ [4 shillings] per diem, including all minor incidental expenses.

I am Sir

Faithfully Yrs.

James I. Thomson

HSS.139.14.27.   *Pollaky to Sanford*

'London 15th Oct 61.'

Pollaky in a hastily written letter reports on the movements of various ships, in particular the *Princess Royal* that departed for Rotterdam. He offered to go there himself in the event that Sanford was alone, and again requested an interview with Sandford.

HSS.139.14.28.   *Pollaky to Sanford*

'18th Oct 61.' [Friday]

Now preparing to keep a close watch on the north-east coast of England, Pollaky reports further on ship movements, and also warns that Yancey, now in Paris, had written to Bulloch that he was making good headway. Bulloch, however, was already on the *Fingal*, en route for America.

HSS.139.14.29.   *Pollaky to Sanford*

London 19th Oct 61. [Saturday]

By enclosed Rpt You will see that 'they are at it again' large quantities of Rifles are deposited at Billiter St. previous their being shipped – They dont give us 'breathing time' and are at it day & night –

Surveillance had become very difficult as the Confederates were aware they were being spied upon. Pollaky still hoped for communication from Sanford:

I am without a letter from You & I hope you will excuse me in referring after to this but I would consider it a personal favour if You could only find time enough for one line to say You receive my letters, as it would do away with caution which I must otherwise necessarly [*sic*] use in my leters [*sic*].

HSS.139.13.2.   *Pollaky to Sanford*

[Undated – Possibly October 1861]

Pollaky reports that a Mr E.N. was trying to buy 120,000 metres of cloth, presumably for making army uniforms:

Mr E.N is still in Paris – he is bearer of letters of Credit on Rothschild of Paris & London and on Peabody amounting altogether to £300,000. He is trying to get at once in England 80,000 meters of Blue army Cloth & 40,000 meters of Blue Grey army Cloth – he offers to give orders intending for a period of 3 months the deliveries to be made monthly – I have not been able yet to ascertain the prices he pays, but shall know it in a few days – If he orders these goods delivered in London, Southampton or Liverpool.

He sent yesterday a dispatch to a friend of his whom I am acquainted with, calling him to Paris – That gentleman left by the mail train last night to return on Friday morning to London. I shall then know the purpose of that journey & will inform you without any delay.

HSS.139.14.30.   *Pollaky to Sanford*

'20th Oct 61.' [Sunday]

Having received two letters from Sanford, and feeling that he was therefore empowered to continue his surveillance, Pollaky wrote detailing more rifle acquisitions. He gives more information about ship movements, and also mentions that Brennan, 'who was so fortunate about the *Fingal*' will proceed to Scarborough and Hartlepool in search of a steamer said to be fitting out there.

HSS.139.14.31.   *Pollaky to Sanford*

'25th October 61' [Friday]

Pollaky used headed writing paper for this letter – not his own, however, but headed 'Mansion House, Justice Rooms, London E.C.' below a crest with the Latin inscription *Domine Dirige Nos*. He did not use this as the header for his letter, however, but turned the paper upside down and wrote on it as if it were a piece of scrap paper.

He had travelled to Leeds on Wednesday 23 October, where he 'discovered a large quantity of blanquets [*sic*] ordered by the Southeners [*sic*] to be shipped in Liverpool', and the next day had gone to Hartlepool, where he had spent the whole day going around the harbour, but without making any discoveries. On Friday he travelled back to London where he discovered that Candler & Sons had received more cases of rifles. It was reported that Bulloch and others were in Liverpool, though in this last piece of information he must have been misinformed by his agent, since Bulloch was by then on the *Fingal* bound for America.

The letter includes his usual advice to Sanford that he should come to England as soon as possible so that they could meet. Pollaky offers to go himself to Ostende or Antwerp to meet Sanford there, should his original suggestion not be possible. Naturally, Sanford remained silent.

HSS.139.14.32.   *Pollaky to Sanford*

[Letter undated, but written on a Saturday at the end of October 1861]

Pollaky enclosed two substantial newspaper cuttings. The first, from a Saturday edition of the *Express* is entitled: 'POLITICAL ESPIONAGE IN LIVERPOOL', and describes in very negative terms the watch that was being kept on Confederate agents:

> For some time past one of the principal topics of conversation in Liverpool, both on 'Change and in private circles, has had relation to a system of political espionage and terrorism which has for some time been exercised in that town

in connexion with gentlemen supposed to be directly or indirectly connected with the Southern or secessionist States of North America. We have heard of one gentleman being constantly dogged by private 'detectives' for many months past. All visitors to his residence and place of business have been carefully scrutinised, and it is supposed that owing to 'information received' from Liverpool many persons, friends of the gentleman above alluded to, have been seized and searched, and in some cases imprisoned, immediately on their arrival at Boston and New York. *Employés*, it is said, have also, in some cases, been tampered with, and even the privacy of correspondence and of business affairs has been mysteriously violated. We have also heard of cases in which goods sent from Liverpool for shipment by 'suspected' firms have been watched from the manufacturing districts to the Liverpool dock quays, and in some instances, it is more than hinted that packages have been opened furtively *en route*, and their contents overhauled and noted. We do not, at present, feel justified in giving publicity to all the rumours which point to the authors of these proceedings, so foreign to English ideas of everything that is fair, honourable, and manly.

The second cutting, from the *Evening Star*, but originally from the *Manchester Examiner*, was reprinted by the *New York Times* (credited as being from the *Liverpool Mercury*). The original title was 'THE POLITICAL SPY SYSTEM IN LIVERPOOL'. The *New York Times*, perhaps surprisingly given its geographical position, entitled it: 'AMERICAN POLITICAL SPIES IN ENGLAND.; THE GRIEVANCE NOT TO BE BORNE.' It was printed in America on 16 November, but must have originally been written in October:

We heard the other day, upon excellent authority, that one of the members of an influential Liverpool firm is watched as systematically and tenaciously [as if] he were known to be hatching some infernal machi[ne] which would annihilate President Lincoln and his whole Cabinet at one blast. Ever a mysterious stranger, in the person of a 'private detective', is on his track. The gentleman cannot leave his office but this odious 'double' is seen shuffling about the doorway. Whether he walks, rides, or visits, he is sure at some turn to encounter the same tormenting and scrutinising gaze. Even at home he is not safe; for when he imagines himself snugly shrouded with his family and Penates, his demon may be noticed peering in at the window, or hovering about the threshold, until the victim re-appears once more to undergo the daily round of dogging and hunting until, as evening approaches, he is again 'earthed' at home. Nor is this all. It is reported that the domestics of the gentleman alluded to have been waylaid and questioned as to his habits and operations; while it is stated that, in his case, as in the case of other 'suspected' persons and firms, goods consigned from the manufacturing districts have been opened on their transit to Liverpool, inspected, and their contents duly noted and reported. In order to show the extent to which these proceedings are carried on, as well as their vindictive character, we may mention that several friends of the merchant in question, and others, have been reported as passengers by a particular steamer, and, on their arrival at New York and Boston, have been searched, and, in some instances, imprisoned. Where these things are known – and during the last few days they have been the theme of much remark in mercantile circles – they have excited general sur[pri]se and indignation.'

These items show the feelings of sympathy held by many in Britain for the Confederacy in its struggle for independence. In his covering letter, Pollaky writes to Sanford that by reading these articles, he will see the necessity for them to meet for discussion. He felt that it was impossible for his men (who were not all as cautious as he himself was) to watch the same person for three or four months, 'without being tumbled too [sic]'. He also includes the information that the Commissioner of Police has been advised anonymously of what was happening, and that he felt that, 'this officious individual will do something to get a slice of popularity'. This description, presumably of Sir Richard Mayne, forms a nice contrast with the deference he would be showing to that official in his letters only a few months later.

This letter will be returned to in Chapter 9, as it contains within it a mysterious paragraph concerning Pollaky's nationality. It continues with Pollaky's assurance that he will continue the task, together with a rare burst of literary expression:

I will fight until I receive Your Orders to withdraw, no matter what the consequences may be – But I am not by nature nor experience a Don Quixote, and will & cannot fight against Mills without a good object in view of –

He concludes:

Let me know if You please Your resolution I am too much a man of buisness [sic] not to take my share of risk where the bargain is good – but You will oblige me to be very plain with me on this subject[.]
Saturday.

HSS.139.14.33.   *Pollaky to Sanford*

'29th Oct.61' [Tuesday]
Having received some instructions from Sanford, Pollaky sent a man to Grimsby and Hartlepool to carry out surveillance in both places. He makes another request for Sanford to come to London so that matters would 'go more smoothly'.

HSS. 139.13.9.   Pollaky to Sanford

Pollaky complains that he has not received his weekly payment:

> 29th 61 [Probably Tuesday 29 October 1861]
>
> Mr. M. did not make his weekly payment to me on last monday (yesterday) in notifying the fact to You I must respectfully but peremptorly [*sic*] demand the keeping of the engagements entered into – As I have to pay my men for whose honesty and Labour I am made answerable if the men are not paid regularly they turn generally traitor.

This last matter shows how reliable, or not, his men were. We find out another reason for his dissatisfaction. It seems that 'Mr M.' (Morse) who was supposed to give Pollaky his money:

> has a fit of indigestion, and makes me go to his residence unnecessarly [*sic*] and sends Mrs. M. to confer with me !!!

Perhaps today we would call Pollaky's objection to having to deal with Mrs Morse instead of her husband sexist. Taken in its context, it reads like material for a novel by Dickens, and we may find a kind of wry amusement in Pollaky's indignant use of three exclamation marks underlined twice.

HSS. 139.14.34.   Pollaky to Sanford

Pollaky had found himself in an invidious position:

> 31 oct 61 [Thursday]
>
> I dont know how to conduct myself nor how to act under the difficulties which have arisen –
>
> I have seen Mr M. yesterday, he told me that he will write to You declining of any further being mixed up in this affair – He also paid me yesterday the weeks money due on Monday; but does not hold out any precise apearance [*sic*] for next week. It appears moreover that Mr Adams [unreadable] has had a conference with Mr M. about this affair.
>
> I again express my belief that Your immediate arrival here would settle & put the whole matter at rest and do away with any objectionable difficulty.

Aware of the other team of agents not only duplicating his work, but getting in his way, Pollaky felt that Sanford would be able best to sort out misunderstandings. Beneath the apparent politeness of this letter lurks restrained annoyance and, perhaps, sarcasm, for he was also now aware of who had employed them, and undoubtedly felt that Sanford knew of the situation too.

The letter ends with details of further Confederate supplies:

There arrived in Billiter St 70 Cases of Rifles yesterday. Large quantities of leather Belts Swords and Blankets were sent to the Great Northern Railway by Campbells & Co for shippment [sic] in a northern port [...]

HSS.139.13.7.   Pollaky to Sanford

The cataloguer of these letters has written brief headings on most of them. Many just read 'Surveillance'. The heading for this letter reads, 'Surveillance – Distressed over lack of Funds – Pollaky'.

> Ventnor [Isle of Wight] Saturday [November]

My dear Sir!

I was indeed astonished to receive a letter from You with the London Postmark; and I suppose You are in London altho' You did not send me Your adres [sic] –

I dont think I misunderstood Your directions –

I discontinued the personal surveillance – but I told You that I will follow B. to Portsmouth. I reported to You the result – I found that B received while in P. several letters from this place and I at once turned my path particularly as the order which he gave will precipitate his return to Southsea on Tuesday next[.] I do all for the best but with no means and with no prospect it is very hard working in such matters. You will be kind enough also to bear in mind that West Hartlepool and Grimsby entailed on me expenses which I was called upon to defray while the Surveillance was Kept up in all its vigour and that no good came of it was no fault of mine. I expect nothing but fairness – and I am sure You will not hesitate to accord me as much –

Please adress [sic] me poste restante at Southsea. I will be there on Tuesday or Wednesday next; and if you desire me to resume my work, I will return to London forthwith, and make arrangements according to the mode of working You think best under prevailing circumstances.

I have it from Mr King that Messrs Mason & Slidell arrived at the Havannah [sic] and will come to England in the ordinary Mail Packet from the Royal Mail Company at Southampton – How this tallies with Your information about letters received in England dispatched by them I cannot understand Yours truly Saturday

HSS.139.14.35.   Pollaky to Sanford

Even Sanford, it would seem, was now expressing doubts as to the advisability of continuing to employ Pollaky and his agents. Pollaky writes, in some confusion, that he is ignoring Sanford's decision as to the future and continuing to carry out surveillance:

> Friday 22th [*sic*] Nobr. 61
>
> Events have been following themselves so quickly, that I do not know where to begin and I still ignore Your decision as to the future; that I dont feel justified to express myself to [*sic*] freely in this Rapport [*sic*].
>
> I arrived at Southsea on Tuesday noon and in the afternoon I picked up BullocK & Yancy and a stranger at the Portland Hotel. They had a long Conference, after which Yancy and Stranger returned to London, & BullocK and myself went to Southampton, where we arrived at 10pm Tuesday.

The next day, he continues, Yancey and Bulloch had exchanged a number of telegrams, and later met with a correspondent from *The Times*. On Thursday morning at eight o'clock the Confederate ship *Nashville* had arrived at Southampton flying the Confederate flag. Pollaky fully expected that this would be reported in the press for all to see. On asking Morse what action he should take, Morse had replied that there was nothing to be done, and Pollaky writes of his disappointment at Morse's indifference.

This is most curious, since Bulloch was in Savannah, Georgia at the time. Pollaky introduces into this letter a Captain Barkley, who meets with the others. This was not a spelling mistake, as there was a Confederate agent of that name. Was Pollaky confusing the names Bulloch with Blakely (or Barkley)? It would seem unlike him to make an error of that sort. Perhaps he was not taking proper care because he felt resentful? The following sentence is telling:

> I am now out of my pocket about 15£ and will go no further. This is therefore virtually my last rapport [*sic*] unless You furnish the means for following up this buisness [*sic*].

But after writing this complaint, he makes it plain that he will continue his surveillance. This letter was written with clear handwriting but evidently at ever increasing speed. Pollaky's illegible signature at the end trails off, almost as if in angry disgust.

HSS. 139.13.5.   *Pollaky to Sanford*

Pollaky gives some information, but also complains that despite having written three letters since he had been sent to the Isle of Wight, he has had no response:

> 25th [November 1861?]
>
> No letter from You since Your [*sic*] sent to me to Ventnor. I have since Written 3 letters to You.

The Pacific Steamer is now loading guns and powder for the South she has been bought for 7500£ by B.

I cannot express my surprise of not hearing from You and I wish You to Know that we are doing absolutely nothing at present[.]

I am 16£ [sic] out of pocket expenses incurred by travelling[.]

Pollaky's oft repeated complaints of not being paid and not having his letters and reports acknowledged show these matters to have been a continuing thorn in his side. He felt that he had invested a lot of time and energy into this investigation, and was plainly annoyed by the disorganisation of his employers. Though trying to be polite so as not to antagonise them, the irritation he felt is obvious from the wording of his next letter:

HSS. 139. 13. 13.   Pollaky to Sanford

Pollaky complains to Sanford that he has received no letters from him, and therefore no instructions. He is still £15 out of pocket, and accuses Sanford of impoliteness:

26th [November 1861?]

No letters, it is certainly a strange way of doing a strange business – I dont find fault with Your not going further in this matter what I complain of, is of Your not telling me plainly Your intentions when last here – and on the contrary by encouraging me to make certain statements which I would not have made; if I had known Your true intentions. You even dont dismiss me with the common politeness in such matters. As I have informed You before I am out of pocket of 15£ – have I to lose them? or will you pay – ? I shall not insist if You decline – but will be more carefull [sic] in the future. Your 2 weeks are now long at end & still there is no answer.

The British authorities were keeping an eye on the proceedings of the Civil War in America. Although, in common with other European governments, the Confederacy was never officially recognised, there were still potential embarrassments between countries to be avoided, both financial and political. As early as 17 June 1861, Lord Somerset, First Lord of the Admiralty had written a letter to Lord John Russell, Foreign Secretary, expressing restrained concern:

I hear by a private letter from the consul at Brest that the French Admiral who is going to the North American station has received orders to salute the flag of the confederate states. We have given no such orders. If however this report be true, our admiral should not be left without orders on the subject. I believe that while we acknowledge the Southern states as belligerents, we are in no way bound to take the further step of saluting their flag. It may be desirable that we should however act in concert with the French and therefore you will perhaps inquire as to the orders given to the French Admiral.

On 27 November 1861, Major Anderson, by now back in America wrote from Savannah to Edmund Molyneux, British Consul at Savannah detailing in no uncertain terms the triumph of the *Fingal's* escape to America, even though:

> [...] the United States' Consuls through detectives employed for the purpose, discovered that she was taking on board munitions of war. This fact was immediately made public through the newspapers, and the ship was closely watched by the detectives sent from London and Liverpool by the American Consuls at those places.

This letter was deemed important enough to be published in the Confidential Cabinet Papers in a book entitled *Papers Relating to the Blockade of the Ports of the Confederate States,* although more probably for the information on the movements of the *Fingal* than for the carryings-on of the detectives. Both this book and Lord Somerset's letter are kept at the National Archives in Kew. As can be seen from Somerset's letter, the British Government was trying to appear unconcerned, trying to blend in with the crowd, so to speak, to appear neutral, though many sympathised with the Southern States and perhaps would have been more vocal if it hadn't been for the issue of slavery. On 8 November, however, Messrs Mason and Slidell, Confederate Commissioners to London, had been captured by a Union ship while they were en route to England and then imprisoned in Boston. It was no wonder then that Anderson might feel the need to write his letter in order to show that things were going well for the Confederacy. Mason and Slidell eventually arrived in England on 29 January 1862.

HSS. 139.14.36. *Pollaky to Sanford*

Still in some confusion as to whether he should continue his work or not, Pollaky wrote to Sanford with a little information, including the hint that he knew Sanford would not let him be out of pocket:

29th Nov. 61 [Friday]

Your letter dtd 27th at hand, you say You wrote to me few days ago, <u>I have received no letters from You</u> – 'You say when You saw me You gave me for fortnight wherewithal to proceed' – true, but Your ulterior Comunication [*sic*] contains the following sentence 'better luck next time' and other words implying that in following the track I was then on, You were satisfied and not likely to let me be out of pocket.

He quotes Sanford's words from a letter written to him, 'You are deserving great Credit for Your activity and intelligence', thus trying to prove it impossible for Sanford to say that he had not done his work properly. He finishes by indicating that if necessary he will make representations to the US Government in Washington. He later did so, but with no success.

That he was upset by the offhand treatment he was getting from Sanford and Morse may be deduced from his handwriting and the fluidity of the language he used as well as what he actually wrote. His signature is completely illegible.

HSS.139.13.15.   *Pollaky to Sanford*

Pollaky had received no reply from Sanford. Unable to withhold his bitterness, he nevertheless encourages Sanford to continue employing him, saying that he has more information (but not saying what that information is).

> Tuesday
>
> I wrote You a letter Friday last but up to this day <u>no</u> reply – Could I suspect the silence, as Your desire to break off the Correspondence I should no more trouble You and end the mater [*sic*] <u>a wiser man</u> – Knowing that American Diplomatists are the same as European – Promise when they require You, and a kick overboard after they have done with you. […]
>
> The feeling here is very warlike, and I think that the time is come for You to employ me rather than dispense with me –
>
> I have tolerable interresting [*sic*] information, my source I let You guess[.] Expecting Your reply[.]

After a carelessly scrawled initial as signature he writes the following postscript:

> I cannot wish more times may be troublesome but will meet You on any point in England or Continent You may desire[.]

One cannot help wondering why Pollaky did not feel that it would be better to cut his losses since everything was being made so difficult for him. But then it is necessary to reflect that he had a reputation at stake, as he was certainly already intending to start out on his own account, separating himself entirely from Field's office. The kudos that he must have expected from being employed by a government (not for the first time if he himself was to be believed) may have been enough to keep him doggedly following the same path as long as he could. When combined with his own self-pride and the fact that he was newly married and needed the work, one may understand his motives better.

HSS.139.14.37.   Pollaky to Sanford

This letter is quoted in full, and shows the depths of Pollaky's feelings:

15th Xbr 61 [Sunday]

Private
Always supposing that my frequent letters have been miscarried and that You therefore could not have answered them, I again adres [*sic*] You – Mr M. writes that he is ill and cannot see anyone. I have a very important communication to make to You but how can I write – if I cannot satisfy my mind that you receive my letters. Or is it possible that You do receive my letters and thro' them into the fire without answering them but than [*sic*] pray say so, in two words – 'don't write' and You may depend upon it I will trouble You no further.

   I cannot believe that You have forgotten all the lavishing promises held out to me – and now that I am 15£ out of my pocket turn away for that reason – This 15£ are spent in consequence of the 2th [*sic*] Grimsby & Hartlepool journey which was undertaken by Your peremptory orders.

   But I easily understand that in the present state of affairs You will not nor need not disquiet Yourself about a vanload more or less of Arms being shipped – neither is it in that direction that my information point.

   Let me know in what light I have to consider our relation, on or off.?
Yrs Sunday
   Should I receive no answer to this letter I will draw my own conclusion and try to reimbourse [sic] me the best I can.

Pollaky was by now thoroughly fed up with the treatment he had received from Sanford and Morse, and was determined to try another tack. On 27 January 1862, he went over Sanford's head and wrote directly to Seward:

WHSP   Pollaky to Seward

Private (Continental) Inquiry Office
14 George St. Mansion House
London 27th January 1862 [Monday]

Strictly Private & Confidential

Sir !

I beg to apologise for addressing You this but I do so in hope that You will give me a patient hearing – I shall not enter into details, and confine myself strictly to facts – I don't adress [*sic*] You as a stranger, since my former reports must have made You familiar with my name and handwriting.

This [*sic*] said Reports I sent to You through Mr. Morse here, and through Mr Sanford Your Ambassador in Belgium – The Reports signed Brennan will be still in Your possession relating to the 'Fingal' – 'Thomas Watson' 'Cheshire' I have worked hard for the interests of the Government of the United States.

It was me who traced BullocK Hughes Anderson BlacKley Yancy & Mann – I had a whole staff working admirably until the whole got wind into the english papers through the indiscretion and bad tact of Messrs Morse and Sanford, I gave way before the public outcry, and declined to go on further; now that the matter has blown over and the Confederates renew their worK with double energy, it would be desirable to begin the surveillance afresh – I am willing to do it by Your direction, under Your immediate guidance, without being compelled to confere [*sic*] with Mr. Morse who confers again with Mrs Morse, before giving a reply – As regards Mr. Sanford he is more of a Diplomat, but very impulsive and utterly unfit to direct such delicate manoevres – There is now arrived in England (Bristol) a Mr Muir who purchase[d] large quantities of gunpowder (100 Tons) with army Clothing and Apothecary wares, which will all be shipped via Havanna to some Southern ports. – The vessel will escape as did the Bermuda & Fingal – I gave Mr Morse timely information about the Bermud[a] and her Cargo, Mr Sanford at that time being in Italy with the Garibaldi business, and it is owing to Mr Morse that the Bermuda got away.

I offer my services, the past will be sufficient guarantie [*sic*] for my tact talent and sincerity, I enclose You a letter of Mr Sanford which will speak for itself – and will do away with the necessity of referring ~~with~~ to him about my Capabilities and will on the other hand enable You to employ me without the Knowledge of any other person in this Country – which would be the most practicable, sure, and in fact only mood and condition, under which I would undertake this most delicate and difficult task of surveillance as I do not know if this letter will ever reach Your hands I confine myself to what I have stated[.] Should you desire to utilise my services in this country in the direct manner

I have stated, it would be necessary to give me an adress [*sic*] <u>less conspicuous</u> than <u>Your name</u> under cover of which I may write to You with full confidence – Mr Morse by the direction of Mr Sanford paid me weeKly a considerable sum for the execution of said services – and it would therefore be advisable if You remit per '<u>BanKers order</u>' under my name the monies so required –

As I have ceased for the last 6 weeKs to worK in this affair it will therefore require that I should employ in the beginning more men than it would otherwise necessitate after the surveillance has been Kept up for some time –

I have great means at my disposal[.] You require them, and if You can afford to pay You will be well served. I speaK plain and will be glad to hear from You soon. Remit me 500 Dollars which will be sufficient for Strict Surveillance, and other incidental expenses <u>for 3 months</u> – <u>I will report to You weekly</u> not only about ships and blankets but something more interesting – which neither Mr. Adams nor Mr Morse nor Mr Sanford can furnish You with[.] I am Your obd Servant

<u>Ig. Pollaky</u>

He enclosed the letter written by Sanford to himself the previous year which he had already quoted back to Sanford the previous November, and annotated it at the foot of the page, 'Mr Sanford's own Handwriting to Mr Pollaky':

WHSP   *Sanford to Pollaky* [Sent on by Pollaky to Seward]

[August 1861 ?]

Dr Sir:

Yours of yesterday recd. It has good news & you are deserving of great credit for your activity & intelligence in the matter. I sent you yesterday name of London Agents of the Liege manufacturer Lemaire for B & Co, Moss Brothers & [?] A. Franklin [?]

Yours

Wednesday

Though he was hopeful that this letter would do the trick of maintaining his employment by hiring himself out directly to Seward, he did not yet want to cut all ties with Sanford in case Seward did not take the bait. He was somewhat naïve if he thought his blatant criticism of Sanford and Morse to Seward would further his prospects. Unable to refrain from further pressuring Seward, he sent another letter to him two days later:

WHSP   Pollaky to Seward

14 George St. Mansion House
London 29th January [1]862 [Wednesday]
Private

Sir !

Enclosed I respectfully beg to hand You, copy of a letter I received to day from the American Legation in this town.

I remitted yesterday into the hands of Mr Moran a communication adressed [*sic*] to You, with 2 enclosures[.] a. letter from Mr. Sanford to me, b. a paragraph from a ministerial paper. – I trust You will receive them in speed and Safety; and beg to say that it will be of the utmost importance no[w] that Messrs Mason & Slidell have arrived, to have an eye upon passing events here – all I require is money and a safe channel of Communication with You. Of course it would be the safest to communicate through Mr Adams. but I fear that Gentleman will object to it – as it is a great favour that he has agreed to forward this communication.

Hoping to hear from You by Return of post

Yours truly

Pollaky

[Postscript]

Mason & Slidell went yesterday evening to Yancy 31 Bury St. This morning Slidell leaves for Paris. Dr Holland who left here by the Fingal, and who was connected with the Honduras Railroad – had several interviews with Sanford at Morley's Hotel and it is through Holland that the whole affair of the Fingal was spoiled –

The above letter was written on 29 January. Pollaky sent it to the United States Legation in London, and received a letter of acknowledgement from Benjamin Moran who forwarded it to Seward in Washington DC where Seward received it on 13 February. Dr Henry Holland was, according to Bulloch's description, 'a spirited Texan who had served in the United States army during the Mexican War', who was 'requested to prepare a big medicine-chest and a case of surgical instruments to take with him'. How Dr Holland spoiled the affair of the Fingal is not clear.

HSS. 139. 14. 38.   Pollaky to Sanford

On Friday, 31 January 1862, the indefatigable Pollaky sent another letter to Sanford. Written on his own headed paper, now that he was established properly with his own business address, he still tried to maintain an interest in Sanford's activities by writing a brief letter indicating that there had been large preparations: '100 Tons of powder 30,000 Rifles, <u>10 privateers</u>'. As a postscript he writes, 'please remit that trifle (15£)'. But it was no good. Pollaky's association with Sanford was almost done.

HSS.139.13.6. *Pollaky to Sanford*

London Coffee House
Sunday

Yancy has returned. The Doctor has seen him this morning – Messrs Mason [&] Slidell are hourly expected at Liverpool – please to see me as soon as possible as many arrangements have to be made, as I intend to go to Liverpool tonight

WHSP *Pollaky to Seward*

Pollaky writes of a meeting between Slidell and Édouard Thouvenel, French Minister of Foreign Affairs with the intention of gaining the sympathies of the French Government. As a gesture of goodwill he gave Thouvenel a letter from the President of the Confederate States of America.

George St. Mansion House
London 11th Febry 62 [Tuesday]

<u>Private</u>
In an audience which Mr Thouvenel gave to Mr Slidell yesterday the question of the ineffective Blockade was freely discussed[.] Slidell handed to Thouvenel an authograph [*sic*] letter from Jeff. Davis.

I am informed that Mr. Thouvenel did no more than promise to lay the facts before the Emperor; but this said that the policy of the French Governemt [*sic*] will shape itself after that of England – with this they parted.

As You will see by the enclosed (which is in Mr Thouvene[l's] own handwriting, I could if You wish be of some service to You in that quarter. But I would require larger means than quoted in my first[.] Please return to me Mr Thouvene[l's] letter.

The english Gov. will now strictly adhere to the principle of '<u>non</u> <u>intervention</u>'
<u>Pollaky</u>

The following day, Pollaky wrote a letter to Seward which seems to show that he desperately needed to remain in charge of surveillance: perhaps for financial reasons after all he not only had a new business, but Mary Ann was now expecting their first child. He had undoubtedly felt that with work such as this, he could afford to start out on his own account, and for his business to fail so early was unthinkable.

The letter contains a half-hearted threat, indeed it amounts to attempted blackmail, and is a rare example of any shady dealings on Pollaky's part, another being the bribing of the postman mentioned above. He was playing a dangerous game. That it was out of character is shown by the evident agitation in his handwriting:

WHSP   Pollaky to Seward

12th February [1862 – Wednesday]

Private

I bg [*sic*] to enclose Your Excy the last Rpt from Bristol the news contained therein are authentical [*sic*] and it would be all to watch the weasels when they arrive at the American Coast[.]

I forwarded to You yesterday through Mr Miller the Dept agent a letter containing a communication with a letter from Mr Thouvenel Mr Sanford & Mr Morse – All I want is money enough to carry on the Surveillance, and I can assure You it will be done effectually, as I understand the work well [.] You will also perceive by Mr Morse Rpt that they are only Duplicates to my Repts, and that it is in my power to stop his supply of information at any time[.] My means at present are nil, and I have spent upwards o[f] 30£ out my own pocket besides 15£ Mr Morse owes me a balance of former service – but I have now nothing to do with him – I want to serve you honestly and energetically a why [?] the letter of Mr Sanford I had the honnor [*sic*] of sending to You in my Communication through Mr Adams, he expressed himself highly satisfied – but through incompatibilty [*sic*] of temper we could not agree, have I through this to be debarred from serving my adopted Country when I have the means and Capacity for doing so.

Hoping that ere this reaches You to have Your reply to former Communications
Yours
Pollaky

Whether his claim that he could easily spoil the surveillance by stopping the supply of Morse's information at source was taken seriously or not is hard to say. Pollaky seems to have regretted his rashness in sending this letter, and three days later sent another. More conciliatory in tone it gave advice and information, and praised Francis Adams, the US Ambassador:

WHSP   Pollaky to Seward

George St. Mansion House London
Saturday 15th Febry [1862]

Private

Strictly Confidential

I just receive [*sic*] the enclosed <u>Rpt</u> and I hasten to forward the same without delay as I can hardly save the post.

You will see the necessity of strictly watching the movements of this ports [*sic*].

There is now talk about Slidell having gained a strong friend in Prince Nap. and of the later [*sic*] accepting the propority [*sic*] of the crown of the Southern Confederacy – all this although freely spoken off [*sic*] is good informed society here lacks every evidence, and the [unreadable] of Prince Nap. who showed Slidell's letter to a friend expresses his Conviction to the contrary

There is a great deal of speculation in all this which is sold here to Morse and Sanford for ready Cash, but which is mere trash and not worthy of one moments consideration –

Mr. Adams here is a man of too good sound sense to attach the slightest value here to this <u>talk</u> and he is therefore little troubled by the number of Dollar Hunters which reap such rich harvest with Mr. Morse

Yours truly

Pollaky

This seems to be his last letter to Seward. He had one more try at raising Sanford's interest in March:

HSS. 139.14.39. *Pollaky to Sanford*

14 George Street
Mansion House
London 12th Ma[rch] 62

Pollaky wrote to Sanford that he had 'some nice bits of information'. He mentions a figure of £1,000, but it is unclear whether this is the value of goods he wishes to tell Sanford of, or whether it is the value of the information he has. If the latter, it would have been a simply enormous amount of money. He asked to meet Sanford, but no meeting was forthcoming. As late as 14 February 1862, Ed Brennan was still reporting to Pollaky, this time from Bristol where he had observed three ships, the *Robert Bruce,* the *Gambia,* and the *Windward* all apparently about to head for the Southern States and attempt to run the blockade. Pollaky forwarded this report, but it did him no good; his association with the American Civil War and the activities of the Confederate agents in London was at an end.

He had not been helped by the fact that even though Morse had been fully aware of his work, Morse and Adams had set up a rival surveillance operation, which had been spotted by the Confederates as early as September 1861. Sanford had not been pleased, particularly when he discovered that Morse and Adams had paid the other team the sum of £270 for the same information about the *Fingal* which had already been supplied by Pollaky; his lack of contact with Pollaky may have in part been due to embarrassment. Sanford himself had complained to William H. Seward, but to no effect. Indeed, Seward had written to Sanford as early as 4 November 1861 informing him that Morse should take charge of the surveillance using his own agents.

The war in America finally ended in 1865, but does not seem to have figured in Pollaky's life any further.

Perhaps the end of Pollaky's association with Sanford was just as well. He had found it very difficult, and it must have taken a huge amount of his time. In addition, Morse's oft-made excuses that he was ill and therefore couldn't communicate with (or pay) him must have seemed very suspicious. Pollaky had spent several nights away from his home and his new wife, and that must have created something of a strained atmosphere, particularly in the light of Mary Ann's condition. One can, however, understand his great anxiety over financial matters, especially if he was not being paid what was owed him. Now he would be free to concentrate on his private practice as an investigator. How successful this was we shall see.

7 Marriage Two

London in the 1860s was the grimy, dirty place of Victorian fame, rather than the beautiful city imagined by Dick Whittington. In 1860 work started on what would become London's underground railway. The first section opened on 9 January 1863, and ran from Paddington Station (already the London terminal for the Great Western Railway,) to Farringdon. Construction caused absolute devastation of the houses along its path. The atmosphere created by the steam trains made the air underground even worse than the air above. Life for a young family was hard, and infant mortality was high. The Pollakys would outlive all but two of their children.

It is hard to imagine how Pollaky maintained a satisfactory home life when he was first married to Mary Ann, bearing in mind how busy he was spying for Sanford. Perhaps it was because he *was* so busy that married life worked out well for him.

Their first child was, unfortunately, stillborn on 27 July 1862. They named her Lily and she was buried at the Kensal Green Cemetery in the family plot. Their next child, another daughter, Pauline (or Lena for short), was born the following year, but died in 1871 aged only eight. The cause of death was given as *scarlatina simplex* (scarlet fever) from which she had been suffering for twenty-three days. Mary Ennis, the children's governess was present at her death.

Altogether they had seven children, whose health must have caused great anxiety to their parents. Lily: stillborn in 1862, Pauline (Lena): 1863–71, Minna Mary Ann: 1864–99, Francis Hughes James: 1866–99, Rose Katherine: 1868–1934, Mabel Mary: 1869–1947, William Ernest: born early in 1872, died later that year aged 5 months. All but Lily and William Ernest were baptised (at St Saviours Church, Paddington). With a large family, the Pollaky's employed a live-in nurse for the children, German-born Marie Burke, 28 and married. Mary Ennis left the Pollaky's employment after Pauline's death.

On the records of his children's births, Pollaky is described variously as 'Continental Agent', 'Foreign Agent', or 'Gentleman'. He was very busy during the 1860s, and his work must have taken him away from home on numerous occasions, both in England and abroad. One can imagine the tired private detective arriving home after a long trip away, back to his own house with his study and his things, the paintings on the wall and the comforts of life to be faced by three or four small children eager to see their papa. Childhood illnesses giving concern to both father and mother, the stress of hard work and lack of appreciation from police officialdom, combined with the fun and scorn made in the press of him and his cases, may have made him irritable. Judging from what he later wrote in his will, though, his marriage seems to have been happy as well as long lasting.

There are no details of their married life together aside from the records of the births and deaths of their children. One might wonder whether Mary Ann cooked food in the English fashion for her husband or whether he had shown her how to cook in the Hungarian style. In 1861, Mrs Beeton's *Book of Household Management* was published. Might that have been a source for recipes, or had Mary Ann learned all that was necessary from her landlady mother? Eventually they were able to afford the services of a live-in cook. In 1871, the Pollakys had two servants living with them: Mary Burke, who doubled domestic duties with that of nurse, and Elizabeth Harbridge, aged 17, the housemaid. The census that year was taken on 2 April. Pauline had died a few weeks earlier on 27 February, which left four young children. The last to be born, William, would begin his short life a few months later. Mary Burke may have been present in the household for some time, and her life would have been a very busy one with four children aged between 2 and 7 to look after now that the oldest was no longer alive. William died suffering from diarrhoea, with a nurse, Louisa Fletcher, in attendance. The grieving parents had now lost three children.

The family lived at a number of addresses over the years. In 1862 they were living at 18 Maida Hill where their first five children were born; Pollaky's inquiry office was at 14 George Street. In December 1864 he would have heard the news that Henry Banister, the husband of his sister-in-law Laura from his first marriage, had died of *phthisis pulmonalis* (tuberculosis) while at work. Banister had been Superintendent of the Chartered Gas Company, Horseferry Road and had been suffering from tuberculosis for five years. It is a sign of those times that one so ill as to be at death's door was working at the gas works he supervised on the very day of his death.

Earlier in 1864 the Pollakys had moved into No. 9 Portsdown Road where Mabel and William Ernest were born and where Pauline died. Nearby, at No.10 Portsdown Road, lived artist John Tenniel, illustrator of *Alice's Adventures in Wonderland* and *Through the Looking-Glass and what Alice Found There*. It seems a shame that he did not draw Pollaky while there was a chance. Tenniel was a member of the congregation of St Saviour's Church, Paddington (donating £20 to the building fund), the same church in which the Pollaky children were baptised.

Meanwhile, Pollaky had been busy trying to improve his prospects by every possible means. Leaving no stone unturned in his efforts to gain influential friends, he became a Freemason, joining the Jerusalem Chapter (No.185). On 13 April 1869 he was appointed Second Assistant Sojourner, not a high rank by any means, at a Convocation which took place at Freemasons' Tavern in Great Queen Street and which was followed by a banquet. The event was reported in the *Era* on 18 April. He was mixing, though, with tradesmen who were not perhaps as influential as he would have liked: one was Adolphe Oberdoerffer, a tobacconist based in Regent Street who had recently become bankrupt, another was Abraham David Loewenstark, founder of a firm of masonic jewellers based near Lincoln's Inn who was wealthier but unlikely to further Pollaky's own career, which was probably the reason he had accepted membership.

The 1861 census shows the family of William Cook living at 13 Paddington Green. By 1871, the occupants were the family of James Bedding, boot maker. From 1863, Pollaky began renting a part of the house for use as his office, and newspapers from 1863 show that this was his business address. He indicated in 1862 that, as a foreigner, he was not entitled to purchase a freehold, but later the legal position must have changed, and his fortunes rise, as in 1872 he was able to buy the freehold. August 1872 finally saw the family in complete occupation of their new home, though the electoral register for 1873 still lists Pollaky at 9 Portsdown Road:

The Times – Tuesday, 27 August 1872
POLLAKY'S PRIVATE INQUIRY OFFICE, 13 Paddington-green. – The rebuilding of these premises being now completed, Mr Pollaky's RESIDENCE is REMOVED to that his sole address.

Records held in the City of Westminster Archives indicate that there were some problems with the drains at No. 13. If so, they were put right in 1871 by Thomas Thompson and Thomas Smith, builders and contractors of 13 Marylands Road, Harrow Road, Paddington the year before the Pollaky family moved there. However, though the builders certainly laid a new drain for the house, their official application for permission for the work indicates that they did considerably more than that, implying that the house was completely rebuilt sometime after October of that year. The 1884 sale advertisement appears in Chapter 11, in which one can read of Pollaky's evident pride in the house he was selling, mentioning, as it does, its three water closets and that 'the sanitary arrangements are of the most approved system', all a result of the work undertaken by Thompson and Smith. That house is now demolished as is the house at 18 Maida Hill (now renamed Maida Avenue); 9 Portsdown Road (now Randolph Avenue) still exists though.

Paddington, once a leafy village, was well known for its railway terminal and its police station. It must have been a convenient base for Pollaky's travels around London and the rest of England. In the 1850s, 13 Paddington Green had been the home of George W. Millichip, 'Omnibus Proprietor', and his family. Once Pollaky was installed there the house became famous (or notorious in the opinion of some) as the address of the best-known private investigator of his time.

The man himself found occasional outlets for his problem-solving skills in the *divertissements* supplied by puzzles in newspapers and journals. The 20 February 1875 edition of *Fun* named him as one of the solvers of the double acrostic which had appeared there two weeks earlier. Judging from the lack of news about him that month, business was slow, otherwise perhaps he would not have indulged in entering this competition.

By 1881 the Pollakys had as servants, a nurse Emily Smith who was 28; and a cook, Elizabeth Gwynne (or Gwynn) who was 24. With four children now aged between 12 and 17, we might wonder at the need for a nurse, and 24 seems young for a household cook, if we judge by television dramas of today, but that is how they are described on the census.

Some of the neighbours in Paddington Green were themselves an unusual collection of characters. Perhaps the most interesting was Richard Metcalfe who kept a 'hydropathic establishment' and Turkish bath at Nos 10 and 11. Metcalfe's establishment was called Priessnitz House, and he ran his business in Paddington Green from 1860 until after 1879. He was a force in establishing baths, wash houses and turkish baths for the working class, and wrote a book, *Sanitas Sanitatum et Omnia Sanitas* (1877) promoting this. Priessnitz House was named after Vincent Priessnitz, founder of hydropathy, now called hydrotherapy. Metcalfe wrote a biography of him in 1898. The comings and goings of clients at Metcalfe's establishment, evidently not one for the working classes, would certainly have added interest to the sights that might have greeted the Pollaky family as they went through their daily routines, which must have included walks for the children on the Green itself, since that plot of land was so conveniently placed.

Metcalfe lived on his business premises with his wife Lucy and son Frederick. The customers and boarders were all listed as either gentlemen or ladies; the ladies often brought their maids with them. Residents at No 12 Paddington Green, between the Pollaky and Metcalfe establishments did not stay there for as long as those two. They included the family of Jonathan Knight, a 'Whitesmith' (a worker in tin), and later of John J. Thomas a 'Wire Worker'.

Sir Richard Mayne

8

etween 1862 and 1863, Pollaky engaged in another highly dramatic and most frustrating one-sided correspondence, this time with the Metropolitan Police and in particular with Sir Richard Mayne, its Chief Commissioner. These letters involve his attempts firstly to be recognised by the police as one willing to assist them should they be in need of his skills, and secondly to gain official status as a British citizen. Although these matters are separate, there can be little doubt that Pollaky hoped that his proposed assistance to the police would help him in his attempt at gaining citizenship. The letters are held by the National Archives in Kew.

Sir Richard Mayne was almost 33-years-old when, in 1829, he became Joint Commissioner of the newly formed Metropolitan Police. The other commissioner, senior to Mayne was Lieutenant Colonel Charles Rowan. The two worked amicably together building the new force. Rowan retired in 1850 aged nearly 68, and Mayne became Chief Commissioner.

In 1829 Mayne wrote:

> The primary object of an efficient police is the prevention of crime: the next that of detection and punishment of offenders if crime is committed. To these ends all the efforts of police must be directed. The protection of life and property, the preservation of public tranquillity, and the absence of crime, will alone prove whether those efforts have been successful and whether the objects for which the police were appointed have been attained.

These words, from the first Metropolitan Police Instruction Book, show him as an idealist, one who must have felt that the newly established Metropolitan Police would be able to put an end to crime for good. His desire to make good these words led him to adopt an authoritarian manner that, with his background as a barrister (he was called to the bar in 1822), made him respected as one not to be trifled with.

On 21 January 1862, Pollaky sent the 'Prospectus' of his new inquiry office to Sir Richard Mayne. Mayne, now 65, would remain Commissioner for another six years. Known from the first for his harsh manner, he was by now a demanding and difficult man, and Pollaky probably regretted that he ever started writing to him.

The Prospectus reads:

<u>Private Continental Inquiry Office</u>

This office, established with the view of protecting the interests of the British public in its social, legal, and commercial relations with foreigners, etc will furnish prompt and reliable information of those residing in England or abroad. Solicitors through this agency will be enabled to serve writs or subpoenas on the continent at less expense; insurance offices will find at any time a special officer prepared to investigate cases of incendiarism abroad. The Private Continental Inquiry Office however will not undertake any cases which properly come within the preserves of the regular police authorities.

Translations from the German; French; Italian; and Spanish will be undertaken.

Letters to be addressed

I.P.Pollaky

14 George Street Mansion House E.C.

His covering letter is as ingratiating as it could possibly be:

21 January 1862

To Sir

Richard Mayne K.C.B.

Commissioner of Police

Sir!

I take the liberty to lay before You enclosed prospectus, and beg to state that it will always be my most earnest wish & desire to assist the Police in forwarding the ends of Justice (if Foreigners are concerned) My long stay in England and Knowledge of the localities and languages will sometimes powerfully assist the Detective Police.

Hoping that You will gracefully pardon me for intruding on Your valuable time I beg to remain Sir

Your most obd Servant

Ig.P.Pollaky

formerly in Mr. Field's office

How could Pollaky know that this communication would be met with as much disdain and metaphorical huffing and puffing as it did? Sir Richard Mayne on reading the contents of Pollaky's enclosure passed it to Inspector Detective Frederick Williamson with a very sniffy note dated 22 January 1862:

Is this person following the same course as on former occasions other Reports were made to this office[?] RM

Williamson replied the same day, writing below Mayne's query:

I beg to report that in December last the writer Ignatius Pollaky advertised stating that on 1st January his connexion with the office of Mr Field would cease, but he is now carrying on a similar kind of business at No.14 George Street, Mansion House.

As noted in Chapter 6, Pollaky had been preparing this new office since as early as September the previous year. It officially opened on 1 January 1862 though. Pollaky's hopes of advantageously placing himself with the official body the of Metropolitan Police as a private investigator, were already running into trouble less than a month later.

On 13 February 1862, Pollaky wrote to Sir Richard Mayne requesting an interview: 'i [sic] am desirous to aquaint [sic] You with certain circumstances which would be interesting to You.' Mayne acceded to this request and Pollaky visited him at his home at 2 p.m. the following afternoon. After the interview, Mayne wrote on the back of the letter:

I saw Mr Pollaky again this morning & he said he thought it unfair to himself & of no public advantage to appear as an accuser, but that he wd. at any time communicate to me any matters coming to his knowledge that he thought wd. be of interest to me[.]

On 15 March 1862, Pollaky wrote again to Mayne. He had, either during the course of his interview with Mayne the previous day, or else in another with Horatio Waddington, made a statement that he had been sent to Europe by the City (of London) Police. Feeling that he had been doubted, Pollaky enclosed a copy of a letter that had been written nearly two years earlier. It is a letter of introduction from the Consul General of the Swiss Confederation in London, John Rapp. This document handwritten in German in old script was translated into English by Pollaky himself. The original was evidently intended to recommend Pollaky to Jonas Furrer, first Swiss Federal President and Chief of the Department of Justice and Police in Bern, as the first line shows:

London, 5 February 1859

To the Councillor of the Federation Mr. Furrer President of the Deptmt of Justice and Police in Bern
Upon the request of the Chief Police Officer in this City I have the honnour [*sic*] to introduce to You by this letter Mr Ignatius Pollaky and to recomend [*sic*] him to Your best reception. You will greatly oblige me if You will assist him in his researches & inquiries with Your good advice & council

Thanking You beforehand for Your Kind attention to him I remain esteemfull [*sic*] & obd.
The Agent & Consul General of the Swiss Confederation

The original German text is signed 'John Rapp.' Pollaky writes beneath his translation:

Please to return the litographed [*sic*] copy as it is the only in existence –

Both the copy and Pollaky's translation were evidently not returned to him as he requested, as they are still held in the collection with the other letters in this series. Pollaky states that the City Police had requested to see a copy of this letter as a reference, and presumably hoped that if the reference was good enough for them, it would be good enough for Sir Richard Mayne.

In his covering letter, Pollaky mentions his work for the Americans, and states that he and Field were engaged in watching the shipping of guns. Thus providing confirmation of Field's involvement in that affair. He concludes:

I will strive to obtain Your good opinion, my intentions are honest and I would consider no sacrifice too great, to obtain Your favourable consideration of my personal honesty.
Permit me Sir Richard to express a hope that I may be useful to the police at the ensuing Exhibition; and if You would appoint me under the Inspector of the H Division I would deserve most fully Your trust.

The International Exhibition of 1862 took place in South Kensington from 1 May to 1 November. Pollaky may have attended, but not in an official capacity, and perhaps not with Mary Ann, who suffered a miscarriage in July, unless it was while she was heavily pregnant.

Pollaky, already making use of international connections, was known to advertise in the foreign press; his name appeared a number of times in Viennese newspapers – there were announcements of his having on at least three occasions in the late 1860s donated about 50 florins to the poor of Vienna. The International Exhibition of 1862 created an ideal opportunity to drum up some business, and one of the most interesting mentions of his name was in a paragraph which appeared on 27 May 1862 in *Der Vaterland*. This was a warning to visitors to the London Exhibition to be careful, in which he is referred to as 'Ignaz Pollaky, richtiger [correctly] Pollak'. Whether this correction of his surname was his own or someone else's is not made clear, but his first name is invariably spelled 'Ignaz' in the Austrian press.

A number of letters were sent from Pollaky to Mayne, and from Mayne to Waddington. Pollaky wrote a second letter on 15 March 1862. He had seen Field in a public house speaking to one Sergeant Robinson of the police. It is evident that Pollaky had some reason for keeping an eye on Field:

> Field treats me cooly and I suppose was informed of my interview with You yesterday.

The cooling of the friendship between Pollaky and Field was not surprising since the former had set up a rival business. Pollaky enclosed a letter from Nicholls, Fields business partner and eventual successor, the contents of which are unknown. Mayne then invited Nicholls for an interview, and asked Waddington if he should bring him over so that they could both speak with him.

On 17 March, Mayne wrote:

> Mr Waddington saw him [Nicholls] & heard what he had to say in reply to question relating to statement by Pollaky.

Pollaky heard of this meeting. It is hard at this distance in time, bearing in mind that the records are incomplete, to know exactly what the problem was. Pollaky seems to have taken it upon himself to investigate corruption in the City Police Force. On 21 March, he wrote a letter to Mayne:

> Sir!
> Enclosed I beg to remit a few facts, if the public would Know what is going on in the City Police, this imitation of the Continental Police would not be tolerated for a week.

Later in the letter:

> Mr. Nicholls has not had anything to say to me so that I stand in very bad odour with him.

Pollaky enclosed with this letter a report dated, 'London 21th March 1862':

Facts collected from Sergt May of the City Police who appears to day before the Police Comité

1. Sergt Russel C.D.P. went in company with an officer from Geneva after a man who run away [sic] with some property belonging to his creditors they found the man in Oxford St. A scuffle issued, and the watchs [sic] fell to the ground (which were picked up by the Geneva Officer ?) This foreigner who saw himself so attacked by strangers, went afterwards to Inspector Hobb (C. Division) and complained of being assaulted and robbed – Russel receiving 2£. Hamilton was promised a watch for this heroic exploit.
2. Sergt Webb C. DVs. was sent down to Southampton in Reference to the 'Nashville' the Mayor of Southampton inquired of Furnell the name of the officer (W) which he (F) declined to giving.
3. Sergt Webb takes a man a foreigner (who could not speak a word English) in the City Road 6 months ago. takes him to Mr Hamilton's Office, they then take all the money from him. Hamilton and Webb each retaining 20£. which they entered in the Gratuity Book after which the foreigner was sent about his business no charge was booked nor was the man brought up before the Magistrate[.]

The CSS *Nashville* was the first warship to fly the Confederate flag while in English waters. Pollaky at the time of this letter had just finished his association with Sanford.

Sir Richard Mayne, though, was already more than a little irritated with Pollaky. On 27 March he instructed Charles Yardley, Chief Clerk of the Commissioners of the Metropolitan Police to:

Write to Mr. Pollaky by my direction that if Sgt. May City Police has any information which it is proper shd. be made known to me request it may be put in writing.

Yardley did as he was directed and Pollaky evidently received this communication, but was not to be put off so easily. On 29 March he wrote another letter to Mayne telling of how:

Srgt Ed. Furnell C.D.J. apprehended yesterday a young man at 4 Newcastle Place Clerkenwell on a charge of Misdemeanour without a Warrant and brought the prisoner Phillipps up this day at the Mansion House, contrary to the Section which makes it compulsory to bring such prisoners up before the District Magistrate particularly as in this case property has been seized.

He also writes that he has received the letter from Mr Yardley, and, perhaps not realising the implication that Mayne wanted no further words on the matter, that he will get Sergeant May to write what he knows.

He concludes:

> I shall do my best; that anything which may come to my Knowledge in the City, which goes to the Direction which will serve to expose the manner in which the City Police discharge their duties. I shall always hasten to aquaint [*sic*] You of, and shall be most happy to be of any service.

There followed a most unusual letter to Mayne purporting to be from Sergeant Daniel May. May writes that he will write, 'a full statement in corroboration of the contents of Mr Pollaky's letters.' But the letter is on Pollaky's headed paper, and is evidently in Pollaky's own handwriting, though the signature might be May's.

In early April 1862, Pollaky tried again, giving further examples of petty corruption and also of nepotism within the City Police. Evidently trying to ingratiate himself with Sir Richard Mayne by giving him (as Chief Commissioner of the Metropolitan Police) information about what Pollaky hoped he would perceive as a rival force, he only added to Mayne's irritation:

1. The 12 police & Sergt of 26 Old Jewry pay to the Comissioner [*sic*] 25% or 5/- out of each pound they receive as gratuities. And it is now stated that the Comissioner [*sic*] has about 500£ of this monies [*sic*]
   The Inspector of detective Department does not however give his share of 5/- in the £.
2. Inspector Hamilton's son is in Stubbs' Trade protection office and all inquiris [*sic*] made in the Country for Stubbs are made through the City Police by the Country Police. Stubbs has also opened a branch in Paris and Stubbs' Clerks are in daily and hourly communication with the Detective Deptmt of the City Police –
3. The Comissioner [*sic*] Harvey's <u>Neveu</u> [*sic*]. is on the Police Pay Sheet as a Supernumerary received £1 p. week he is a lad between 17 and 18 years of age – and is commonly called Master Harvey

Later in the same letter:

> Although animated by the purest desire to serve You I am exposed to the grossest treatment from the detective officers in Scotland Yard which proves to me that all that passed between me and Yourself is well known to them, the following is an <u>illustration</u>

Last Thursday I returned to my office My Clerk told me that Mr. Thomas called. I supposed it was Sergt Thomas and took a cab to Scotland Yard. I then saw Thompson and asked if he knew that Thomas wants me, he said <u>no</u>. I then met Thomas on the Street near Leicester Sq. on Saturday when he grossly abused me for calling at Scotland Yard. And he said <u>I dont care for Sir Richard, he is nothing to me.</u> But all this will not make me abstain from acting as I do upon Public Grounds, as long as You consider my services of any good to You
I am Your truly
Ob Ser.
'Pollaky'

On 16 April, he wrote another letter of the same kind. It seems that there was much talk about misappropriation of police funds by an Inspector Mitchell of the City Police. Pollaky points out that though this would have resulted in instant dismissal in Mayne's Metropolitan Police, Mitchell was instead promoted:

If such a case would have occurred in the Metropolitan Police (everybody says) he would have been sumarly [*sic*] dismissed. [He] takes 25% of the 12 Detective Srgts of all their Gratuity Monies; which now amounts I am told to about 700£ without ever accounting for it, then it becomes a matter of wise discussion of the said Commissioner, not to be too hard on a Sinner.

He goes on to warn of demonstrations he has heard were being organised for the next visit to London of the Emperor of France:

Yesterday I heard from a person generally well informed in all such matters, that a Comité has formed itself here for the purpose of getting up demonstrations at the next visit of the Emperor of the French to London. I am willing to give up to You the name of the party, who is bye the bye or better <u>was</u> for a long time Honorary Secretary of the <u>Deutsches Vaterland here.</u>

He concludes:

Should you desire to see me I am at Your disposal at any time by day or night and You know I hope by this time it is not for the filthy lucre.

Pollaky trying even harder to prove his value, wrote yet another letter on 25 April to Mayne enclosing a paragraph from that day's *Times*. Ever hopeful, he writes, 'I hope You will not consider me too officious in intruding on Your valuable time.'

The enclosure concerned the police investigation of a murder and robbery in Holborn, London. The newspaper clipping ends with the following sentence which Pollaky highlighted with two crosses:

They [the jury at the inquest] also added that they desired the authorities should be made acquainted with the fact that the police had left the widow of the deceased for an entire week unacquainted with his condition, although from his pocketbook and papers they must have been aware of his address.

With this emphasis he evidently was trying to help the police improve their own image by making Mayne aware of what was being said. This itself would have probably been enough to annoy Mayne still further.

⏝

Having now irritated Sir Richard Mayne, who was not known for his tolerance of private investigators, with clumsy and tactless attempts to ingratiate himself, Pollaky tried to move forward with his life in a new way. This was something he must have been contemplating for some considerable time, but would cause him more trouble and anxiety than almost anything else in his professional or personal life; something which is inextricably bound up with his correspondence with Sir Richard Mayne, the Metropolitan Police Force, and Horatio Waddington, Permanent Under-Secretary of State to the Home Office.

On 29 April 1862, Ignatius Paul Pollaky went to the Mansion House in the City of London, and formally made his application for British Citizenship.

9 1862 Naturalisation Application — 'It would be monstrous'

On 3 May 1862, Pollaky's application for British nationality, written a few days earlier was formally received by the Home Office. He describes himself as having been born, 'at Presburg [*sic*] in the Empire of Austria in the Month of April One thousand Eight Hundred and Twenty Nine'. (This date would be contradicted in 1914, when he wrote that he was born on 19 February 1828.)

That Pollaky not only felt frustrated but also deeply upset by the treatment he would now receive is evident from the way he expressed himself in the letters that followed, and also from his handwriting, which becomes more and more agitated in some of them. A great outpouring of astonishment at the lack of understanding shown by the authorities, despite his protestations of sincerity and loyalty, is also present in abundance.

He states that he first came to England in 1852, and this, if true, would explain why he does not appear on the 1851 census. Four friends gave references: Henry William Sewell, Thomas Kelham Minchell, Edward Hunot and Alfred Wynne. They made their declarations at the Mansion House in front of William Cubitt, Lord Mayor of London.

Henry William Sewell (1796–1872) was elected to the post of Swordbearer to the Lord Mayor of London in 1860, a post in existence since at least 1420. His predecessor had held that office for twenty-eight years until his death in 1860 at the age 94. The Swordbearer, the most senior of the Mayor's staff officers, supervises the protocol of ceremonial events. He wears a type of fur hat called a 'Cap of Maintenance' and, as his title implies, carries the Lord Mayor's sword.

Thomas Kelham Minchell (1815–70) was, according to the 1861 census, the son of a 'mariner'. He married for the second time in 1842 and was a messenger working at the Mansion House at the time of Pollaky's application.

Lawyer's clerk, Edward Hunot (1839–1915) was 24 when he acted as a referee. At the age of 40, by then a merchant, he married the exotically named Eugenie Victoire Leonce de Brignola, daughter of an Italian count, resident in England. Lest it should be considered that Hunot moved in exalted circles, it should be pointed out that Count Angelo de Brignola had in 1857 applied for financial relief as an insolvent debtor. Alfred Wynne was a clerk in the City of London.

In the meantime, Pollaky was still working hard to get on the right side of Sir Richard Mayne by informing him of the misdeeds of the City Police. On 5 May 1862, he wrote Mayne a letter which he must have supposed would be helpful, but can only have given rise to ire.

Pollaky enclosed a clipping of a letter published that day in *The Times*. He tells of what appears to have been an expenses-paid trip to the West Indies for the interestingly named Sergeant Jack Spittle of the City Police, officially on police business, but in fact, according to Pollaky, 'it was a private business in which D.W. Harvey and a certain public company had some interest in'. (Daniel Whittle Harvey was the first Commissioner of the City Police.) He continues: 'I shall shortly be able to lay before You a case of such flagrant malpractice which will doubtless appear to You sufficiently important for intervention.'

The enclosed newspaper paragraph, tactlessly sent with his letter is entitled: 'ARE THE POLICE TO BE BETTER PAID AND CARED FOR?'

It begins fairly enough, urging the public to sympathise with poorly paid police constables in the hope that they might be better paid, but it then continues to compare Mayne unfavourably with Harvey:

> Day duty in the metropolitan police is so badly arranged, and so very tedious, that it is dreaded by everyone in the service; and this arrangement only to suit the caprice of the commissioners, whose despotic rule is predominant in the police. Had Sir R. Mayne have been as charitable to the men of the metropolitan police as Daniel W. Harvey was to the officers of the city police, the men of both services would have been equally considered. [...] There is no division in the metropolitan police where so much tyranny exists as in the police of your locality.

The letter is signed 'A Police Constable'.

As noted previously Pollaky had already written to Mayne about corruption in the City of London Police. This mention of Harvey's name was now so blatant that he must have felt it impossible for Mayne to ignore it. It was, indeed, Harvey that he had accused the previous month of taking 25 per cent of his men's gratuities, amounting to about £700, just as it had been Harvey who had employed his own unqualified young nephew in an overt act of nepotism. At that time policemen were allowed to accept gratuities from members of the public in gratitude for their work.

On 22 May 1862 Pollaky wrote a letter to Mayne requesting an interview to discuss a robbery of £800 worth of diamonds. He received in reply a letter from Chief Clerk Mr Yardley informing him that any information he had should be put in writing. Pollaky evidently felt, rightly it would seem, that this was a snub, he responded to Mayne with the information on 26 May, but insisted in his letter that he was acting in 'perfect good faith' and that his sole object was to gain Mayne's good opinion, feeling certain that one day Mayne would appreciate him. The information Pollaky sent is a newspaper article from the *Telegraph*: A story of how a London jeweller was robbed by a German and an American in a complex fraud. The American used a seal with the initials 'R.M.' to seal a box of jewels, but aside from this coincidence, there seems to be no reason for Sir Richard Mayne to have deemed the story of particular significance, and it is hard to see why Pollaky should have thought he would. Pollaky seems to be clutching at straws in his attempt to make himself indispensable to Mayne.

To return the question of naturalisation: one can see things as they really stood between Sir Richard Mayne and Pollaky. On 27 May, Pollaky's solicitor wrote a letter to Horatio Waddington. It had been about four weeks since Pollaky's application for a Certificate of Naturalisation had been sent to the Home Office. Frederick Browne asked Waddington to inform him if Pollaky's application might be entertained. Waddington sent the letter to Sir Richard Mayne for comment. Mayne's written response regarding Pollaky was: 'This is a man of very indifferent character, an agent of Field, the Ex-Police Officer – shall his application be refused to him.'

So now it becomes clear that Pollaky's correspondence with Mayne had done him more harm than good. Things would not get any better. On 2 June 1862 a letter was written to Sir Richard Mayne by a police detective regarding Pollaky's application, which is quoted here in full:

Detection Dept
2 June 1862

Confidential

I beg to report with ref. to Ignatius Pollaky who has petitioned for a certificate of Naturalization that I have known him for the last 4 or 5 years as a person obtaining his living by his wits, but occasionally acting as an Interpreter. He has frequently tendered his services to this Dept. but has never received any encouragement being always considered a dangerous man, but he asserts that he is well known at the Foreign Office & that he has been confidentially employed by the Government on important political matters on the continent.

He was recently connected with a private Enquiring Office kept by the late Inspector Field, and styled Supt. of the Foreign Dept. of the Bureau de Sureté, but he has since left these & opened a private Enquiry office for himself at 14 George St. Mansion House City which he still carries on.

Enquiry has also been made respecting the persons who have made declarations in support of his petition with the following result.

1er. Henry William Sewell is a householder & resides at address given. He bears a respectable character & acts as Sword bearer to the City Corporation

2nd. Thomas Kirkham [Kelham] Minchell is a householder & resides at the address given. He bears a good character, & is a Messenger at Mansion House City.

3rd. Alfred Wynne is a householder & resides at Address given. He is a Clerk in the City, & bears a good character.

4th. Edward Hunot resides at address given & is by profession a lawyer's clerk. He bears a good character. He is not the proprietor of the house but lodges there with his mother.

Signed
J. Whicher
Inspt.

He found nothing bad to say about the referees, but this faintly damning report into Pollaky's character was written by none other than that Inspector Jonathan Whicher who had investigated the Road House Murder in 1860. He undoubtedly had an axe to grind after Pollaky's unwanted presence at one of the official examinations into that case, which had added to the stress that he was already under from the problematic inquiry he was making and the hard time he was given by the press and his superiors. Inspector Whicher, the hero of both Kate Summerscale's excellent book and the television dramatisation of the investigation into the Road House murder, is here shown in a less than sympathetic light, finally able to vent his resentment of Pollaky.

Mayne sent the report to the Home Office with a covering letter dated 5 June. Various hands made their comments on the back of this letter: 'Are we to naturalize adventurers of this description?'

To which the response of someone identified only as 'SS' was:

As he says he is well known at the F.O. it may be as well to inquire there what is known of him & whether Ld. R. thinks it desirable that he should have a certificate of naturalization.

The final letter in this series was written on 16 June by one I. Hammond of the Foreign Office to Waddington:

In reply to your letter of the 11th instant, I am directed by Earl Russell to request that you will inform Secretary Sir George Grey that in His Lordship's opinion it will be better to decline to grant a Certificate of Naturalization to Mr. Ignatius Pollaky.

(Lord John Russell, one time Prime Minister, was at that time Foreign Secretary. It was Sir George Grey to whom the original naturalisation application had been made.) On the back of this letter there were two further unsigned remarks in different hands.

Mr Pollaky should not be naturalized –

No – of course not – it would be monstrous.

Pollaky was sent a negative response to his application on 18 June 1862.

⟜

Pollaky was deeply hurt and upset by the refusal of British nationality, and instantly began to canvass for the decision to be overturned. Writing to Sir George Grey on 20 June, he tried to begin calmly:

> 18 Maida Hill West & 14 George St
> Mansion House
> London 20th June 1862

The Rt Honbl. Sir George Grey Brt, ect [sic]

Sir.
I have the honor to aknowledge [sic] the receipt of a letter signed H. Waddington dated the 18 inst written by Yr. direction and refusing me a Certificate of Naturalization.

I should feel greatly obliged if You would do me the favour of stating on what grounds my application is denied me, whether from any informality in the documents sent You, or from any objections as to the Gentleman, making the declaration or from motives of policy; taking into consideration my antecedents – and whether I will always remain at any future period incapable of becoming a naturalized British Subject; the refusal of which to myself personally is a matter of indifference; but as I have in the month of June 1861 contracted Matrimony with an english Lady and am in hourly expectation of the birth of a child I am most desirous that any offspring may desire that advantage they otherwise would not possess, should I not become a naturalized Bts Subject

I have been a householder at the address above named for some time and consequently pay all assessed and other Taxes demanded and as the want of a Certificate of Naturalization debars me from being a purchaser of any freehold property I am of Course most anxious for my Childrens sake, to become a natural British Subject.

I trust and hope that the above facts may induce You to reconsider my application and alter the Decision contained as Your letter of the 18th inst.

Anxiously waiting Your earliest reply, I have the honor to be

Sir

Your Obd Servant

Ignatius Pollaky

The child referred to in the letter would be the stillborn Lily.

Upon receipt of this letter 'SS' wrote on the back of the second page:

We need be in no alarm as to his children – if they are born in England, they are British Subjects. So inform him.

On 2 July, Waddington wrote to Pollaky informing him of this.

Pollaky responded with a letter to Sir George Grey on 4 July showing a little more of his hurt feelings. He now understood the situation with regard to any children he might have, but reaffirmed his need, 'to be informed on what grounds the Certificate is refused to myself personally, and whether at a future time my application for the same will meet with the same objections.'

Part of the final sentence of this letter is underlined:

Believing that You would not be a party to anything so grossly unfair, as the refusal of my Certificate upon mere 'on dits' [on dits: gossip] and that You will be good enough to reconsider Your decision of Your letter of the 18th June.

This had evidently become a matter of great personal import. Note Pollaky's description of the Certificate of Naturalisation as '_my certificate_'. There is something almost childlike about this sentence, or like Gollum's description of his ring as 'my precious' (_The Hobbit_ – J.R.R. Tolkien). Of course the decision had not been made by Grey, but Pollaky would not have known that.

A note in an anonymous hand on the reverse of the second page reads: 'No further notice – We cannot allow the discretion of the Sect of State in this matter to be questioned.' And so no response was sent.

Pollaky, of course, was not going to leave things there. On 31 July, he wrote to Sir Richard Mayne complaining of his treatment:

I now have no other alternative but to address myself to Your well known sense of justice; Knowing as I do that You have no formal feeling in this matter, and that You only advised the Secretary of State upon Reports made to You.

How wrong he was! Mayne was, unknown to Pollaky, strongly antagonistic to him. Pollaky in this letter tries everything he can to persuade Mayne to intervene on his behalf.

He affirms that he was never tried or convicted of any crime in London, England or Europe.

He mentions his work for Lord Palmerston in 1854 and his good reference from Mr Hodgson to the Austrian Ambassador in 1858. He states that he is certain that Mayne could not be 'a party to anything unjust and unfair', and that he would give the matter 'Kind and Favourable consideration'. After expressing the hope that he might have better chance of success if he reapplied in three or four years he adds some over-the-top admiration of Mayne's qualities:

> I will than [sic] patiently wait and will moreover ever be thankfull [sic] to You; whom I believe in this matter solely actuated by the strict observance of Your duty which although I suffer I cannot help admiring.

He then makes the following extraordinary offer:

> Should you wish me to shut up my office, I will do so after one month notice as a proof that I do not intend to act in any way against the wish & interest of Her Majesty's Government.

He restates his wish to:

> … assist the Police whenever the opportunity presents itself and to serve Her Majesty's Government with all sincerity and honesty, and in this manner show my gratitude for the Grant of the Certificate of Naturalization should I ever obtain such.

His agitation, evident in this letter both from the language and the handwriting, would grow far more acute over the next few weeks.

Another letter followed on 31 July 1862. Pollaky protested that people far less respectable than himself had been granted Certificates of Naturalization, and gave three examples:

1. Baron v Essen formerly in the foreign Legion – is no Baron at all, and is now an inmate of a prison in the Duchy of Baden on a charge of forgery.
2. On the 19th inst the Certificate was granted to a Captain Kastner, who has no visible means of existence who lives on the charity of the Massonic [sic] Lodges, and who would not dare to make his appeerence [sic] in Glasgow.

3. Napoleon de Chorlakovsky a person of bad repute once in custody at Malborough [sic] Police Court for obtaining money under false pretences.

In the lines that follow, his handwriting very noticeably becomes still more and more agitated, larger and less legible. Furthermore his usual care with regard to grammar slips a bit: 'I am not engaged in anything what is [sic] unlawfull [sic],' he writes near the start of this letter. 'Mr Mullens Solicitor could give further information about [him].' He adds, 'to all this 3 persons [sic] the Grant of Certificate was allowed and to me a householder who pays his rates and taxes it is refused. I trust however that it is not to [sic] late and that I will yet find justice.'

One cannot but sympathise with such deep feelings.

There followed a half-hearted attempt to show that he was still trying to be of assistance to the police, in the form of two letters with some fairly uninteresting information about 'evil-disposed persons [who] have lately fraudulently possessed themselves of the tenancy of certain fisheries', mixed in with hints about his naturalisation. Then, on 4 August, he wrote a letter to Horatio Waddington, re-rehearsing matters from the 31 July letter to Mayne, and asking Waddington to intercede with Sir George Grey on his behalf, since Mayne had written declining to interfere with matters to which Pollaky had referred.

The letter of 4 August is the last existing communication on the subject of Pollaky's desire for a Certificate of Naturalization at that time. Those words 'Certificate of Naturalization' or 'my Certificate of Naturalization' occur in those letters almost like a mantra repeated in each one with an insistence which is still almost embarrassingly unbearable to read.

Pollaky's desperate and ultimately unsuccessful attempt to obtain British citizenship implies great sincerity on his part, and yet there is a mystery, and for this we must return to the letters written by Pollaky to Henry Sanford.

From the letter to Sanford at the end of October 1861 (ref. HSS 14.32):

I have during the whole time acted with the utmost good faith towards the U.S. Governement [sic] particularly as I have already informed You, I myself am an American Citizen – But although in possession of my first papers of Naturalisation I did not reside the required 5 years in America to obtain [seco]nd papers, and can therefore not in case of any steps being taken by the British Governement [sic] claim by right the protection of the U.S. altho I should[,] such protection ought to to be given to me 'par faveur' under this [sic] peculiar circumstances.

And in the letter to Seward of 12 February 1862 he refers to America as, 'my adopted Country'. Had he made the required 'Declaration of Intent' to become an American citizen at some earlier time? Had he at one time tried to apply for American citizenship and then transferred his loyalty to Great Britain? As usual, the more one discovers about this mysterious man, the more questions there are to answer.

On 23 October 1856, an Ignatius Pollaky listed as a merchant from Germany aged 19, arrived in Philadelphia, Pennsylvania and stated his intention of becoming an American citizen. Could this be Ignatius Paul Pollaky – though the age, occupation and origin are wrong? In 1856 Pollaky would have been 28. Mistakes like this are known on the most official of documents. Six days later, according to the *Evening Star* of Washington DC, a J. Pollaky of Pennsylvania booked into the Willard Hotel in that city. If it had been he who went to America in 1856, he was certainly not there for the required five years. Unfortunately, these two records are the only ones of an Ignatius (or J.) Pollaky in the United States at the correct period.

~~~

However, he continued in his attempts to make himself indispensable to the Metropolitan Police with another series of letters. These began on 30 December 1862, in the usual way of sending information culled from the press or from his own observations. These include a letter clipped from *The Times* of 10 February 1863 about a foreigner being overcharged by a London cabman with the apparent connivance of a policeman. Pollaky also writes to Mayne on 10 March 1863, declaring that, 'since I left Mr Field I scrupulously abstained from acting in cases which properly belong to the police'. Field himself was inconsistent in this kind of matter, sometimes interfering, and sometimes not, but on the whole was evidently less scrupulous than Pollaky. The implication seems to be that Pollaky too had been less scrupulous when he was working with Field.

Finally, on 16 March 1863, Pollaky managed to have an interview with Sir Richard Mayne. Yardley, the Chief Clerk was also present at Mayne's request. Pollaky refused to speak in front of Yardley as what he had to say was a private matter. Yardley noted that following this, 'Sir R Mayne then wished him good morning & Mr Pollaky left'.

That it was deemed necessary to compare his handwriting later that month with that of an anonymous letter sent to Lord Palmerston (as mentioned in Chapter 3), is indicative of the complete lack of trust that Mayne (who had asked for the comparison to be made), had in Pollaky. He had been writing to Mayne, oblivious to the complete contempt that Mayne had for him. A small number of undated letters from this period show Pollaky indicating that certain members of the police force were passing information to Field's office, but these too led nowhere.

An undated letter of 1862 or 1863 shows that Pollaky thought that Mayne's desire would be, 'to smash the City Police', though why he believed this is not recorded.

It is only right to give another view of Pollaky's motives. In his book *Policing Victorian London* (Greenwood Press, 1985), Philip Thurmond Smith writes with apparent scorn of Pollaky and his self-styled 'grandiloquent title – "Superintendent of the Foreign Department" with his offices in the "Foreign Department Bureau of Sûreté, Temple."' He also seems to find Pollaky's accusations of police corruption in the City Police, and in particular Commissioner Harvey's 'pocketing' £700 of gratuity money and using his force for his personal use rather unbelievable.

Actually it was Whicher who mentioned that Pollaky had been 'styled Supt. of the Foreign Dept. of the Bureau de Sûrété [*sic*],' and that while Pollaky was working for Field, not for himself. Pollaky himself does not mention the Sûreté at all.

Smith feels that Pollaky's motives were an attempt to make himself as helpful to the police as possible in order to secure his naturalization. The following paragraph finishes: 'The fact that there were regular police detectives, did not, as we have seen, obviate the need for informers, however unreliable they might have been.'

While these observations may have some element of truth about them, thorough analysis of the letters themselves show Pollaky to have acted also from a genuine desire to be helpful, though as detective work was his profession he would have felt the need for financial reward and must also have felt that it was only right and fair that he should gain British nationality. It seems unfair, however, to put Pollaky in the category of *unreliable informer*. While the information he gave may not always have been exact, he only made use of information he had received himself, passing it on to Mayne in good faith, with his own commentary it is true, but with the knowledge that Mayne would make whatever use of it he wished. And from a viewpoint in the twenty-first century, we can see that accusations of police corruption are not unusual, and whether well-founded or not, they deserve investigation now as they did then. The difference is that in Pollaky's day, allegations of this sort were unlikely to be taken seriously by those in authority. A mighty police corruption case would, however, erupt in 1877, in which an attempt would be made to blacken Pollaky's name.

Despite his difficulties establishing a relationship with the police force, Pollaky still felt it part of the responsibility of one living in England to carry out civic duties when required, and so in 1867 he was sworn in as a Special Constable in the X Division of the Metropolitan Police.

On 29 June and 2 July 1866 the Hyde Park Riots had taken place. Demonstrators wishing to meet in the park as part of their campaign for suffrage for all men had found the gates locked, and this had resulted in a riot in which stones were thrown at the police, including Sir Richard Mayne, and a policeman had been killed. The following April there were further meetings, and the park was more strongly policed. Pollaky wrote in a letter to *The Times* in 1911 that he became a Special Constable in 1867, though in 1914 he wrote in his naturalisation application that he served during the Hyde Park Riots. Special Constables would be in great need later in 1867 as well to help bolster the regular force. A Special Constable was an unpaid police volunteer, who would have police powers when on duty. It is not known whether Pollaky's services were much in demand in this capacity.

On 13 December 1867 the Middlesex House of Detention, Clerkenwell was bombed in a botched attempt by the Fenians to free an agent of theirs named Richard O'Sullivan-Burke. A huge hole was blown in the prison wall; twelve people were killed and many others injured. Mayne was heavily criticised for ignoring a warning that such an action might happen, and he offered to resign. His resignation was not accepted. The Fenian Movement created great antagonism against themselves by this action from the general public in England, and it did their cause – establishing an independent Ireland – no good. Michael Barrett, charged with causing the explosion, was the last person to be publicly executed in England, being hanged outside Newgate Prison. In the aftermath of this event, some 50,000 Special Constables were enrolled into the Metropolitan Police Force. Pollaky was already a Special Constable by that time, but doesn't mention this affair in any surviving documents.

It is impossible to say what Mayne's reaction would have been had he known of Pollaky's inclusion as a Special Constable. Sir Richard Mayne KCB died on 26 December 1868; Pollaky continued as a private investigator for another thirteen and a half years.

The Casebook of Ignatius Pollaky

10

'Newspapers are the most neglected of historical materials', writes Patrick Pringle in his introduction to Henry Goddard's *Memoirs of a Bow Street Runner* (first published in 1956 but written in the late 1870s). Whether this is still true is open to discussion. In any case, a number of newspaper reports are included in this chapter. Some of them are extraordinary, and many refer to matters still relevant today.

It should be noted that Pollaky was not a private detective in exactly the same mould as Sherlock Holmes. Not for him the analysing of abstruse clues in order to piece together the solution to a mystery. His method was to go out and watch, to observe what others did, or to employ others to watch for him. He would place advertisements in newspapers in the hope that they would be answered by those with the information he needed, and we can deduce from the success of his practice that such information was often forthcoming.

He was quick-minded and able to make deductions from his information, and this sharpness, combined with a knowledge of human behaviour gained him many results. He was less successful in understanding behaviour, however, when his own personal interests were concerned, and it is this which gave rise to some of the problems that beset him – his relationships with difficult employers such as Sanford; with those he wanted to impress such as Mayne; and with those who would threaten him including Lomax, who we shall meet in this chapter.

Between 1862 and 1884 when he retired, Pollaky worked on numerous cases as a self-employed private investigator. Many were reported in the press, or can be deduced from his communications in the 'Agony Column' of *The Times*. The 'Agony Column' was the nickname for what was officially called the 'Second Column'. To avoid confusion, it will be referred to as the 'Agony Column' from here on.

Many different papers from New York to Australia reported Pollaky's exploits. Australian newspapers in particular had a great hunger for news from London. Pollaky was often mentioned in the national press, and advertisements for his inquiry office appeared on the front page of *The Times* very frequently. Some of these were in other languages so as to attract foreign clients. In short, Pollaky was soon a household name, admired, mocked, and hated by turn depending on the points of view of individuals and the newspapers they read. On 9 September 1865, the *Berkshire Chronicle*'s London correspondent wrote of Pollaky's advertisements for missing young ladies, 'I don't of course imply that Mr Pollaky's are fancy sketches, but I should like to know if I am entitled by law to stop and take into custody on suspicion any young lady I may happen to meet answering at all to that worthy description of the lost one.' On 7 June 1871, the *Western Daily Press* referred to 'Mr Pollaky, of the private detective persuasion', lending a quasi-religious overtone to its brief report on his warning over one Joan Georges aka. the Bishop of Ourmea aka Lazarus Bar Chuchaga who was collecting money from clergymen all over Europe for the 'pretended building of a cathedral'. These two reports, written in a somewhat quizzical manner, were comparatively gentle in their approach.

Pollaky's use of cryptic and other advertisements in *The Times* 'Agony Column' became notorious. Over the years, he advertised there on numerous occasions for missing persons or those who knew their whereabouts. Advertisements would frequently appear in codes and ciphers, often with the appearance of gibberish to the casual reader.

In his *Handy-Book of Literary Curiosities* (1893) William S. Walsh writes of *The Times* 'Agony Column', 'even ciphers have been found dangerous. There are everywhere certain ingenious busybodies [...] that make a study of this column, and, finding a key to the cipher in which a clandestine correspondence is carried on, insert a marplot advertisement, – sometimes for the mere fun of the thing, sometimes to stop an intrigue that is nearly ripe for execution.' And indeed examples of this can be found: hardly surprising when some of the ciphers used are so disingenuous in their structure. Pollaky's ciphers, however, when he chose to use them, count among the most difficult to break. Some of them remain unsolved to this day. He found ample opportunity for increasing the mysterious atmosphere that seemed to surround him, unconsciously, though, making himself something of a figure of fun at the same time.

A selection of the many reports involving Pollaky's cases and advertisements is given here to provide a flavour of his activities in the years 1861 to 1884. Though some of them are more exciting than others, taken as a whole, if the image of a busy and alert man should appear before our eyes we should not be surprised. He had his finger in so many pies one might wonder at his ability to keep track of everything. This may be the closest we can come to a case note diary. Many items appeared a number of times. The reports, some quoted in full, show the various opinions of their authors, some critical, some approving, and some overtly hostile. Some of them may cause a smile; others show examples of humanity at its very worst.

The Old Bailey, otherwise known as the Central Criminal Court, was the scene of some of the most celebrated and notorious trials in London. Pollaky's name first appears in the records of the trial of Edward Segers in 1861, which went to court shortly before his employment by Sanford to watch Confederate activities. Pollaky's involvement would be criticised by both police and judge.

Edward (or Edouard) Segers was born near Ghent, Belgium in 1825. Describing himself as either merchant or gentleman, he travelled between Belgium and England probably on business, first arriving in Dover in 1847, and then making a number of trips to and fro.

He was arrested in early 1861 and appeared at the Guildhall Magistrates' Court in early April. According to *The Times* of 6 April, he was charged, together with one Elizabeth Smith and a cab proprietor called Gilbert, with 'conspiring together, and with other persons not yet in custody, to obtain goods by means of false pretences to a very considerable amount, with intent to cheat and defraud a number of foreign firms in almost every branch of trade and manufacture'. The report described Segers as appearing to trade 'for nefarious purposes', and mentioned a letter given as evidence by the wonderfully named Mr John Ulric Meili, an importer of foreign goods.

Pollaky then gave evidence (as reported in the same article):

I am acquainted with the handwriting of the prisoner Segers. I have known him by that name for the last 18 months. He formerly had an office at 38, St. Mary Axe, where he carried on business under the name of Edward Segers and Co., as general merchants and importers, but I never saw any signs of business going on upon any of the occasions that I have been there. Since then I received a communication from him addressed from Lime-street. The letter produced by the last witness, dated the 28th of January, is in the handwriting of the prisoner Segers, and the purport of it is that he was in the receipt of a letter from M. P. Tory-Cadet, dated the 24th of January, and considered the prices for certain goods named were too high, but that if Mr. Tory-Cadet would accept the terms he (Segers) proposed, subject to a discount of 10 per cent., he would take a quantity equal to the value of 116*l*[£]. The letter also urged expedition in the execution of the order, as trade was too dull to admit of doing a brilliant business, and that any unnecessary delay in forwarding the goods might lose him a good market. The letter produced dated the 9th of February is in English, and in the prisoner Segers's handwriting; it is the order for delivery of the goods by Messrs. Horne and Co., of Moorgate-street, to Charles Reil and Co.'s agent. I believe that since Segers has been in London he has obtained goods of various foreign houses to the amount of not less than 20,000*l*.; and had it not been for the information and assistance derived from Stubbs's Trade Protection Institution, the prisoner Segers would not have been arrested, as he was, for claims amounting to nearly 1,000*l*., and consequently would not have been forthcoming to answer the criminal charges which are about to be provided against him

When, a day later, on 7 April 1861 the census was taken in England, Segers was listed as a 'General Merchant', married, aged 36, and a resident of Newgate Gaol. When arrested he had among his papers (available at the National Archives, Kew) an advertisement for strongboxes.

On 8 April, Pollaky placed the following advertisement:

The Times – Monday, 8 April 1861
NOTICE. – Whereas, Edward Segers, formerly in the Queen's Bench Prison, now under remand for Friday next. 12th inst. at the Guildhall Police Court, stands CHARGED with CONSPIRING with others, to CHEAT and DEFRAUD numerous CONTINENTAL MERCHANTS, all parties who have been so defrauded are requested to call on Mr. Pollaky, Superintendent, Private Inquiry-office. 20, Devereux-court, Temple, W.C.

This together with the recognition of Segers's handwriting would become a bone of contention.

On 21 April, Segers was brought before the Guildhall Magistrates' Court again. The charge was more defined this time: 'Obtaining goods under false pretences to the value of 70l. of Mr Cozzi of Paris; 120l. of Mr Tory Cadet of Nice; and 500l. of Mr Bernstein of Hamburg.'

At the conclusion, Inspector Knight produced Pollaky's advertisement of 8 April, in order to draw it to the attention of the magistrate as he considered it, 'a most unjustifiable interference with the police and the regularly-constituted authorities'.

The Times, which had printed the advertisement, continued with the rest of Inspector Knight's complaint. He described Pollaky's method as:

… a very irregular mode of conducting or getting up prosecutions, and one very much calculated to divert important information from the regular course, and defeat the ends of justice, by which means the recognised police, if the objectionable system were not checked, would be entirely superseded by a dangerous, secret, and irresponsible institution, for the properly constituted authorities had not the slightest control over the private inquiry offices. Foreigners were often led into the mistake that such offices were connected with the regular police, and it was therefore most desirable that they and the public generally should be protected from such an erroneous impression.

The magistrate, Sir F.G. Moon, evidently agreed saying that he 'had noticed the advertisement, and he thought Inspector Knight's observations were very proper, as it was quite clear that advantage was taken of this case to advertise a private inquiry office, instituted exclusively for private purposes'.

Segers was kept on remand, and his case came to trial on Monday, 6 May 1861 at the Old Bailey (the original record incorrectly records it as the 5 May which was a Sunday), where he was charged with, 'Feloniously forging and uttering an order for the delivery of 60 bonnets, with intent to defraud'. Pollaky (who appears on the Old Bailey records in this case as Ignatius Polaki) was among those who appeared as witnesses. A transcript of part of the trial can be found at Old Bailey Online:

MESSRS. KEMP and PATER conducted the Prosecution.

IGNATIUS POLAKI. I am superintendent of the office of Mr. Field, the detective, and live at 20, Devereux – court, Temple – I have known the prisoner about eighteen months – the signature to this letter (produced) looks like his writing, but it is "Ryle and Co.," and not "Segers and Co.," that I am accustomed to see – I swore before under the impression that I had, but I will not now swear positively, that it is the prisoner's writing – I have seen so many persons writing that I would not swear to any one's.

COURT. Have you corresponded with him?

IGNATIUS POLAKI. Yes – I saw him write on one occasion – I have received five or six letters from him, and have acquired a knowledge of his writing – I am able to form a judgment whether writing is his or not, when I look at it – the name signed to this letter may be his, but I will not swear it – it seems to be all in one writing; the signature and all – I believe it to be the prisoner's writing, but I should not, like to swear to it positively – I have received letters from him very much like this; so like this that I believe this to be his writing.

MR KEMP. Now look at this other letter.

IGNATIUS POLAKI. I can form no opinion of the writing by the signature, but I can form an opinion by the body of the letter in extensor – here are only three lines of writings and I should not like to swear to them – my belief can only be formed on experience, and three lines might be forged – it looks much like the prisoner's writing – it might be his and it might not.

Cross-examined by MR METCALFE.

MR METCALFE. Have you had sufficient opportunity of seeing the prisoner write to enable you to say with any degree of certainty whether any of the letters are his?

IGNATIUS POLAKI. The only time I ever saw him write was his signature, "Edward Seagers" [sic] – I believe the first letter to be his writing, because, if I look at each letter independently, there is a great similarity – the prisoner carried on business as a general merchant in St. Mary Axe some time ago.

MR PATER. Did you know him when he carried on business at St. Mary Axe?

IGNATIUS POLAKI. Yes; because I had a civil suit against him, under the name of Seagers and Co. – we had no business transactions with him, except what our clients instructed us – we have had written communications with him subsequently – none of the letters were addressed to me, but I have received many communications from him – according to my belief, this letter is in his writing, but I should not like to swear to it.

MR KEMP. Looking at the second document, do you not believe that it is in the same writing as the first.

IGNATIUS POLAKI. Yes.

COURT. Are you the same Ignatius Polaki that was examined before the Magistrate?

IGNATIUS POLAKI. Yes; this is my signature (Looking at his deposition) – the answer that I there made referred to the second letter – I now believe that the second letter is in the handwriting of the prisoner.

Segers was found guilty and sentenced to 18 months' hard labour. The jury gave their opinion that Monsieur Tory-Cadet had behaved very incautiously. The report of the trial in *The Times* gave a few more details with regard to Pollaky, pointing out that it was only when pressed by the judge that he had overcome the doubts he had begun to have over the identification of Segers's handwriting. The judge himself had commented on this:

The Times – Wednesday, 8 May 1861
The learned judge, in passing sentence, observed that the charge had been clearly established, and the only difficulty presented in it was in consequence of the witness Pollaky declining, when he was now examined, to give the same evidence he did before the magistrate, as to the handwriting of the prisoner.

The following advertisements were placed when Pollaky was on the cusp of leaving Field's employment and officially opening his own office. They are included here, as they play a part later on in this chapter.

1861

The Times – Thursday, 5 December 1861
05100. – Moribond. – 3rd Dec. 1861. Abruzzi, 13. – Hotel des Ambassadeurs. – Ig. Pollaky

The Times – Tuesday, 10 December 1861
05100. – Moribond. – Abruzzi, 9th December, 1861. Tempora mutantur, et nos mutamur in illis. Ab uno disce omnes. – IGNATIUS POLLAKY
(Translation of the Latin: Times are changing, and we change with them. From one learn all.)

There were a number of advertisements addressed to Moribond. After that Pollaky used *The Times* as a frequent method of communication, although there does remain the question as to whether this was just a good publicity stunt to drum up business and keep the public aware of his office. We will return to the Moribond series later. After setting up for himself, his advertisements became far more frequent. Some aroused suspicion or were made fun of, and there were a number of imitations and burlesques. Indeed, Pollaky's use of the 'Agony Column' was well known enough to be burlesqued as early as the 1860s. Although he was not the only person to insert cryptic messages for all to read.

1862

January 1862 was an important month. He was featured on the front page of *The Times* in a new capacity. Firstly, Field's advertisement, and then that of Pollaky which appeared immediately below:

The Times – Thursday, 23 January 1862
PRIVATE INQUIRY OFFICE, established 1852,
20, Devereux-court, Temple, under the direction of CHARLES FREDERICK FIELD (late chief Inspector of the Detective Police of the Metropolis). Confidential inquiries made for noblemen, gentlemen, solicitors, railway and insurance companies. Evidence collected in divorce and other cases. This office is unconnected with the police.

(Note the disclaimer at the end that Field was careful to include.)

PRIVATE CONTINENTAL INQUIRY OFFICE.
– Mr. Pollaky, formerly superintendent of the foreign department in Mr Field's office, and who has been entrusted during the last 12 years with the most delicate and confidential inquiries in this country and abroad, has OPENED the above ESTABLISHMENT with the view of protecting the interests of the British public in its social, legal, and commercial relations with foreigners. Inquiries of every description, which do not come within the province of the regular police authorities can be made through this office on any part of the continent. Offices at 14, George-street, Mansion-house, E.C.

Pollaky, in the above advertisement, like Field, is shown to be distancing himself from the police. By May, Pollaky's advertisements had occasional descriptions of himself in French: '*ancien surintendant du départment de l'étranger*' (former superintendent of the foreign department) and offered 'prompt and reliable information of foreigners and others.' By June, information was also added that he had 'agents in all the principal towns on the continent'. From a report of proceedings at Bow Street Magistrates Court:

The *Standard* – Saturday, 25 January 1862

THE LATE EXTENSIVE SWINDLING BY FICTITIOUS FIRMS. – [...]
Ignatius Polaki [*sic*]. – I carry on business at No. 14 George-street, Mansion House, where I keep a Continental Inquiry Office. I know the prisoner Shine by the name of Keeling. In June or July, 1860, I had occasion to offer a reward of 100*l*. for the apprehension of the members of the firm of Dodson and Son, 27, Newman-street, Oxford-street, merchants and brokers. The prisoner came to me at Mr Field's office, and said he had been clerk to those persons. He told me there was no such person as Dodson, but he mentioned the names of several persons who he said were engaged in trying to find them. He said his name was Keeling.

Pollaky was not immune from attempts to impersonate him, and as early as 1862, his apparent success caused him to advertise this fact:

The *Times*, London – Thursday, 30 January 1862
CAUTION. – Whereas a certain person (a foreigner) has been going about the metropolis applying to different mercantile firms for money upon representation that he was connected with Mr POLLAKY's PRIVATE CONTINENTAL INQUIRY OFFICE. The object of this caution now made is to inform the public that this proceeding is entirely unauthorized, and it is hoped that the effect of this announcement will be to put a stop to the deception and fraud that is being practised by the individual referred to.

The irony of this surely cannot have escaped him. He the (foreign) expert on foreigners having a problem of this sort with a foreigner.

One of the most important and best-known types of Pollaky's endeavours was the detection and prevention of the abduction of young women, for purposes known at that time as 'white slavery' – a euphemism for sex-trafficking of women. The next item is the first of a number of examples quoted here:

The Times – Thursday, 13 March 1862

ONE HUNDRED and TWENTY-FIVE POUNDS REWARD. – Whereas, a matronly-looking woman, tall, and of good figure, persuasive voice, piercing black eyes, wearing a profusion of jewellery, and ordinarily dressed in black, speaking the English language with the German accent, and styling herself Baroness de FREIBERG or STEINBERG, is going about the metropolis with the nefarious design of enticing young, innocent, good-looking English girls, to proceed to the continent, under the promise of placing them in respectable and lucrative situations; and as the young females so ensnared, on arriving at their destination, invariably find themselves detained in houses of ill-fame, from which their escape is almost impracticable, the authorities abroad, being desirous of effectually stopping this infamous traffic, £100 reward will be given to any one who shall furnish such INFORMATION as will lead to the apprehension and conviction of the said spurious Baroness and her accomplices, either in London or abroad. £25 will be given to such person as shall inform of the house which is said to serve as a depot somewhere in the neighbourhood of the South Eastern Railway Station. Information to be given to Mr Ignatius Pollaky, private continental inquiry-office, 14 George-street, Mansion-house, E.C. Description of dress of the pseudo 'Baroness' when last seen in Bond-street:- Black glacé silk dress, full train skirt trimmed with narrow flounces, black velvet mantle with guipure collar, black velvet bonnet with violet flowers, and violet kid gloves fitting very tightly.

The Times – Saturday, 13 September 1862

INFORMATION WANTED of a LITTLE BOY, five years old, black eyes and rosy cheeks, with a small scar on the left temple, who has been decoyed away from his parents in Germany, and supposed to have been brought to England. – IGNATIUS POLLAKY. No. 14, George-street, Mansion-house.

The Times – Saturday, 11 October 1862

NOTICE. – On the 15th instant, a special employé of this office will leave for France, Germany, and Switzerland, who will undertake PRIVATE INQUIRIES (on the above route) at fixed charges. – IGNATIUS POLLAKY (Home and Foreign Inquiry-office). 14, George-street, Mansion-house.

1863

This item, one of Pollaky's longer advertisements, contains information not seen elsewhere regarding his own perception of his office, as well as the length of his career as an investigator up to that time:

The Times – Thursday, 1 January 1863
THE HOME and FOREIGN INQUIRY OFFICE, 14 George-street, Mansion-house. E.C. – Mr. Pollaky, who founded the above establishment in 1861 for the purpose of furnishing prompt and authentic information of the past career and character of foreigners and others in this country and abroad, will continue to make private inquiries, with the view of testing the respectability of persons who, under fictitious, high-sounding titles, introduce themselves into English society; as shown by numerous reports in the daily press. The system of espionage, so justly condemned and so firmly repudiated by the British public, forms no element in the important as well as legitimate prosecution of these delicate investigations. Since the opening of this office the desirability of its permanent existence has been demonstrated by the numerous cases in which its assistance has been sought by all classes of society. Mr Pollaky in strictly adhering to these principles hopes for a continuation of the confidence of the public, to obtain which he has striven during the past 10 years. On the 15th of every month a special employé of this office will leave for the continent to execute confidential inquiries at these places where no constituted agent of the establishment resides. – Jan. 1863

The sending of an agent to the continent every month is a continuation of working practice developed at Field's office (possibly by Pollaky himself). Confirmation of the establishing of his own office during 1861, before his departure from Devereux Court can be seen in the first sentence. Most of the rest speaks for itself – but hidden away there is a little gem of information: the implication that he has been working as a private investigator for ten years. It is possible, therefore, that he began working for Field in 1853, the year after Field left the police force and opened his private inquiry office, where, as seen, it took Pollaky a while to gain recognition for his work. On the other hand, his claim that espionage would play no part in his work must mean that he had changed his methods since the days of spying on the Confederates – unless he was simply being disingenuous.

The Times – Friday, 30 January 1863
CONSPIRACY. – Whereas several evil-disposed PERSONS, principally foreigners, are constantly conspiring, with others out of this country, to ALLURE young and innocent ENGLISH GIRLS to PROCEED to the CONTINENT, under promise of lucrative employment (especially in the

capacity of governesses) have succeeded in many instances by these false representations in inveigling honest, industrious, young persons to quit their home and proceed abroad, where they invariably find themselves entrapped into houses of ill-fame without the means of escape. This infamous traffic has of late so alarmingly increased and baffled all endeavours to check it, that recourse is had to this public notice, in the hope that it will prevent English girls from too readily listening to any such proposals proceeding from questionable parties, and in all such cases they are requested to notify the same without delay to Mr Pollaky, who is instructed by Mr G.B. Talbot (the secretary of the London Society for the Protection of Young Females, 28, New Broad-street), to investigate, free of charge, the character of parties in England and abroad, holding out such inducements. – IGNATIUS POLLAKY, Home and Foreign Inquiry-office, 14, George-street, Mansion-house.

The Times – Tuesday, 10 February 1863
THE HOME and FOREIGN INQUIRY OFFICE. – No Espionage. – Confidential inquiries and legitimate investigations privately instituted. On the 15th of every month a special employé will leave for the continent on private missions. – Mr. POLLAKY, 14, George-street, Mansion-house, E.C.

In February 1863, two letters appeared in the *Standard* under the heading, 'INFAMOUS TRAFFIC IN YOUNG GIRLS'. The first was an introduction by J.B. Talbot, Secretary of the London Society for the Protection of Young Females, of a letter received by him written by Pollaky, asking for that letter to be published. Pollaky's letter was as follows:

The *Standard* – Thursday, 12 February 1863
To J.B. TALBOT, ESQ.
Home and Foreign Inquiry Office, 14 George-street, Mansion House, Feb.9.
Sir, – It is my desire to bring to your notice the result of the advertisement headed 'Conspiracy', for the information of the board of your society.

Since the publication of said advertisement there have been numerous applications at my office, for the purpose of inquiry into the respectability of parties abroad, who, through advertisements and other channels, proffer situations to English Girls. To all applicants – and the greater part were governesses – I am happy to say I have been able to render great assistance; some are now on their way to really good and lucrative engagements, whilst others are fortunately deterred from proceeding to the Continent, and falling an easy prey to scheming adventurers.

It is my firm conviction that, as I mentioned to you in our last conversation on this subject, publicity alone will be the means of putting an end to this infamous traffic; but I regret to say, at the same time, that my limited means debar me from carrying out the required publicity, especially as the inquiries have entailed on me a certain amount of expense, having in no case, even when offered, accepted payment from the applicants, who, though generally poor, were anxious, some of them, to testify their gratitude by some remuneration. I hope, therefore, the board of your society will, after mature consideration, see in the above statement sufficient encouragement to induce them to defray the expense of a monthly advertisement, and I shall be glad to continue my services gratuitously.

Yours truly,

(Signed) IG. POLLAKY

Ironically, the term *adventurer* had been applied to Pollaky himself, as mentioned in Chapter 9. Pollaky's call for his expenses to be defrayed is again heard in this letter, nevertheless, in this worthwhile cause, he considered that he would work for no payment. Does not this letter put one in mind of Sherlock Holmes in *The Adventure of the Copper Beeches* (1892)? Holmes aids a young lady who has doubts about whether she should accept a job as a governess. *The Adventure of the Solitary Cyclist* also comes to mind. It has been suggested that Pollaky was a prototype for Holmes, though there are obvious differences. Pollaky was Hungarian, energetic and with a moustache. Holmes is very much an Englishman, clean shaven and given to bouts of drug-induced lethargy. Undoubtedly Arthur Conan Doyle would have heard of Pollaky; several other candidates have been put forward, though, the most important of which was forensic surgeon, and Doyle's mentor, Dr Joseph Bell. Others who have been suggested as models for Holmes have mostly been policemen, or one-time policemen. Pollaky was a private detective, and only that. There seems little doubt that his cases, which may very well have been read about by Doyle, form a model for some of the cases of Sherlock Holmes, furthermore, both have an interest in the 'Agony Column' of *The Times*, as well as with codes and cyphers. The legend of Sherlock Homes of Baker Street is not far from the legend of Ignatius Pollaky of Paddington Green, the addresses themselves are within comfortable walking distance of each other. Doyle's full name was Arthur Ignatius Conan Doyle, his second name may have no bearing on his interests, but it is a nice coincidence.

A report in the *Middlesex Chronicle* on Saturday, 7 March 1863 mentions that Pollaky was trying to find, in England, a man who had murdered a French judge in a railway carriage between Paris and Lyons some three of four years earlier, the victim having been robbed of 40,000 francs. The French police had sent him a photograph of the suspect.

On 23 March 1863, an item appeared in the *Dundee Courier and Argus* entitled:

'ENTRAPPING WOMEN FOR PROSTITUTION':
Dundee Courier and Argus – Monday, 23 March 1863

At the Mansion House, last week, Mr Beard, attorney, addressing Alderman Sir Robert Carden, the magistrate for the day, said, in effect, he was instructed by the London Society for the Protection of Young Women to call attention in the public interest to certain systematic attempts which were being made to prevail upon young women in this country, chiefly governesses, to go to France, by holding out to them tempting offers of employment and remuneration, but with the real though secret intention, as there was reason to believe, of entrapping them for the purposes of prostitution. A few weeks ago many very respectable young women of the class alluded to were induced to reply to an advertisement which appeared in the 'Times,' the result of which was to bring them into communication with a Mr F. Robertson, who was supposed to be a Frenchman, though he bore or assumed an English surname. He (Mr Beard) had letters which this Mr Robertson had addressed to three young women, and all of which were to the same purport. Writing from an address in the Rue Paradis-Poissoniere, he stated that he could introduce his correspondent as a governess to a highly respectable French family, where it would be her duty to instruct, chiefly in English, two young ladies, about 13 and 15 years of age. The salary would be L[£]72 a year, and she would be 'privileged to use her employer's carriage and a separate apartment.' Her travelling expenses would be paid 'in a first-class department', and she would be guaranteed an engagement of three years certain. The writer added, that the condition of "our firm" were – commission L4, to be paid in four months at L1 a month, and she would be expected to send immediately a post-office order for L1, the first month's commission, with her references. In one case he offered one of his correspondents a situation in the family of a Countess in Paris, with a salary of 2,000f., on her paying him 100f. as commission, 25f. of which were to be in advance. There was reason to believe, from inquiries made by M. Pollaky at the instance of the Society, that about 20 young women had been induced to embrace the offers held out to them and to go to Paris; but on arriving there they discovered that they had been allured from their home for immoral purposes. On Monday last, this Mr. Robertson being then in London, about as many more young women met him by his appointment at an office in Lower Thames Street, in the occupation of a countryman of his, to make arrangements for going to Paris to situations which he had undertaken to procure them. The housekeeper, a man in charge of the offices there, surprised at seeing so many well-dressed, lady-like women, and strongly suspecting something amiss, entered the room and mentioned his suspicions to the Frenchmen. Robertson, unable to speak English, was then conversing with them through his son, but, on the interference of the housekeeper, he left the place, and had not been seen there, nor had the man in the occupation of the office in which the interview took place. The society for which he (Mr Beard) appeared, believing that this man, with others, was systematically engaged in inveigling young women abroad for purposes of prostitution had desired him to make this statement in the hope that, by the publicity which would probably be given to it through the press, it might operate as a warning.

Sir Robert Carden said he would go further than that, and advise the society to make a representation, through the Foreign Office, to the English Ambassador in Paris, who would probably, with the assistance of the French Government, institute inquiries into the matter.

On 25 March 1863, a similar, though slightly shorter item, appeared in the *Cork Examiner* entitled: 'DECOYING FEMALES FROM LONDON TO FRANCE'.

Though Pollaky's name appears in the article only in passing, it would not be the last time that he would be engaged in investigating the disappearances of young girls and women, actually rescuing them, preventing them from being abducted, or actively taking an interest in their welfare.

On 3 October 1864, the *Morning Post* published a letter from J.B. Talbot, Secretary of the London Society for the Protection of Young Females, correcting an item published by them on 31 September which mentioned that Pollaky was the honorary secretary of that society, whereas this position was held by Talbot himself. He writes, 'I feel it right to say that Mr Pollaky is sanctioned by this society in his efforts.'

In 1862, Henry Mayhew had published the fourth volume of his *London Labour and the London Poor*. Mayhew discusses traffic of foreign women: 'One of the most disgraceful, horrible and revolting practices [...] carried on by Europeans is the importation of girls into England from foreign countries to swell the ranks of prostitution.' He then moves to the subject of 'English Women [who] are also taken to foreign parts by designing speculators', and gives examples of interviews he had with two victims and of the terrible experiences of the second. Since these matters were documented then, one might have expected this issue to have been solved by the twenty-first century, but news items even today show that there has been little change.

Pollaky became famous (or infamous) for investigations leading to divorce cases. The *Standard* of Monday, 13 July 1863 reported on the case of John Pym Yeatman, a barrister, who lost his case for divorce on the grounds of the adultery of his wife with 'a person passing as prince Hohenlohe, at Handschuksheim, in Germany'. It transpired during the proceedings that this was not the first time Yeatman had sought a divorce from his wife. In 1858 he had falsely cited insanity

as grounds, having previously sent her to a lunatic asylum from which she had
escaped. Yeatman had then accompanied his wife to Germany where he had
then deserted her. After this, she had found 'that a detective named Pollaki [*sic*],
not present, had been dogging her steps, and that these unknown persons from
Germany were fixed upon by Pollaki to prove an act which there was no other
single act to lead up to or support'.

This next report, though Pollaky is not mentioned till the end, is included here
as it is a wonderfully told story, that ought not to be lost to posterity. Indeed, it
almost feels like it belongs in the collection of the *1001 Nights*, so fragrant is the
language used by the writer:

The *Empire*, Sydney – Monday, 31 August 1863

A MISER'S CAREER. – The extraordinary circumstances connected with the
death of an old miser named Crepin, which took place on the 11th August,
1858, in Lyons, are still undoubtedly fresh in the recollection of many of
our readers. Crepin was an old *bonhomme*, from whom nobody would have
withheld a penny in the streets if he had asked for it, and who, if it had been
offered, would certainly not have refused it. Having retired from business with
about 100,000f., which he had accumulated in the space of a few years, thanks
to lucky and certain speculations of every description, he raised that sum to a
fortune considerably exceeding a million. But the great source of his riches
was his sordid avarice, which even induced him to tear down bills posted up
on the streets in order to write his receipts upon the back, instead of making
use of stamps, as the law exacts; and yet these receipts represented the rent of
several houses which brought him a decent income. Dressed in a coat which a
superb burnish of grease and dirt rendered proof against all weathers, and his
head sheltered from the sun and rain by a hat that outlived the storm of the
first revolution, one would have taken him for a fugitive pauper. But every
one residing in his quarter knew that he was the millionaire Crepin, possessing
superb mansions in the best quarters of Lyons, the rent of which he made his
tenant[s] pay nine months in advance, while all were expelled – the clause
was inserted in the agreement in every case – who required any repairs to be
done. But the deity who caused the destruction of Troy also caused that of pere
Crepin; not that the wronged and artful deity ever succeeded in loosening his
purse-strings, but he gifted a cunning woman with charms sufficient to induce
Crepin to live with her and her husband, and that woman eventually managed
so completely to wind him round her finger that in his will he made her his
heiress. Finding, however, that he did not die soon enough, she had recourse
to poison in order to hasten the opening of the will, which made her twice
a millionaire. The indiscretion of an accomplice, who did not think himself
sufficiently well-paid, let the public know the horrible crime committed upon

the person of the deceased, and all the turpitude which had preceded it. Since the Dumollard [a French serial killer] case the public has not been so impressed by any judicial drama, and it is the tribunal of Lyons which had the honor of finally condemning the guilty trio, namely, the man Favre and his wife – (the inheritors of Old Crepin's fortune of 1,700,00f.) – the woman to twelve years, and the husband to five years' hard labour, and the accomplice, Claude Charel, also to twelve years. After the trial the property was of course sequestered. But on the day the verdict was given the heirs of Crepin commenced proceedings in the civil court to have the will revoked, and Mr. Pollaky is now conducting the inquiries on their behalf as next of kin of old Crepin in England with a view to support these proceedings in the Justice Civile (Common Pleas) which is about to give its decision on the affair of old Crepin, by application *en declaration d'idignite* made by the legitimate heirs of the late Mr Crepin against the convict Favre, according to the provisions of the article 727 of the *Code Napoleon*, at the First Chamber of the Tribunal Civile of Lyons.

A number of interesting facts emerge from the next report. The descriptions of Pollaky, firstly as mysterious and then as indefatigable, give some light both as to his character as well as to the opinion that the public and press had of him. He had evidently been approached by reporters to give a statement, but had refused to give them any information. Inspector Hamilton and Sergeant Webb both appeared in Pollaky's correspondence with the Metropolitan Police the previous year:

Morning Post – Wednesday, 7 October 1863

Owing to a report which appeared in the papers yesterday stating that the fugitive Sigmund Dietichstein [incorrectly spelled!], for whose apprehension it will be remembered, a warrant was issued from the Mansion-house, charging him with defrauding one of the banks of about 10,000*l.*, had been taken into custody in Austria, long before the hour arrived for the commencement of the business of the court a number of persons had assembled before the gate leading to the steps of the police-court, expecting that the prisoner had arrived, and would be brought up for examination. It will be remembered that Ditrichstein left this country on the 29th August last, and almost simultaneously with his flight the mysterious Pollaky also disappeared, and a notice was issued to the effect that he had gone on the continent for a fortnight, which naturally led to the belief that the services of this indefatigable foreigner had been engaged to trace the fugitive. For the last two days his reappearance in London has caused considerable curiosity, but nothing could be gained from him respecting the matter, though there is not the slightest doubt that the surmise was a true one, and moreover that the apprehension of the fugitive is beyond a doubt.

The following facts which may be relied upon, may be given. Mr Pollaky and Sergeant Moss, a detective of the City of London police force, under the direction of Mr Hamilton the inspector of the detective staff, who with Sergeant Webb has been unremitting in his exertions to gain information in town, proceeded to Ostend, where they had reason to believe Mrs Ditrichstein was staying. On arriving there, however, they found she had left, but they ascertained that she had paid her hotel bill with some money which formed part of the proceeds of the alleged fraud, thus establishing beyond a doubt that there had been some communication between her and her husband. From inquiries they made at Ostend, they had no doubt that Mrs Ditrichstein had proceeded over the North German lines to Austria, and her movements led to the belief that she would proceed to Hungary, where in all probability it was thought she would meet her husband, that being the native country of both. They succeeded in tracing Mrs Ditrichstein to Vienna, where, having communicated with the Austrian police, Moss was furnished with their ready assistance. Mrs Ditrichstein was then traced to Pesth, in Hungary, where, as was expected, she met her husband, Sigmund Ditrichstein, who was apprehended by Moss, after an interview with his wife. Owing to some formalities which had to be gone through in respect to the Austrian police some delay has taken place in handing the prisoner over to the English authorities. Great credit is due to the officer Moss, and also to Inspector Hamilton and Webb. Pollaky is himself a native of Hungary. The prisoner cannot possibly arrive for a day or two.

The police had made use of his ability and experience in a case that took them to the continent. Austria and Hungary were, of course, home territory to Pollaky. Three days later further information about the course of the investigation was reported in the *Liverpool Mercury*:

Liverpool Mercury – Saturday, 10 October 1863

Some additional particulars of the arrest of the now notorious Sigismund [*sic*] Ditrichstein have transpired [...] The persons most actively engaged in the search for the fugitive were Detective Moss of the City Police, and Mr Pollaky, of George-street, Mansion-house, the latter having been employed by Messrs. Mullins, the solicitors of the Poultry [a street in the City of London], to accompany the officer as interpreter. In the course of their inquiries they found that a photographer in the neighbourhood of Worthing, where the prisoner resided, had portraits in the negative shape as well of him as of his wife and child, and from these about 1500 copies have since been taken and largely distributed both here and abroad, accompanied by a detailed description in print of the prisoner's personal appearance. [...] Having communicated with the Austrian police, they continued their pursuit to Presburg [*sic*], a Hungarian

town some 35 miles east of Vienna. They soon discovered that the wife of
Ditrichstein had been living there, and also that her husband had been seen
in the neighbourhood; but on inquiry it was found they had quitted the place,
when and how no one could tell. A clue after much difficulty was discovered,
and the officer and Pollaky left Presburg and proceeded to a town on the
frontiers of Austria, from thence to Pesth, in Hungary, where Ditrichstein's wife
was found to have joined her husband [...]

This is the only record of Pollaky visiting his home town. He had not been in
Pressburg for at least thirteen years. Did he visit his old haunts? Were his parents
still alive? Did he see other members of his family or old friends? There is no
way of knowing how he felt about going back to the place he had left behind.

The fraud in which Ditrichstein was involved caused payment on a number
of high currency banknotes, including two £500 notes, to be stopped, and for
this fact to be advertised as far away as Australia. He was finally brought to trial
the following September, and cleared of wrongdoing, claiming that others had
been responsible for the fraud. Ditrichstein (or Dietrichstin), Hungarian or
Austrian by birth, had married Theresa Elizabeth May in Richmond, Surrey
in 1858 when he was 28 and she 21. After his capture, he had written a letter
to his prosecutors from Vienna offering to assist in the recovery of the missing
money. About £6,000 was recovered as a result. After the trial, they disappear
from the records.

Finally, Pollaky installed himself into 13 Paddington Green, the address for
which he is best known. The family were still living at 9 Portsdown Road, though.

The Times – Wednesday, 21 October 1863
AUDI, VIDE, TACE. – Private Inquiries in England and Abroad. – Evidence
for Divorce Court. – City firms and others are waited upon personally by Mr
POLLAKY (late of George-street, Mansion-house) or if more agreeable, may
consult with him at No. 13, Paddington-green. W.

1864

The Times – Monday, 18 January 1864
INFAMOUS TRAFFIC. – Several advertisements headed 'Corps de Ballet'
having lately appeared in many English and foreign newspapers, which upon
investigation, turn out to be only a cloak for the purpose of inveigling English
girls to the continent for nefarious motives, virtuous GIRLS are herewith
CAUTIONED against this new scheme. – POLLAKY, Private Inquiry-office,
13, Paddington-green W.

The Times – Thursday, 28 January 1864
LADIES of the ARISTOCRACY and others are herewith CAUTIONED against a woman, who (by some means at present unknown) has possessed herself of the visiting cards of various ladies of distinction; and, by using them as a means of introduction at their friends', has succeeded in inducing the latter to make purchases of worthless Chinese silks, &c. She is a stout, fair person, wearing a brown dress and black velvet bonnet with white feathers. – POLLAKY, Private Inquiry-office, 13, Paddington-green, W.

The matter of police supplying information about private individuals upon request to private investigators was raised in a debate in the House of Commons. Sir George Grey responded that he was putting in place steps to 'prevent the continuation of the practice'. This was reported in *Hansard* on Thursday, 3 March 1864.

The Times – Monday, 11 April 1864
Sans CŒUR. – Owing to my unavoidable absence from England for a fortnight, I shall be unable to attend to your business till my return. – Mr. Pollaky, Private Inquiry-office, No. 13, Paddington-green.

There follows a spoof advertisement from *Fun*. Offensive in its snide use of Pollaky's name, the remarks that follow the fake advertisement combine the popular song *Polly Perkins of Paddington Green*, with the implication that Pollaky was one who might 'pry' into affairs that did not concern him.

Fun – Saturday, 7 May 1864
FROM THE SECOND COLUMN
ALL advertisements are funny, and the following is no exception to the rule: –
SANS COEUR. – I am returned, and now at your disposal. – MR. POLLAKY, P.I.O – 13, Paddington-green.
This has a deep political meaning. MR. PAUL (PRY)LAKY is returned – for a county or borough, of course – and is now at the disposal of whom? *Time will show,* and in the meantime we advise all England to keep its weather eye open. What is the meaning of the mysterious letters P.I.O? Is it POPE PIO? No, no, it can't be that. The last sentence is probably intended to be read thus: MR POLLA(KY) P(ERKINS) I(nhabiting) O(f) 13, Paddington-green. That's it.

In 1886, Pollaky's name would again be associated with the expression 'Paul Pry' (referring to private detectives), in *An Iron-Bound City* – a novel by John Augustus O'Shea. *Paul Pry* was a three-act farce by John Poole first performed in London in 1825. The central character is an interfering busybody.

A short paragraph in the *Cheshire Observer* quoted another item from *Fun*. The misspelling of Pollaky's name is intentional. The writer, attempting to criticise using humour, manages instead to be snooty and crude:

Cheshire Observer – Saturday, 2 July 1864

HI, SPY, HI! – The spy system is not a favourite in England: consequently it was with feelings of intense gratification we observed that Sir James Wilde had dismissed a case with costs in the Divorce Court, principally on account of the employal by the petitioner of one of those disreputable evidence-hunters. For our own parts – and in this we believe we're expressing the feelings of the whole people of England – we rejoice particularly at any failure of obtaining even justice, when caused by such means, and we wish that the whole spy business as of late years introduced into our island, whether disguised under the title of Grubb's Trade Protection Society, or Rollaky's [*sic*] Private Inquiry Office, were – – We leave a space for the exact fate we desire for the fellows, but our readers can supply it for themselves by inserting anything very unpleasant indeed. – *Fun*.

The Times – Monday, 18 July 1864

ANONYMA. – FIVE THOUSAND FRANCS REWARD. Whereas some evil disposed persons did maliciously write and unlawfully print and circulate a pamphlet (French) containing libellous accusations against the fair fame of an English Lady residing in Paris, the above reward will be given to any one who shall furnish the names of the parties so offending to Mr Pollaky, private inquiry office, 13, Paddington-green, W.

Morning Post – Tuesday 9 August 1864

Pieter Broughsmann, a German described as a cattle minder on board ships, was brought before the Lord Mayor yesterday, charged with having committed an indecent assault upon Mary Anne Eliza Williams, a little girl nine years of age, residing with her father at 15, Love-lane, City.

Mr Pollaky was present to watch the case on behalf of the Society for the Protection of Young Females, 28, Old Broad-street.

The evidence left no doubt that the prisoner had committed the offence imputed to him, and further that he attempted to allure the child on board the boat by telling her that her father was on board and wanted her.

Mr Pollaky informed the Lord Mayor that it was not the first attempt of a similar character that had been made about Tower-hill.

There had been previous complaints of this sort against the accused, and the Lord Mayor described it as, 'a very bad case'; Broughsmann was sentenced to six months with hard labour.

1. *Pollaky* by Faustin Betbeder. 1874. (Courtesy of the Ohio State University Billy Ireland Cartoon Library & Museum)

2. Pressburg Castle. De Kaai from *De Aarde en haar Volken*, 1867. (Author's collection)

3. Charles Frederick Field, *Illustrated News of the World*, 1855. (Courtesy of Wikipedia)

4. Two cigarette cards of Inspector Bucket from Charles Dickens' *Bleak House*, with illustrations looking remarkably like Field. The first image is dated around 1900 and the second around 1912. (Author's collection)

5. Lord Edward Bulwer Lytton (1803–1873), *Illustrated London News Extra Supplement*, 25 January 1873. (Author's Collection)

6. James Dunwoody Bulloch. Image from *Battles and Leaders of the Civil War.* (Courtest of the Century Co.,1888)

7. Henry Shelton Sanford (1823–1891), Library of Congress, Washington DC.

8. Image and obituary of Sir Richard Mayne, *Illustrated London News*, 9 January 1869. Mayne's severe countenance may be an indication of his personality, however, it would only be fair to point out that this formal expression was the fashion for official portraits of the time. (Author's collection)

9. Inspector Jonathan 'Jack' Whicher, 1865. Powell of Charing Cross wrote a report to Mayne stating Pollaky was 'always considered a dangerous man'. (Courtesy of Hampshire County Council Arts and Museum Service, ref. HMCMS: FA2004.141.135)

10. Meikeljohn, Druscovich, Palmer and Froggatt in the dock at the Old Bailey, *The Graphic*, Saturday, 1 September 1877. (Author's collection)

11. Numbers 11, 12 and 13 Paddington Green taken in 1956. (Courtesy of the City of London, London Metropolitan Archives)

12. *Left*: Number 13 Paddington Green (centre) in 2010, shortly before demolition. (Courtesy of Pre-Constuct Archaeology Limited)

13. *Below*: Back cover of *Benjamin D. His Little Dinner*, 1876. Pollaky's advertisement, showing only his name and address, is at the top of the page. (Author's collection)

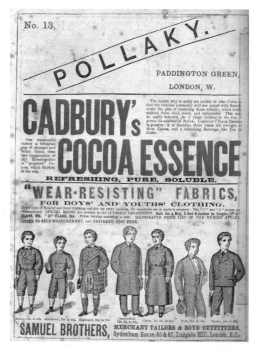

14. *Above*: Caricature of Pollaky by 'Whew' from *Benjamin D. His Little Dinner*, 1876. (Author's collection)

15. *Right*: Number 33 Stanford Avenue, 2014. (Courtesy of K.P. and S.N.)

16. Pollaky family gravestone at the Kensal Green Cemetery. (Photograph by the author)

17. Darrell Fancourt as Colonel Calverley. Photograph taken by H.C. Hughes in the early 1920s. No image of a uniformed Richard Temple, the creator of the role, seems to exist. Fancourt was a famous interpreter of the role for the D'Oyly Carte Opera Company. (Courtesy of David Stone)

18. Photograph of Pollaky in his later years from the Toni and Gustav Stolper Collection, ref. F12249. The verso reads: 'Mr. (or Sir?) Polacki grand-uncle of Toni. Noted British detective.' (Courtesy of the Leo Baeck Institute, New York)

The Times – Friday, 19 August 1864
ANONYMA. – Through the discovery of the names of the writer and printer of a certain libellous French pamphlet, entitled 'Anonyma' the REWARD of £200 offered in The Times is herewith WITHDRAWN. – Pollaky's Private Inquiry Office, 13, Paddington-green, W.

A strange item appeared in the *Wells Journal* – Saturday, 29 October 1864, and the *Newsman* – Sunday, 30 October 1864. It seems that on 19 October a letter had been, 'extensively circulated among bankers' and merchant's clerks and also medical men', which had been signed 'pro Pollarky [*sic*] and Co., N.U.E.' The letter was an attempt to extort money from the recipients; it asked them to inform on their employers if they believed them to be working illegally. Pollaky had instructed his solicitors, Lewis and Lewis, to deny any connection with it and the matter had been reported to the presiding alderman at the Guildhall. Mr Lewis, junior, said, 'the signature is a forgery, and [...] Mr Pollaky's name is not spelt so; he has no partner, and never under any circumstances, sanctioned his name being used; [...] he believes that [...] these letters are sent in consequence of the prominent part taken by Mr Pollaky lately in exposing the nefarious practices of certain employment agencies.'

That Pollaky's name was already known enough to be used by fraudsters in this fashion must be an indication of the amount of attention his work had already received. It is interesting to note that he had no partners in his firm, although he employed agents to work for him when necessary.

The *Newsman* reports the matter impartially. The *Wells Journal* reporter, on the other hand, manages to have a few digs at Pollaky, stating that the writer of the letter came 'from that dreary neighbourhood, which only "pretty Polly Perkins" has made famous – Paddington Green', that the solicitor had 'of course' taken advantage of the occasion to 'puff' Pollaky, and that 'Mr Pollaky, (a Hungarian refugee, I believe) in fact, makes a very good advertisement out of this application'. The reporter denigrates the work of private detectives, calling it 'un-English', and further, states, 'the whole detective system requires legislative interference'.

Pollaky's solicitors, Lewis and Lewis, were a highly respected firm. Mr Lewis, junior, George Henry Lewis (1833–1911), who spoke for him in this matter would later become well known for his cross-examinations in a number of high-profile cases such as the Bravo case of 1876. (The still unsolved case of Charles Bravo who was poisoned with antimony.) Lewis was knighted in 1893, and nine years later became a baronet. At the time of this matter, he was yet to make a name for himself. The 'Lewis and Lewis' of the firm refer to his father and his uncle.

1865

The *Morpeth Herald*, (Northumberland) of Saturday, 29 April 1865 reported that two foreigners, Edmund Renard, 16, and Nicholas Lion Pruvot, 27, had been 'charged with stealing a watch and ten silver spoons'. Renard was 'very respectably connected' and had been 'enticed away from his friends' by Pruvot. Pollaky had been asked by Renard's friends to find him. He did so, and took him 'under his own care at his residence', after which he was 'placed to board at the house of Mr Bucknell, in Martin's-court, Cannon Street'. Unfortunately, while Mr Bucknell was out, Renard left his house with the above mentioned watch and spoons. The two men were caught and fined £20 each.

Mystery of mysteries. The following advertisement has never been decoded. We can deduce that Pollaky was again abroad, but he must have wanted to keep his whereabouts a deep secret. There is not enough information to decipher the lines and dots, but it forms an amusing challenge, and is just one of the ciphers he used – others involved rows of numbers, sometimes intermingled with foreign and invented words. It is, perhaps, of little wonder that his motives might be doubted by some:

The Times – Tuesday, 16 May 1865

T.—Your telegram was duly forwarded, and fortunately in time to ⎯⎯ :|: ≡≡≡ : ⎯⎯ ·.·|· ⎯⎯ (:) ⎯⎯ ≑ :||| · I shall return to England about the middle of June.—Pollaky.

Of all criticisms of Pollaky, the following (which arises out of the previous extract) is one of the most vituperative. It does, however, give cause to wonder about the style of his dress.

Cardiff Times – Friday, 19 May 1865

OUR LONDON CORRESPONDENT

[…] I confess to […] doubts when I look in an advertisement in the second column of the Times of Tuesday. Not that I doubt the existence of 'Pollaky,' for I have seen him in the flesh, and very common flesh it is, though adorned with all the flashy jewellery that bad taste can heap upon it. But I doubt the existence of any meaning to those lines and dots which form so conspicuous a feature in the advertisement. They may mean something of course, but I much doubt whether they do; and I have a shrewd suspicion that the only notion is that out of the many thousands of readers who peruse that advertisement the majority may think, 'Bless my soul, what a wonderfully clever and artful man that private-inquiry man, Pollaky, must be.' But some equally clever reader of this may exclaim, 'Ah! but I thought the Times always insisted on being told the meaning of these mysterious advertisements.' So they may; but still nothing can be easier than to affix an imaginary meaning to it before insertion.

The London Correspondent of the *Cardiff Times* was in favour of abolishing all private inquiry offices, not just Pollaky's. On 13 April 1866 he made this plain, referring to Pollaky in passing as 'the usurper of Paddington-green'.

There are a number of series of advertisements in *The Times* in which one can almost follow a story from start to finish. One involved messages to the mysterious Heart of Stone. The first appeared on 9 September 1859, though Pollaky's name was not attached to it. They do not make happy reading. Pollaky's name appears involved, apparently not for the first time, in the following advertisement of October 1865, one of the series of four which appeared that month:

The Times – Tuesday, 3 October 1865

THE HEART OF STONE – Why torture the victim longer? Bright prospects shine if you meet at once. Present conduct very suspicious to him who knows all; indicates also desire to delude, and exhibits all the past professions to have been for the same purpose. The 'Martyr' can no longer endure such ungenerous, petty insult; it out-Herods all. Address, as before, under cover, to Mr Pollaky, Private Inquiry-office, 13, Paddington-green, W.

The next example reads like an extract from a melodrama, showing, we imagine, a young lady who wears her heart on her sleeve. This was published for all to read, and it is therefore no wonder that with such material as this, *The Times* 'Second Column' was as popular as it was, and that it continued to be on the front page for many years, nor that Sherlock Holmes should find it a source of so much to interest him.

The Times – Monday, 13 November 1865

GASTON. I have seen you at last; but alas! too late, for I am now the wife of another, and from henceforth, should we ever chance to meet, it must be as strangers. Let me implore you to return my letters under cover to Mr Pollaky, private inquiry office, 13, Paddington-green; and my last prayer is, that you leave England at once, and in other climes endeavour to forget that 'Rosebud' ever existed. – Farewell.

Some were in doubt as to the genuineness of this advertisement and others like it:

The *Worcester Journal* quoted the *Pall Mall Gazette's* opinion of the 'Gaston' advertisement under the heading: 'MR. POLLAKY RIGGING THE MARKET'. In the view of that paper:

Worcester Journal – Sunday, 25 November 1865
Much as we wish to believe in the reality of that little bit of romance, we cannot do so. Reason rebukes the desire, and we feel bound to make known the suspicion that the letter sprang from a brain fertile but unfeminine, and probably quite unromantic: namely that of Mr Pollaky himself. We doubt whether a real 'Rosebud' advertises her real agony: we question whether Mr Pollaky does not simply advertise his utterly abominable and most mischievous business.

This description of Pollaky's business, 'abominable and most mischievous', feels like an echo from the anonymous comments made on the back of the letter of 16 June 1862 about his abortive attempt at naturalisation. That he left himself open to this criticism must be put down to his need to push himself forward in a way that would irritate others: unconsciously on his part no doubt.

1866

Meanwhile, the advertisements continued:

The Times – Friday, 9 February 1866
ANONYMOUS LETER. – Whereas, some evil-disposed person did maliciously write and send an anonymous letter, bearing the London post mark, February 24, W. district, to a lady in Bayswater. A proper REWARD will be given to whoever shall furnish INFORMATION to enable the law being put in force against the person so offending. – Pollaky's private inquiry office, No. 13, Paddington-green, W.

The Times – Monday, 2 April 1866
G. – Having prolonged my stay in Austria longer than expected, will you MAKE a SECOND APPOINTMENT for one day next week? – Pollaky, 13, Paddington-green, W.

The Times – Saturday, 21 April 1866
CLANDESTINELY LEFT her HOME, a YOUNG LADY, 15 years of age; has light brown hair, large brown eyes, a cicatrice over the right temple, regular features and is of remarkably pale complexion; speaks French, but very little English; was dressed in a black and white striped silk dress, short black velvet mantle, and white straw bonnet; linen marked, 'F.H'. INFORMATION to Mr Pollaky. Private Inquiry-office, 13, Paddington-green, W. [cicatrice: a small scar or pockmark]

Pollaky reacted strongly when he felt others were taking advantage of his good nature, as can be seen from his method of dealing with a trifling, but highly irritating matter:

The Times – Friday, 8 June 1866

A.B. – Mine is not a receiving office, where letters can be left at call; nor do I hold myself answerable if any person or persons, unauthorised and without my sanction, choose to make my office the medium of their correspondence. All such letters go into the waste paper basket, and from thence into the fire. – POLLAKY, Private Inquiry-office, 13, Paddington-green.

The next item includes the only example of an actual report as made by Pollaky. According to this, he discovered that reported cases of abduction in Hull were unfounded:

The Times – Thursday, 4 October 1866

There has recently been going the rounds of the newspapers a paragraph stating that at Hull a most nefarious traffic in abducting young girls from their homes and conveying them to Germany for immoral purposes was being carried on. In consequence of that statement the London Society for the Protection of Young Women took the matter up and placed it in the hands of Mr Pollaky to investigate, and the following is an official report of the facts upon which the rumour was founded:– 'I have examined the occurrence-book respecting young girls reported missing from their homes or situations, and have ascertained that six were reported missing between the 19th and 24th of September last, three of them from home and three from situations. Three of them were of the age of 14 years, one 15, one 17, and one 18 years. Two of them returned home, having been to some relatives; one was found at Cottingham with her relatives; one at Beverley with her friends, one was found by Police-constable Clay among some prostitutes in Manor-street and taken home, and the other has been heard of at Grimsby, and her mother is going there in search of her. The above was the only account they had of girls missing during the month of September." Mr. Pollaky produced a letter from the Mayor of Hull expressing his surprise at such a report having gained publicity, and requesting him to get the published statement contradicted.'

The Times of Saturday, 8 December reported of a mission undertaken to Basle, Switzerland by Sergeant Webb accompanied by Pollaky in order to affect the arrest of one Lionel Holdsworth who had plotted to defraud various insurance companies by destroying the British ship Severn, while it was on the high seas. Holdsworth had been detained by the Swiss authorities and had 'expressed his willingness to proceed to England to answer the charge against him'. Sergeant

Webb and Pollaky, 'in their search for him had not been in bed for seven consecutive nights, to have one day's rest'. Pollaky is described in the article as an 'officer', though he would not become a Special Constable attached to Division X until the following year.

1867

The *Argus*, Melbourne – Wednesday, 18 October 1867
ARTHUR TOMS. – Should this meet the eye of ARTHUR TOMS, son of the Rev. William Toms, a native of Devonshire, who left England November, 1863, and was last heard of at Adelaide, South Australia, he is requested to communicate immediately with Mr Pollaky, Private Inquiry Office, 13 Paddington-green, London, where a communication of vast importance is awaiting him.'

The Lomax Affair – Part 1

The Lomax Affair was thoroughly horrific – a case of appalling child abuse. It caused Pollaky a considerable amount of trouble and personal anxiety, even though he seems to have had no part in the matter except as an observer during the court proceedings:

Blackburn Standard – Wednesday, 23 October 1867
REVOLTING CRUELTY TO A CHILD. A case in which a mother was charged with gross cruelty to her daughter has been heard before the magistrates at Margate. The defendant was Adelaide Lomax, wife of John Lomax, of East Cliff Villa; and it was alleged that she assaulted Agnes Lomax otherwise Agnes Bailey. Mary Ann Petley, a servant, who had lived in the employment of Mrs Lomax from the 9th of February to the 20th of July last, described the treatment to which the child had been subject. She said – About a month after I went there one of the children, named Agnes Lomax, was placed in the sink by Mrs. Lomax, who threw several jugs of cold water over her for being dirty. She is between six and seven years of age. Since then she has always had her hands tied behind or in front of her with string, and rice and mustard have been rubbed in her.

The report continues with the servant's description of Mrs Lomax's inhumane and brutal treatment of her daughter. Rebecca Kennedy, another domestic who had also been employed by Mrs Lomax confirmed the testimony of Mary Ann Petley, adding that Mrs Lomax had told her that the reason for her ill-treatment of Agnes, 'was because she was afraid Mr Lomax would die, and leave her [Agnes] more than she [Mrs Lomax] would wish him to do'. The beatings she had given her daughter had caused at one time or another, bleeding from her fingernails, toenails and tongue. The case was adjourned. Other papers also reported the matter:

South Eastern Gazette – Tuesday, 29 October 1867
ALLEGED CRUELTY TO A CHILD. – At the Borough Police Court, on Wednesday last, Adelaide Lomax was placed at the bar, charged on remand with cruelly assaulting and beating her child, Agnes Lomax. [...] The court was densely crowded during the whole of the hearing, and considerable manifestations of approval and disapproval were made by the public.[...] Mr Pollaky watched the case on behalf of the London Society for the Protection of Young Females.

And that is the only mention of Pollaky's connection with this case. These dreadful events were described in this paper as being 'of the more revolting character'. Among other abuses, Little Agnes had been tied up to some hat pegs in the hall of her parents' house, with her hands tied behind her all night long. She was wearing a 'chemise', but no shoes or socks. Robert Lewis Wardell, aged 14, who with his brother was lodging in the Lomax house, as they went to school nearby, gave evidence that Mr and Mrs Lomax were both in the house at the time. Mr Sicklemore (one of the magistrates) commented, 'The way in which the child was tied prevented it from lying down.' A dozen witnesses for the defence gave evidence that they had never seen the mother treat the child cruelly, but that the child had been bruised when her parents were away in Brussels, during which time she had been left in the charge of the servant, Rebecca Kennedy. The report continues:

One witness for the defence deposed that during their [the Lomaxes'] absence he found the girl naked and tied to the kitchen doorpost by a rope that was fastened round her waist. [...] Other acts of cruelty were proved against this servant, and the excuse she made was that she had been told to do so by her mistress [...] to prevent it [the child] getting into trouble.

In a very full report on the trial, which took place at the Dover Sessions on 30 December 1867, the *Whitstable Times and Herne Bay Herald* of 4 January 1868 gave further details. Adelaide Lomax had pleaded not guilty. Mary Ann Petley had deposed that Agnes had been compelled on many occasions to eat bread with mustard or cayenne pepper spread on it; the audience had hissed at this revelation, and hissed again when told of how blood had flowed from the child's fingernails. A neighbour had heard, 'lamentable cries of a child issuing from the defendant's house'. According to Rebecca Kennedy, Mr and Mrs Lomax called all their servants 'Ann', and Agnes had been told to tell the Wardell brothers, who had discovered her tied up, that 'Ann' had tied her. Rebecca left her employment because Mr Lomax struck her, and had heard him say to his wife, 'If you are not careful, Adelaide, we shall be served the same here as in Boulogne'. Robert Wardell confirmed that when asked who had tied her up in the hall passage, Agnes replied, 'Ann'. Mr Lomax had tried to put it about that it was the servants who had abused his daughter, and the counsel for the defence made it plain that he felt that the servants had grudges against the Lomaxes as they had been dismissed, saying that they had conspired 'to take away the fair fame of, and consign this woman to imprisonment'. Defendants at that time were not allowed to give evidence, neither were their spouses allowed to do so, and the counsel for the defence hoped that the law would be reformed so as to allow accused parties to give evidence in future cases.

The outcome on 30 December 1867 was that Adelaide Lomax was found guilty and sentenced at the Dover Quarter Session of the Peace, to twelve months imprisonment with hard labour for assault. And that should have been the end of the matter, at least as far as Pollaky was concerned. Meanwhile, he had plenty of other work to occupy him.

1868

The next advertisement (one of a number of identical ones placed over a few days) was placed at the request of the agents for the Tichborne family. Pollaky had been asked to find witnesses to the last sightings of Sir Roger Tichborne who disappeared in 1854 after the ship *Bella* sank near Rio de Janeiro. The notorious case of the Tichborne Claimant, which finally came to court in the 1870s, resulted in the jailing of the claimant, Arthur Orton, who claimed to be Roger Tichborne, heir to the Tichborne baronetcy and fortune. He first came forward in 1866, and was recognised as the missing man, despite the difference in physical appearance, by Roger Tichborne's mother. The other members of the family were not convinced and sought to disprove the Claimant's identity. Pollaky was engaged by the family to find the necessary proof that Roger Tichborne had not survived:

The Times – Thursday, 23 January 1868
BELLA. – Any of the CREW SAVED from the ship BELLA, lost off Rio in 1854, are requested to COMMUNICATE with Mr. Pollaky, Private Inquiry-office, 13, Paddington-green.

Dr Edward Kenealy, the claimant's defending counsel at his trial for perjury in 1874, wrote in his account of the trial, 'It affords matter for curious speculation whether, if any of the crew had turned up, Mr Pollaky would have sent them to the claimant or his advisors.' Kenealy's book presents a very biased picture of the claimant.

After the trial Kenealy was disbarred as a result of his abusive interrogations of some of the witnesses. The claimant was released in 1884, and in 1895 admitted that he was Arthur Orton, but then withdrew his admission. It seems remarkable that Pollaky was asked to advertise for this information, as a member of the family had already hired Jonathan Whicher, now working as a private investigator, to investigate the origins of the claimant. Whicher's reward was £2,000; according to the book about the case by Kenealy's son, he was astute and unscrupulous and had employed 'derelicts from Wapping, and a number of other needy East-enders' to spy on the claimant's family.

The *Illustrated Photographer* – Friday, 29 May 1868

Photography is the best detective! The Viennese Neue Freie Presse [*New Free Press*] relates the following respecting the capture of an Englishman, named Grey, who by means of forged cheques on the Union Bank of London, swindled the house [of] Rosenbaum of a large amount of money. Through accident, the said banker, Mr Rosenbaum, became possessed of a photograph of the fugitive, and gave the same to the police inspector Breitenfield, at Vienna, who remitted it to Mr Pollaky, an Austrian detective resident in London, who caused the necessary inquiries to be made in London, as it was supposed Grey made direct for England with his booty. Last week it happened, however, that Mr Pollaky, on his way to Vienna, passed through Hamburg, and there visited the theatre, and during the entr'acte passed his time by inspecting the audience, when to his great surprise and no less satisfaction, he discovered in one of the visitors the most striking resemblance to the photo sent to him some months ago from Vienna. Of course this man was at once closely watched, and a telegram dispatched to Vienna; upon which the firm dispatched their cashier, who recognised the swindler, although a great change in his appearance had taken place since his debut at Vienna.

The news item goes on to report that Grey was arrested and sent to Vienna to be dealt with, and also that he was in fact French not English. A not uncommon type of case for the international detective that Pollaky was, this report is nevertheless interesting for pointing out that Pollaky was a theatre-goer, and this is something which will be considered in Chapter 12. A similar item appears in the *Nashville Union and Dispatch* of 14 June with the added information that 'Grey, whose real name is Freyer, is a Frenchman, and the head of the band, which has operated for many years at Odessa, St. Petersburg, Munich, and other places'.

The following two items tell another tale unfortunately still relevant today. This case had, at least, a happy ending. Not all cases of kidnapping are resolved as satisfactorily as this, although the kidnapped child had been kept away from his parents for a very long time:

The Times – Tuesday, 15 September 1868
HIDDEN, and Kept by Two Ladies from his Parents, a Boy, nine years of age, &c. – The ADVERTISEMENT which has appeared under the above heading in The Times for the last three days, and in which a reward of £20 was offered for the recovery of the said long-lost child, is herewith WITHDRAWN, the boy having been found, poorly clad, at a modest watering place within 40 miles of London, and restored by Mr Pollaky himself to the bereaved mother after a separation of several years. Mr Pollaky begs to return publicly his sincere thanks to that section of his numerous correspondents on this subject who, actuated by humane motives alone, volunteered their services and information. – Private Inquiry office, 13, Paddington-green.

Lloyds Weekly London Newspaper – Sunday, 20 September 1868
THE LOST CHILD. – The quiet watering-place of Southend was thrown into a good deal of commotion on Saturday by the following circumstance: – An advertisement had appeared during the last few days, offering a reward of twenty pounds for the recovery of a child who had been removed from his parents for a considerable time, and his whereabouts could not be discovered. The matter, it appeared, was placed in the hand of the well-known Mr Pollaky. It appears that information was received that the missing child was at Southend, and thither Mr Pollaky proceeded, accompanied by the mother. Inquiries had been made which resulted in steps being taken to watch the post-office, which is opposite the 'Royal hotel', and about eleven o'clock a boy, about nine years old, was seen to go to the post-office, and he was recognised by the lady who accompanied Mr Pollaky as the lost child. He was at once laid hold of, and handed to the lady, and placed in a carriage that was in readiness and driven off much to the surprise of the bystanders. What further steps will be taken in the matter remains to be seen, as the long-lost child is at present safe in the charge of its parents, who, it is said, are person of considerable position.

As a result of the last sentence, we can probably assume that in this case Pollaky received a proper fee for his services – after all, this was his profession.

The Lomax Affair – Part 2

The Lomax case was deemed interesting enough for details to be published as far away as Australia. The Lomaxes had been considered quite respectable. Lomax was a journalist, and visitors to their home included Police Superintendent Saunders and his wife, who were given roses from the garden by their hosts. They had three children of whom Agnes was the eldest. Lomax took great exception to his wife's conviction, and seems in some measure to have held Pollaky responsible. The following report speaks for itself:

Daily News – Monday, 26 October 1868

[Marylebone Police Court]

John Gordon Lomax was summoned for using abusive and threatening language to Ignatius Paul Pollaky, and there was also a cross summons against Pollaky for abusive words towards Lomax.

Mr Lewis, jun., appeared for Mr Pollaky, and Mr Wilding for Mr Lomax.

The summons against Mr Lomax having been first taken out, Mr Pollaky appeared as first complainant.

Mr Lewis said – I am afraid, from the well-known character of the man, that unless some stringent measures are adopted some serious consequences will arise. Mr Pollaky has been engaged for a number of years as a private inquiry officer, and is well-known to the public. It appears that he is also a non-paid officer of the Society for the Suppression of Vice and for the Protection of Young Women. It seems that defendant's [Lomax] wife or mistress, whichever she may be, was charged with violently assaulting a child at Margate. My client, in his capacity of an officer of the society, had to make inquiries into the case. She was sent to trial and convicted, and sentenced to twelve months' hard labour. Ever since the defendant has been in the habit of assailing Mr Pollaky with most gross and filthy language as he goes about. In addition to this he has sent a number of letters containing most abominable language and holding out threats. One I have here, commencing, 'Now, my cock, I have started and intend to go in against you and all the provincial and London press, and do not intend to leave you until all matters are finished.' This is the sort of language he makes use of towards my client. I may inform you, sir, that since the affair at Margate the defendant has been convicted and sentenced to 14 days. The offence that we now complain of took place in the street. Now what we want is that he be bound over in some large amount of bail to prevent him committing any violence upon Mr Pollaky.

Mr Pollaky's evidence was then taken. It bore out the statement of his counsel as to letters having been received, and threatening language used. He expressed his belief that his life was not safe while Lomax remained at large.

The defendant denied having sent the letters complained of, and stated on his oath that they were not in his handwriting. He also swore that he had never used threats toward Pollaky, against whom he brought a counter charge of being abusive.

Mr Mansfield said the case ought not to have been brought into court. He believed there was no danger of a breach of the peace and dismissed both summonses.

That Lomax was deeply upset by the events cannot be doubted; there were tragic consequences. On Saturday 16 May 1868, the *Leeds Times* reported that, while in prison, Adelaide Lomax had given birth to a child which had died there. Of Adelaide, continued the report, 'she has become insane, and has recently been removed to a lunatic asylum'.

The fact remains that Pollaky said he felt he was in danger. In Chapter 13 we will see how this kind of fear seemed to worry him in his old age, long after he had retired. However respectable Lomax had been considered to be, the rude and abusive language he used paints an unsavoury picture of a man used to making threats.

By 1870, John Gordon Lomax and Adelaide were together again and living in West London where he described himself as a 'Gentleman'. Records show that they had a son in July of that year. That made a total of three children in their household, for there is no sign of Agnes.

In reading news from so many years ago, one can not help but reflect how little society has changed. So many of the same problems still exist in one form or another today, and this despite the work carried out by people who would change things for the better. Pollaky was such a one. What could his motive have been? A desire to do good for its own sake? A need to improve his own standing in the eyes of authority? A need for publicity to further his career? By mid-1868 he had four living children – three were girls – did this give him a need to show protectiveness not just for his own family, but for any who were potentially vulnerable? Or had his younger days in Hungary affected his character so as to make him sensitive to the evils of the world?

Public figures, then as now, often had fun made of them. Nowadays we have *Private Eye*. One of the satirical journals of the late 1860s was the *Tomahawk*:

The Tomahawk: A Saturday Journal of Satire – Saturday, 14 November 1868

POLLACK'S CHRISTMAS ANNUAL

POLLAKY, the Benefactor of Mysterious Mankind, is evidently under the impression that he is not so well known as he deserves to be. He is consequently publishing in the daily papers condensed romances, which will make hum-drum prosers shudder, and suggest whole plots to the mind of a Boucicault or a Byron. One day we have the startling incident of an elderly nobleman of the British type, with projecting teeth and fair whiskers, running off with a young French lady of engaging exterior: another day brings us intelligence of a heart-rending occurrence on the Rhine, a young lady who plunges into the river from the deck of a steamer – we are left in suspense as to whether she is picked up or remains with the Loreley. What an admirable idea this would be for obtaining stories for a Christmas Annual. Advertise for parties who witnessed such and such fancy circumstances, and immediately you would receive dozens of letters from individuals who imagined they had been witnesses to the acts described. For instance, we insert the following advertisement:

SWALLOWS. – Any lady or gentleman who was present at the Charing-cross Terminus, when a Spanish-looking volunteer, of Herculean mould, swallowed a small black and tan carpet-bag, will be rendering great service to the heartbroken advertisers by forwarding his or her name to Rollicky, Colney-Hatch.

Two days after, a shoal of letters arrives from persons of both sexes who have been witnesses to different acts of deglutition at various railway stations in London. Though, of course, not one has any reference to the absolute fact of a volunteer swallowing a carpet-bag, all detail something more or less curious; and, putting the ideas together, would, in the hands of experienced writers, make very good sensation.

After this hint, if Pollaky brings out an Annual, he will be expected to leave a copy at our office, with the half of any profits in the sale thereof; and should he supply Mr Dion Reade or Mr Charles Boucicault with the ingredients of an original drama, perhaps he will let us know at his earliest convenience.

The *Tomahawk* was founded by Arthur William à Beckett in London in 1867 and ran until 1870. It was frequently very scathing in its burlesque of political and other public figures, far more so than *Fun*. In November 1868 its price was threepence. In 1869, the year after this article appeared, novelist Charles Reade (1814–84), together with Irish playwright Dion Boucicault (1820–90), their first names having been cleverly(!) exchanged by the *Tomahawk* writer, wrote a novel called *Foul Play*, a story about a clergyman transported to Australia for a crime he did not commit. This was dramatised by novelist Marcus Clarke (1846–81) with the title *Foul Play or The Wreck of the Prosperine*. The novel itself has an anonymous detective as a character, but in the play, the detective is given a name – Alexander Ignatius Paul Pollaky Wolouski. Dion Boucicault, like Pollaky, gets a mention in the Colonel's song in W.S. Gilbert's lyric: 'The pathos of Paddy, as rendered by Boucicault' (See Appendix 2). Colney-Hatch, given as the address for Rollicky, was famous for its lunatic asylum.

1869

The *Tomahawk*, with its usual cutting humour, suggests Pollaky as a replacement for the late Sir Richard Mayne as Chief Commissioner of the Metropolitan Police, saying of Pollaky:

The Tomahawk: A Saturday Journal of Satire – Saturday, 9 January 1869
This gentleman thinks that he is now sufficiently well known – thanks to the large sums he has expended in sensational advertisements – to entitle him to the confidence and respect of the community. He would undertake to conduct his business on reasonable terms.

The *South Eastern Gazette* – Monday, 15 February 1869
Taunton Courier – 17 February 1869
EXTRAORDINARY CHARGE AGAINST A CLERGYMAN. – At Worcester, on Friday, a clergyman, the Rev. J. Merest, appeared to a summons at the instance of Mr Workman, of London charging him with having, on the 5th October last, sent a letter to him demanding money with menaces. [...] Evidence was then given to identify the defendant's handwriting with the letter in question; and the testimony of Detective Bates, from Pollaky's private inquiry office, and other witnesses was given.

Merest was committed for trial. Bates was evidently one of Pollaky's agents. Mysterious men who flit in and out of the records but with little information about them.

The Times – Wednesday, 23 June 1869
FLED from their HOMES, on Thursday, the 17th inst., with the supposed intention of proceeding to Rome, for the purpose of conversion, TWO YOUNG LADIES, both under 19 years of age – one, 5 feet 3 inches in height, slender built, chestnut-brown hair, finely chiselled features, and mole on left cheek; the other, 5 ft. 5in., pale complexion, dark eyes and hair, and inclined to 'embonpoint'. Both dressed in dark clothes, and having little or no luggage. A REWARD of ONE HUNDRED POUNDS will be given for information as to their whereabouts, provided such information is furnished within 10 days from this 22nd day of June, 1869. – I. POLLAKY, Private Inquiry-office, 13, Paddington-green, W.

Public Ledger, Memphis, Tennessee – Wednesday Evening, 23 June 1869
Royalty. – Any one giving information which shall lead to the discovery of the writer of an anonymous letter, signed 'Royalty,' and addressed to a lady, Saturday last, 15th inst, shall receive a reward of £50, on application to Mr Pollaky, Private Inquiry Office, 13 Paddington Green.

The Times – Saturday, 7 August 1869
'SIROCCO.' – Mistaken kindness! Have you forgotten the cavern? – Pollaky, Paddington-green.

The Times – Friday, 24 September 1869

MYSTERIOUSLY DISAPPEARED from his home, on the afternoon of the 22nd April, the only child of a wealthy citizen of Frankfurt-on-the-Main, a lad named FRIEDRICH MAXIMILIAN FREIEISEN, 15 years of age, middle stature, strong built, full face, ruddy complexion, thick light hair, and light eyebrows; has a large swelling on the left hip. Was dressed in black coat and vest, black necktie, dark speckled trousers, and small hat. Up to his disappearance he bore a most exemplary character. Information to be given to Mr Pollaky, Private Inquiry Office, 13 Paddington-green.

On 3 January 1870, at the Reading Quarter Sessions, Elizabeth Barry was sentenced to five months' imprisonment for Child Stealing. Even those in Pollaky's employ might be less than pure, as this item shows:

Shields Gazette and Daily Telegraph – Saturday, 23 October 1869

THE RECENT ABDUCTION OF A CHILD.

Mr Pollaky, who keeps a private inquiry office, says that Elizabeth Barry, the abductionist, was in his service for a month, as cook, but it was not through him that she got a character, as his wife declined to see any lady in her behalf.

1870

The Times – Friday, 7 January 1870

HALFPENNY KITE. – Trauernde Mutter sucht ihr Kind. – POLLAKY. Private Inquiry-office, 13, Paddington-green, W.

[*Trauernde Mutter sucht ihr Kind* = Sorrowing mother searches for her child.]

The *Courier*, Brisbane – Monday, 17 January 1870

MYSTERIOUSLY disappeared from her home, near Wilton-crescent, London, Friday, 15th instant, a young lady, twenty years of age, middle stature, glossy dark-brown hair, coffee-colored [*sic*] brown eyes, small mouth, and good teeth; was last seen (in plaid poplin walking dress and black hat with raven feather) at Victoria Station, carrying small red 'necessaire'; supposed no other luggage. Information to Mr Pollaky, Private Inquiry Office, 13 Paddington-green, London. – Advertisement in the Times.

The Times – Tuesday, 8 March 1870

SECULAR (Rome). – Nos. 50, 52, 53 safe – 51, 52 ominous fingermarks! 51, struggled nobly. – POLLAKY, 13, Paddington-green.

The Times – Monday, 28 March 1870

G (Paris). – Like a gentleman with whom however I claim no acquaintance, I am not so black as painted. In the case alluded to, I have not done half that is imputed to me, but a man in my position must learn to bear unmerited criticism. – Pollaky, Paddington-green.

County Observer and Monmouthshire Central Advertiser – Saturday, 18 June 1870

POLLAKY, the great private detective, whose 'private inquiry office' is as well-known to the reader of the Times as the hatch-match and dispatch column, has gone to Oxford on business connected with the recent outrage in Christchurch. It was to have been hoped that the matter would have been allowed to drop. The offence of the undergraduates was not nearly so bad as at first supposed, and in the majority of instances the sentences pronounced by the authorities of the college were sufficiently severe.

The Franco-Prussian War began on July 1870 and lasted until May 1871. As is the case today the supplying of arms to one side or another was a controversial issue. There had been rumours that armaments were being supplied to the French by a Birmingham-based company. Philip Henry Muntz (1811–88), Liberal Member of Parliament who had been Mayor of Birmingham in 1839 wrote to *The Times* stating that no rifles had been sent out of that town. Many were sceptical. Shortly afterwards, according to the *Engineer* (16 September 1870), 'Mr Pollaky, of private inquiry celebrity, advertised for information upon the subject and in a few days wrote to the Times refuting Mr Muntz, and stating that on the 6th inst. 227 cases, containing 4540 Sniders [rifles] were despatched to Havre.' The newspapers were highly exercised by this, as the following articles show:

The *Standard* – Wednesday, 7 September 1870

The ingenious Mr. POLLAKY, of Private Inquiry Office fame, whose announcements regarding missing young ladies of sixteen with fair tresses and alpaca frocks, absconding clerks of short stature with villainous countenances and singular moles, and other interesting individuals who are 'wanted', are so familiar to the public, has come out with an advertisement of a decidedly novel kind. On behalf of some person or persons unknown, or on his own behalf, he has offered fifty pounds reward for information as to certain rifles or 'other contraband of war', said to 'have been purchased in this country for immediate exportation in neutral bottoms on behalf of one of the belligerents', &c. The 'strictest secrecy' to be observed regarding the informant, and the reward only to 'stand good for 21 days after this date'. Is the 'active and intelligent' POLLAKY instructed by some private patriotic individual, or some more than ordinarily weak member of the British Government; or is it by the astute BISMARCK, in search of a casus beli or a grievance against England? Has it struck Mr POLLAKY or his mysterious and not over wise, if English, patron, that if any person were in a position to earn this reward it could lead to nothing under the present state of the British law? It is for German cruisers to seize arms if they can find them on the high seas.

Amidst the active correspondence which took place about this subject, the following article appeared relaying in no uncertain terms its criticism of Pollaky with heaviest sarcasm the writer could muster, feeling that Pollaky's letters were written purely to advertise, or puff, his business:

The *Northern Echo* – Monday, 12 September 1870

Paddington-green is twice famous. It was once the home of one POLLY PERKINS, who was 'as beautiful as a butterfly – as proud as a queen'. Now it is the haunt of one 'POLLAKY', the prince of private detectives. The famous 'green', which now has no verdure, and where metaphorical greenness is unknown, is the headquarters of inquisitiveness. Mr POLLAKY – or plain 'POLLAKY', as he signs himself, as if he were a Lord or a Bishop – undertakes for a consideration to investigate the private affairs of the domestic circle, or to worm out the secrets of the State, and to impart them to the inquisitive persons who employ him. Has your fair-haired, blue-eyed daughter run off with a penniless young scamp? – you go to Paddington-green and POLLAKY will tell you where the birds have made their nest. Has your spouse eloped? – POLLAKY will get you to pounce upon the villain who has decoyed her, and will prepare the evidence that will enable you to rid yourself of the faithless one. Has your cashier deranged your accounts and levanted with your cashbox? – POLLAKY will direct you where to seek him. Does a Birmingham manufacturer seek to involve the nation in the Continental war by supplying the belligerents with rifles and other warlike munitions? – POLLAKY, of Paddington-green will tell you the precise number of cases that have been sent, and the precise number each case contained. POLLAKY is the Old Boguey of every one who has anything to conceal, the bosom friend of every one who is inquisitive and can afford to pay. The utmost reliance can be placed upon POLLAKY'S discretion. He informs his client that 'the strictest secrecy will be ensured'. Once, and once only has POLLAKY been known to divulge a secret imparted to him. Mr Muntz wrote to the Times to say he could not hear of any 40,000 rifles having been sent from Birmingham; whereupon POLLAKY, with a professional pride which overcame both his patriotism and the rules of his profession, rushed into print to show that POLLAKY was not so easily to be bamboozled as the hon. member for Birmingham. 'I also made inquiries', he wrote, 'and find that 227 cases, containing 4,540 Sniders (each rifle fitted with bayonet), have been received at Southampton Docks from Birmingham, which said rifles were dispatched by steamer Fannie, for Havre, on the night of the 6th inst'. But it will be observed that the name of the Birmingham manufacturer was not imparted to the public. POLLAKY prudently conceals that important part of the nefarious transaction, perhaps until he has traced the remaining 35,460 rifles which have yet to be accounted for. In the meantime the public may be excused if they regard the statement that a certain number of rifles have been sent from some unknown person in Birmingham to an unknown shipper at Southampton, as a 'bold advertisement' of POLLAKY'S Inquiry Office.

London Daily News – Wednesday, 14 September 1870
TO THE EDITOR OF THE DAILY NEWS
SIR. – Will Mr. Pollaky explain for whom are the field pieces and siege guns intended that are made at Sir W. Armstrong's Works, and shipped to Rotterdam, thence re-shipped into barges and delivered at Cologne? – I am, &c., FAIRPLAY. Sept. 13.

The *Southern Reporter* – Thursday, 22 September 1870
THE ALLEGED EXPORT OF ARMS TO FRANCE.
Mr Pollaky, the private detective, continues to advertise himself by giving asserted particulars respecting the export of arms to France; and some people are beginning to believe that he is employed by the Prussian Government to make discoveries and publish them.

This last item has a ring of truth about it, for it may have been as a result of Pollaky's investigation into this affair, that on 4 September 1871 he was awarded the Ritterkreuz (Knight's Cross) Second Class of the Saxe-Ernestine House Order, a German Ducal award founded in 1833 by Duke Friedrich of Saxe-Altenburg, Duke Ernst I of Saxe-Coburg-Gotha and Duke Bernhard II of Saxe-Meiningen. The award was given as a 'special mark of Princely goodwill', and the cost was paid for out of the Ducal private fund. He was very proud of this award, and often referred to it in later years. In 1897, the Minister of State for Gotha, Karl Friedrich von Strenge, tried to find out whether Pollaky and two other recipients of the award were still alive. The British minister in Coburg, Alexander Condie Stephen, could find no information on Pollaky, who had retired long before and was living in Brighton. The records are held in the Gotha State Archives.

And if you look carefully at Faustin Betbeder's illustration of Pollaky (see plate No. 1), you will notice that he is pictured wearing the medal on his left lapel.

1871

Pollaky's advertisements were so interesting to the public that some were expanded into little short stories so that readers could link them together and discover the outcome. The following case tells an old story:

Teesdale Mercury – Wednesday, 8 November 1871
LIGHT ON THE RAMSGATE MYSTERY.
Some sensation was created last week at Ramsgate by the mysterious disappearance of a gentleman named Esdale, who was supposed to be drowned. [...] Mr Esdale, who, it seems, had been married only 18 months, went to Ramsgate and put up at the Granville Hotel. [...] In the course of the evening he left the hotel to take a stroll, but he never returned. The next morning Mr Esdale's clothes were found scattered about the beach saturated with sea-water, but the owner of them was nowhere to be found.

Thus the exposition. But many doubted that Esdale had drowned. The report continues:

The following advertisements appeared in a morning paper: –
'Mary to Willie. – For God's sake let me see you. Write at any rate. The way is smooth to return.'
'Willie. – I for one do not believe you are drowned, notwithstanding your sea-water saturated clothes have been found scattered on the beach. You had better return at once, to save your friends trouble and expense. – Pollaky.'
'Mysteriously disappeared from Ramsgate, since the evening of Monday, the 16th inst., a young gentleman, 23 years of age, 5 ft. 11in. in height, athletic figure, of fair complexion, dark brown hair, parted in the middle, slight brown whiskers and moustache, thin face, one front tooth in the lower jaw missing. – Information to Mr Pollaky, Private Inquiry office, No. 13 Paddington-green.'
In consequence of these advertisements, and inquiries that were made, it was ascertained that Mr Esdale was not dead, but that he had returned to London the same night, and had since taken his passage in the Golden Fleece to the Cape of Good Hope under an assumed name.

From the most unattractive picture painted in the description of 'Willie' Esdale, one might suppose that his wife would be glad to see the back of him. This case of a fake suicide may refer to William Esdale, listed on the 1871 census as a timber merchant who lived with his wife Mary in Golders Green, London, He was in fact 22 and she was 20. However, if it was indeed this particular couple, she appears to have taken him back and had four children by him. William Crowder Esdaile, as his name was properly spelled, was born in 1849 in Shoreditch, London. He appears to have married Mary Dobell while she was still a minor, and to have lied on his application for a wedding licence by falsely swearing that her father had given his consent. Their marriage was announced in the *British Medical Journal* on 14 May 1870. They emigrated to Australia in about 1878, and after her death, he remarried and had two more children. He died in 1926 in New Zealand.

We seem to be in the realms of comedy. In 1847 John Madison Morton's farce, *Box and Cox*, was given its first performance at the Lyceum Theatre in London. In 1866 this was turned into a comic opera, *Cox and Box*, with music by Arthur Sullivan and words by F.C. Burnand; it features at one point one of the protagonists explaining how he managed to avoid getting married by faking his own suicide by drowning. Burnand's lyric is better known than Morton's dialogue. Here is Morton's version:

> Box: I left my home early one morning, with one suit of clothes on my back, and another tied up in a bundle, under my arm – I arrived on the cliffs – opened my bundle – deposited the suit of clothes on the very verge of the precipice – took one look down into the yawning gulph beneath me, and walked off in the opposite direction.

And here is Burnand's (as set by Sullivan):

> Box: Listen: I solemnly walked to the cliff.
> And singing a sort of a dulcet dirge,
> Put down my bundle upon the verge,
> Heard the wild seagulls mournful cry,
> Look'd all around, there was nobody nigh,
> None but I on the cliff so high,
> And all save the sea was bare and dry,
> And I took one look on the wave below,
> And I raised my hands in an agony throe,
> And I stood on the edge of the rock so steep,
> And I gaz'd like a maniac on the deep …
> I cried: 'Farewell, farewell to earth,
> Farewell, farewell to the land of my birth,
> Farewell, farewell to my only love,
> To the sea below, and the sky above.'
> With a glance at the sea of wild despair,
> I cried, 'I come.' My bundle lay there.
> At the edge, where the coastguard's way was chalk'd,
> Then away
> In the opposite way I walk'd.

(The saucy French farce *Frisette* 1846 by Labiche and Lefranc on which Morton based *Box and Cox* does not have an equivalent scene.)

So well known was the 'Agony Column' that there was even a song about it. Published by 'S. Brainardes Sons of New York' after 1871 (before then the firm was simply called 'S. Brainard'), in their *Second Series of Comic and Humorous Songs*, 'The Agony Column' or 'Little Di', was written by W. Burnot, and composed, to a polka rhythm, by T. Roberts. The first verse had the following lyrics:

> One day not far from Regent Street,
> Where cabs and buses whirl,
> I saw beneath a horse's feet
> A fascinating girl.
> To save her life I risk'd my own,
> What mortal could do less,
> She thank'd me warmly but refused
> To give me her address.

SPOKEN after first verse.
I persuaded her but she would only consent to advertise in one of the papers making an appointment with me she said she would head it with her name Little Di – I asked her whether she would put it in the Agony Column of –

CHORUS
The Standard or the Telegraph, the Echo or the Times,
Observer, Reynolds, Judy, Punch, or Bow Bells, or the Chimes,
The Hornet, Lloyds, or Figaro, or one of the Reviews,
The Globe or Sun, Dispatch or Fun, or Illustrated News.

(Sheet music for this song can be found in Appendix 2.)

1872

The Times – Friday, 8 March 1872
CARDINALS-HAT. – Will meet you at the place appointed on Tuesday next; and will there and then pay the REWARD. – POLLAKY, private inquiry office, 13, Paddington-green.

The Times – Friday, 29 March 1872
Ανδρωπoθαγων Νησων. – Shall be happy to see you any day next week. 1 to 2 p.m. – POLLAKY, private inquiry office, No. 13, Paddington-green.
[Ανδρωπoθαγων Νησων = Andropothagon Islands]

The Times – Wednesday, 17 April 1872

P.P. – Consider Hedgehog's terrible position, and the parents' anguish, and forward your present ADDRESS to Mr Pollaky, Private Inquiry-office, 13, Paddington-green, W.

The Times – Thursday, 25 April 1872

P.P. – Hedgehog's position becomes daily more embarrassing. Where is your conscience? – POLLAKY.

The Times – Thursday, 16 May 1872

E.M. – In a German capital has arrived a young English lady, apparently between 18 and 19 years of age, destitute and without friends. She is tall, very slight, and good-looking, having short, dark hair and Spanish eyes, small face, bad teeth. Her linen is very fine and marked E.M. According to her statement, she was secretly married in April, 1870, at an hotel in Battersea. The circumstance that her head has been recently shaved, and her incoherent expressions, lead to the supposition that she has escaped the care of friends in this country, for which reason this advertisement. INFORMATION will be gratefully received by Mr Pollaky, 13, Paddington-green.

On Saturday, 5 October 1872 the *Examiner*, discussing the trade in obscene materials, suggests that the Society for the Suppression of Vice employ Pollaky to, 'catch and convict dealers in obscene prints at so much per head'. The article suggests that the London centre of this trade is in Old Bond Street.

Fun found further sources of amusement in the 'Heart of Stone' and missing person advertisements in 1872:

Fun – Saturday, 9 November 1872

A Girl of Metal.

The immortal POLLAKY wants to hear of a girl who stole – let us say, did steel – away from home: – MYSTERIOUSLY LEFT her HOME, on Sunday last, a YOUNG LADY, 21 years of age, 5ft. 2, golden hair, clear steel blue eyes, and remarkably fair complexion. It should have been stated whether she had also an iron constitution and if – being further mentioned that she is in widow's attire – she had a heart of lead. The tin will probably be forthcoming for those who find her, for POLLAKY is no common 'copper', but knows how to employ his pen and his zinc in description.

Fun was a satirical weekly magazine published between 1861 and 1901. Contributors included W.S. Gilbert. Its humour was not usually as acid as the *Tomahawk*. The heavy-handed humour in this last piece lays too much stress on the pun steal/steel, and then tries to fit in as many types of metal as possible.

The Ladies was a very short-lived journal that wrote of 'court, fashion, and society. It was founded in March 1872 and its last issue was the following January:

The Ladies – Saturday, 30 November 1872

MR POLLAKY, the private inquiry agent and detective, announces that he is looking out for a missing young gentleman possessed of very strange and dangerous characteristics: and we hope he will soon be found, for terrible things may occur if he is at large for a considerable time. He has escaped from a Maison de Santé at Paris; and is described as being 'most intellectually gifted, but in his paroxysms has no moral perception whatever, his vanity then becomes excessive, and his irresponsible acts criminal'. As he is young, good looking, fond of uttering high sounding names, and speaks French admirably, this intellectual person who has no moral perception whatever, is a kind of Mephistopheles, and may perpetuate a fearful amount of mischief unless restrained. Intellect without conscience is the Satanic attribute, and we never heard of a human being who so nearly approached the ideal as this young gentleman who has escaped from the French asylum. Very likely Mr Pollaky will have competitors in the search, for, no doubt, there are some lines of business where this peculiar combination of qualities might be found useful.

1873

Evidence that Pollaky's name was now conjured when the occasion called, comes from a letter of 1873 written by the poet Dante Gabriel Rossetti to Lucy Madox Brown who would marry his brother William Michel Rossetti the following year. As Assistant Secretary in the Excise Division of the Inland Revenue Office, he had been engaged on some investigation connected with his work. The poet wrote to Lucy of 'William's début as the Pollaky of official life'.

The Times – Wednesday, 27 August 1873
ANNOUNCEMENT. – After a prolonged absence on foreign mission Mr POLLAKY has RETURNED, and his offices, at 13, Paddington-green, will be open to the public on and after the 1st September.

1874

This item was reprinted almost word for word on 28 November 1874 by the *Otago Witness*, New Zealand, showing how stories about Pollaky travelled round the world:

> *Herald and Planter* (Hallettsville, Texas) – Thursday, 8 October 1874
> The London Art Journal is responsible for the following story: A somewhat curious circumstance occurred lately, which is strangely illustrative of modern manners. A nobleman passing through a West-End street saw a fine but very dilapidated picture in a broker's shop. He purchased it, and inquired the painter's name, but was unable to discover more than the initials. Confident that the picture – a seaside view with a rocky shore – was modern, he was anxious to discover the painter. In vain he tried all the picture dealers. They knew the style and the initials, but were unacquainted with the man. They were confident the painter was alive, but they knew nothing of his home or his haunts. The nobleman piqued at being so balked, determined to find the painter, and at last, in despair, applied to Pollaky, the foreign detective. Pollaky knew nothing about art or artist, but he undertook to find the man. And find him he did, after some trouble, in the midst of the direst poverty, in a little court in Soho. The discovery of the artist was the turning point in his fortunes. The nobleman employed him, and at this moment there is a picture of his in the Academy marked 'sold.'

From London to Texas to New Zealand – even the most unassuming of Pollaky's cases seemed to be of interest to the newspaper-reading public. The *Otago Witness* entitled this piece 'A Pretty Story'. And indeed it is – of course, that title may have been given with its sarcastic meaning implied – a 'pretty story' is a euphemism for a 'tall tale' or a lie; either way, the title works.

> The *Argus*, Melbourne – Tuesday, 15 December 1874
> RICHARD SPARROW, the son of the late Nathaniel Sparrow, of Wexford, Ireland, now somewhere in Australia or New Zealand, will hear something to his advantage on applying to Mr Pollaky, Private Inquiry Office, 13 Paddington-green, London.

1875

> *Shields Gazette and Daily Telegraph* – Friday, 26 February 1875
> RESCUE OF A YOUNG LADY FROM A CONVENT.
> The Morning Advertiser states that on Tuesday afternoon the new convent at Windsor was the scene of some strange proceedings. A party of gentlemen applied to the Superioress to hand over to their custody a young lady who had recently

disappeared from her home suddenly, and had been traced to the convent. A clergyman appeared on the scene, who was immediately charged with decoying the young lady away. A scuffle ensued, during which several of the party entered the vestibule of the convent, and the young lady immediately came forward and volunteered to return at once to her friends. It appears she is entitled to a large sum of money, and is highly connected with some of the leading families of the county. Legal proceedings have been threatened against the friends of the young lady by the convent authorities, and Mr Pollaky, the private detective, who forcibly entered the institution, is also likely to be proceeded against. There was great excitement in the town on the matter becoming known.

Pollaky – knight in shining armour – rescues damsel in distress! This reads like a scene from Malory's *Morte d'Arthur*. We want to know how it all started, and how it ended, but we will probably never find either out.

1877

The *Argus*, Melbourne – Tuesday, 6 February 1877
The *Sydney Morning Herald* – Monday, 12 February 1877
MYSTERIOUSLY left his home in Leeds, on Friday, the 24th ultimo, a MARRIED GENTLEMAN, 40 years of age, 5 feet 9 inches in height, dark hair and beard tinged with grey, sallow complexion, small nose: supposed to be in company with a lady (not his wife), about 30, middle stature, very thin face, and red hair worn in plaits; may possibly have gone to Melbourne or Sydney. Information of their present whereabouts to Mr POLLAKY, Private Inquiry Office, 13 Paddington-green, London.

One imagines that the married gentleman who 'mysteriously left his home' would probably never be heard of again as he was evidently running away from his wife. Interesting that this gentleman is not named in the advertisement. Was there some element of personal shame on the part of his wife who wished for anonymity? Also interesting to note the description of the mistress, presumably supplied by the wife – 'very thin face, and red hair worn in plaits'. She could not bring herself to describe her rival in complimentary fashion, and has painted a most unattractive picture of her – and who can blame her?

The Turf Fraud Scandal

From June 1877 to June 1878, Pollaky was out of England. What he was doing during that time is currently unknown, except that in September 1877 he was in

Germany, possibly holidaying with his family in the mountainous Taunus region. However, while he was away, his name was being mentioned in connection with the most notorious case of police corruption yet heard at the Old Bailey.

The Trial of the Detectives – or The Turf Fraud Scandal – took place in 1877. Four senior police officers, Inspector John Meiklejohn, Chief Inspector William Palmer, Chief Inspector Nathaniel Druscovich, and Chief Inspector George Clarke together with solicitor Edward Froggatt were indicted on charges involving fraudulent betting and of warning criminals of imminent arrest, thus allowing them to escape. Pollaky did not appear as a witness during this case, he was abroad, but his ears must have burned.

Two men, Harry Benson and William Kurr had defrauded a French lady, Mme de Goncourt, of £30,000 with a confidence trick using horse racing bets and producing a non-existent sporting paper to back up their propositions. They had managed to evade arrest for some time, but were eventually caught.

On 28 July 1877, *Sheldrake's Aldershot Military Gazette* reported that Druscovich, while on remand, had attempted suicide in his cell by making a rope out of his bed sheet, tying one end to a bar in the cell window and trying to hang himself, but was discovered, and was cut down and revived by the prison surgeon. This story, which had originally appeared in the *Standard* had already been refuted by Druscovich's lawyer, Mr St John Wontner, as a libel upon his client and on the prison service.

On 7 September, at the initial inquiry, Mr Wontner, acting for Druscovich and Froggatt, questioned one Detective Sergeant William Reimers. Reimers had started in the Metropolitan Police as a police constable, had risen to the rank of detective inspector but at the end of 1876 had been demoted to detective sergeant as a result of a complaint made about him by Pollaky to whom he had given some information, and who he had apparently assaulted in October that year. According to the evidence of Superintendent (Dolly) Williamson, Reimers, who was suspended for two months, had been reported eight times in the period April to August, his defaults including disobedience, incivility, drunkenness, as well as the assault on Pollaky. Williamson stated that 'Reimers was reduced in rank for writing a letter to Mr Pollaky and giving him private information out of the office. It was an improper act. I cannot say that Druscovich had anything to do with it. Pollaky said he had not, and that Druscovich had exerted his utmost to prevent it.' According to Reimers, he and Pollaky had been on friendly terms at one time:

Mr Wontner: How did you come to be a sergeant?
Reimers: Through a dirty conspiracy on the part of your client and a Mr Pollaky.
Mr Wontner: Now we can understand your reasons.
Reimers: I am very glad you have introduced the subject.

This exchange was reported in *The Times* the following day. The report of the proceedings in *The Times* of 15 September 1877 included the following statement from Pollaky who wrote from Falkenstein in Taunus, Germany:

> I read in The Times of the 8th inst. that Sergeant W. Reimers, in his sworn evidence, says 'that he was degraded through a dirty conspiracy between Inspector Druscovich and a Mr Pollaky.' In justice to Mr Druscovich I feel bound to say that there is no truth whatever in the allegation, which I herewith flatly contradict. Mr Druscovich not only did not urge me in any way pressing my charges against Reimers; but he even interceded with me on behalf of Reimers, in consequence of which I wrote a letter to the Chief Commissioner, Colonel Henderson, asking that Sergeant Reimers should not be dismissed from the force. Said letters must still be in existence.

Meiklejohn, Palmer, Druscovich, Clarke and Froggatt stood trial at the Old Bailey in October 1877 for perverting the course of justice. Damning evidence was given by William Kurr who had been sent to prison earlier that year.

On 2 November Reimers was cross-examined by Mr Straight, defending Druscovich. The exchange was again published the following day in *The Times*:

> Mr Straight: Have you ever been charged with an assault before a magistrate?
> Reimers: Yes, when you prosecuted and failed to get a conviction. (Laughter.)
> Mr Straight: Did the magistrate on that occasion reprimand you for your conduct and say that you had shown great want of discretion?
> Reimers: No.
> Mr Straight: You were at one time an inspector, I believe?
> Reimers: Yes, I was reduced to the position of a sergeant on the 24th of December, 1876. I was not first of all called upon to resign by the Commissioners of Police. It was alleged by Mr Pollaky, who was investigated by Druscovich, that I had furnished him with a rough draught [*sic*] of my Bremerhaven report.
> Mr. Straight: Was it not alleged that you gave information to Pollaky who is a private inquiry agent?
> Reimers: It was alleged.
> Mr. Straight: Were you at one time friendly with this man Pollaky?
> Reimers: Yes.
> Mr Straight: And in December last, for some reasons between yourselves, had you quarrelled?
> Reimers: No; we were good friends.
> Mr Straight: Then your story is that Druscovich set Pollaky to inform against you?
> Reimers: That is it.

Mr Straight: And that, in consequence of Druscovich, Pollaky gave information to Scotland-yard about information which you had given him?

Reimers: That is it. The matter was investigated by Colonel Henderson and afterwards by the Home Secretary. I was suspended while the proceedings were going on, and then I was reduced. I allege that there was a conspiracy between Pollaky and Druscovich to ruin me and I have proof of it.

Reimers, whose part in the case was knowledge of some of Druscovich's actions, and who, it seems was aware of the turf swindle, was not asked to produce his proofs of the conspiracy he alleged had been made against him. It is hard to see at this distance in time why it was necessary for Pollaky's name to be mentioned at all in this case; it would seem that the defending counsels were trying to discredit him and the damaging testimony he gave against the defendants. Reimers was evidently using an opportunity to try to revenge himself on Pollaky by getting him into trouble. This was not the first time that Pollaky had caused resentment against himself. The examples of Whicher, Mayne, and Lomax have already been seen. Doubtless there were others, and it seems likely that this must have caused him some anxiety over the years. Michael Abrahams of Abrahams and Roffey, Mme de Goncourt's solicitor, had hired private investigators as he felt the police were dragging their feet over the investigation, but there seems to be no record of which firm he hired.

All the defendants but Clarke were found guilty, and sentenced to two years in prison. Meiklejohn, Palmer and Druscovich had accepted bribes from Kurr to give him warning that he might be arrested for his fraudulent dealings. Clarke, it seems, had not been involved.

1878

In June 1878, the announcement of Pollaky's return to London appeared in *The Times*:

The Times – Wednesday, 5 June 1878
POLLAKY'S PRIVATE INQUIRY OFFICE.
Mr Pollaky can be personally consulted daily, before 11 a.m. and after 3.p.m. – 13, Paddington-green, W.
CORRESPONDENTS who have communicated with my office during my absence from England, from June 1877 to the present day are requested in their own interest to ADDRESS me without delay in case of urgency. – I. Pollaky, 13, Paddington-green, June 1st, 1878.

1879

The Times – Tuesday, 8 April 1879
VAMPYR, not for me! – Pollaky.

Pollaky, an indefatigable writer of letters, wrote to *The Times* more than once in 1879 recommending that greater protection would be given to both servants and their employers if an act of parliament were passed making it a requirement for all servants to have a record of employment. This would follow a system already in use in Germany and other countries where the record book was known as a *Dienstbuch*. All references would be entered into this book, which the servant would take from employment to employment. Pollaky described it as a 'servant's license', and while aware of the difficulties in policing such a system, he felt that fraudulent references would be thus eliminated. Pollaky was, though, unaware of the problems that often beset this system in Germany, where employers had been known to confiscate these books so as to prevent servants from leaving, resulting in acrimonious court cases as the servants tried to retrieve their references.

1880

The ex-policemen found guilty of the 'Turf Fraud' were released in 1879. Nathaniel Druscovich turned to a new career and this announcement soon appeared:

Shields Daily Gazette and Shipping Telegraph – Friday, 9 January 1880
Druscovich, one of the recently released ex-detectives, has opened a private inquiry office in Lambeth Road.

Druscovich born in England to an English mother and a Romanian father, had spent some of his youth in Romania and was a good linguist although his English was not perfect. He became yet another rival in the private investigation business. According to the *Shields Daily Gazette and Shipping Telegraph*, these firms all seemed to be doing well: 'chiefly, in the opinion of Pollaky, through advertising', stated the article. (Pollaky evidently overlooked the fact of his own advertisements.) Somewhat shamelessly, considering his disgrace, Druscovich advertised his business in *The Times*, making use of his experience as a police inspector:

The Times – Friday, 20 August 1880
DRUSCOVICH'S PRIVATE INQUIRY OFFICE, British and Foreign. Conducted exclusively by Mr. N. Druscovich, late Chief Inspector of the Metropolitan Detective Police, No. 64, South Lambeth-road, N.W.

Druscovich's practice as an inquiry agent was short-lived. He died in 1881, aged 39.

1881

Pollaky's communications to *The Times* included a letter to the editor, published on 24 March, expressing his concern at the apparent disappearance of another correspondent. 'Warhawk' was the pen-name of an anonymous correspondent who wrote letters about political and terrorist events, and who had claimed in 1876 to have been, 'for the last 10 years initiated into the mysteries of the most important secret societies.' Pollaky claimed to know him personally, but worried that nothing had been heard of him since 1877. He should have been relieved, therefore, when, on 27 April, a letter from the missing Warhawk was published. Another, written at the end of May, followed on 6 June, with information on the political situation in Turkey where he had been living since his disappearance. However, the same edition of *The Times* carried a report on a Mr Palmer, otherwise known as 'Warhawk' who had been arrested, the day after writing his letter, in Constantinople, Turkey, on suspicion of being the chief conspirator in a plot to blow up the Turkish fleet. Palmer, however, claimed to have been engaged in secret missions on behalf of Turkey, and denied the accusation.

According to *The Times* of 5 November 1866, Hugh P.F. Palmer was by profession a marine engineer, who called himself 'captain' and owned a yacht called *Warhawk*. He claimed to have been instrumental in exposing the 'Bremerhaven Plot'. On 11 December 1875, a bomb had exploded on the dock at Bremerhaven, Germany, killing eighty people. This was apparently part of an insurance scam that went wrong. The man responsible, Alexander Keith Jnr, who had a chequered background, committed suicide when he heard of the number of deaths; the bomb had exploded earlier than he had intended.

The Times – Monday, 29 August 1881

MISSING, since Wednesday, August the 17th, at 11 p.m., from her situation in Durham-terrace, Westbourne-park, a YOUNG ENGLISH COUNTRY GIRL, supposed to have been decoyed away for the purpose of being taken to the Continent. Description – age 18, middle stature, very good looking, neat figure; wore black dress and jacket, cream-coloured plush hat, carried a blue waterproof. Was last seen in Westbourne-grove in company of a middle-aged gentlemanly-dressed man wearing an eyeglass, tall hat, and black coat. The man bought a new black Gladstone bag. INFORMATION of their whereabouts to be given to Mr Pollaky, 13 Paddington-green, W.

The Times – Saturday, 17 September 1881

CLANDESTINELY LEFT their HOMES, in Staffordshire, on the 8th instant, a LADY (single) and a GENTLEMAN (married), in company with a lad seven years old, not their child, with the intention of sailing to America, having, however, their luggage labelled for the Cape. Description of gentleman: – 33 years, 5ft. 8–9 inches, complexion dark, hair black, slightly waved on forehead, narrow face, clean shaven, nose particularly well shaped. INFORMATION of their present whereabouts will be rewarded by Mr Pollaky, 13 Paddington-green, W.

This last advertisement is particularly moving because of the abducted child. One wonders if any of these lost people were ever found, or if any communicated with Pollaky to find out what information he had that was to their 'advantage'. There is a wealth of stories here, each a sorrowful feast for the imagination if one so chooses.

1882

Busy man that he was, Pollaky's advertisements now stated that, 'Personal interviews can only be assured by previous appointment by letter or telegram'. He had become choosy with regard to the cases he would undertake, and shunned the chancer who might turn up at unwelcome times and possibly try to take advantage.

The Wilson Affair

The longest running series of advertisements which ever appeared in the 'Agony Column' was an extraordinary business which involved a certain Mr E.J. Wilson of Ennis, Ireland. Eventually, Mr Wilson decided to use the services of Pollaky's inquiry office. But to begin at (or at least near) the beginning:

> The Times – Tuesday, 11 January 1859
> Mr. E.J. Wilson, Ennis, Ireland, Author of the Decimal System at Her Majesty's Customs, and pronounced by the late S.G. Walford, Esq., Head Solicitor to Her Majesty's Customs, London to be 'extremely clever and equal to anything'. OFFERS his SERVICES to merchants and solicitors having important disputes with the Commissioners of Her Majesty's Customs.

This fairly innocuous item, though it seems of dubious merit, being an offer by someone with inside knowledge, to help those in need of advice on how to escape being fined for smuggling, is but the tip of a mountain of advertisements placed in *The Times* 'Agony Column' by Mr Wilson. It has been estimated that he wrote over 400 messages in the personal column, more than anyone else in its history, and some of a deeply personal nature. They began in 1851, and tell a woeful tale which leaves us with another deep mystery, as the end has never been told.

The messages began with no intimation as to what would happen: a simple message referring to the writer's willingness to wear a particular set of new clothes. As we proceed through the months, Wilson's messages become somewhat poetic in tone and a little obscure: 'Thy star in conjunction with mine against the great globe itself!' is the opening of the message of 7 July 1852. Others follow in the same fashion. A number of these messages seem to refer to the fortunes of his business importing goods and speculating in the City, and he was evidently having quite a hard time. And then, on 1 May 1854, the tone changes:

MY DAUGHTER! O, my daughter! – E.J.W.

In 1852 his daughter, Alice Jane Wilson, had been sent to a boarding school in Boxmoor, Hertfordshire. From reading the messages that follow this, it seems that she had been abducted and removed to a place where her father could not find her. Messages about his daughter, expressing great anguish, occur often, as do others about his failing business. It is possible that Alice had been removed by her mother whose name was apparently Alexis. The state of the relationship between the parents leaves little to the imagination if that is true.

In 1859, she was still missing, and on 13 March he wrote:

CAUTION. – All persons assisting in secreting my daughter, ALICE JANE WILSON, 10 years old, are liable to seven years' imprisonment. – E.J. Wilson, Ennis, Ireland.

A month later he offered a reward of £200. This seems to have had no effect. He must have been reunited with Alice at some point, for on 9 May the following appears:

To B.C.Z. You don't know their antecedents (rouge et noir). I have never seen any of my money from the day I nobly signed it away; and I did not see my child for five years, and yet I respected the laws of Humanity; and you see the return – I have lost my daughter a second time.

The outpouring continued through the years. (It is also possible that the 'Heart of Stone' advertisements form part of the Wilson series.) He was still speculating large amounts of money, and things were not going well there either. In July 1859, he wrote that he had not heard from his daughter for eighteen months.

Finally, in 1861, he went to Ignatius Pollaky to ask for his help. Initial communications with Pollaky used the codeword 'Moribond', and so we have come full circle. The Moribond messages left by Pollaky (see page 115) were communications with Wilson. They sent a number of messages to each other, each using cryptic language. Wilson's messages end in 1869 or 1870. It is hard to be specific about which message is his last as he changed the name he used many times, using some fairly fanciful ones at times: 'Flybynight' and 'Cheops' are just two of a long list. What is certain is that even after eight or nine years of Pollaky's off-and-on investigation of the matter, no one knows whether or not Wilson was ever reunited with his daughter.

That Arthur Conan Doyle in his Sherlock Holmes stories makes use of the 'Agony Column' is perhaps hardly surprising. Examples can be found in *The Sign of Four*, 1890 – Holmes places an advertisement to ascertain the whereabouts of a missing boatman and his steam launch, *The Adventure of the Engineer's Thumb*, 1892 – Holmes is discovered, 'reading the agony column of The Times and smoking his before-breakfast pipe', *The Adventure of the Noble Bachelor*, 1892 – in which he states that he reads, 'nothing except the criminal news and the agony column. The latter is always instructive', *The Adventure of the Red Circle*, 1911 – in which he comments upon reading various agony columns, 'Dear me! […] what a chorus of groans, cries, and bleatings! What a rag-bag of singular happenings! But surely the most valuable hunting-ground that ever was given to a student of the unusual!' and *The Valley of Fear*, 1914 – in which he decodes a mysterious cipher largely made up of a series of numbers.

An Interview with Pollaky

The 1860s had been a busy time for Pollaky. He had become very well known, and his name was often used in conversation. In March 1867 he was even mentioned in Parliament when Mr Beresford Hope, member for Stoke-upon-Trent (as it was known in 1867), moved a resolution in favour of suspending the search of baggage of passengers arriving from France during the French Exhibition of 1867, since this practice, he felt, was due only to red tape and gave rise to resentment by Her Majesty's subjects when they as passengers were searched for non-existent items for which customs duties did not exist. His long speech included his opinion that, 'surveillance, if not of a very vexatious kind, was not objected to, and so [if] smuggling was carried on by passengers there would be no difficulty in detecting it by means of a police system, exercised, not by companies of Mr Pollaky's inquiry officers, as the Treasury seemed to suppose, but by their own Customs officers.' (*Hansard*, 8 March 1867.) After some discussion, with opinion against voiced by Benjamin Disraeli, who at that time was Chancellor of the Exchequer, and William Gladstone, Beresford Hope withdrew his proposal. Public duties carried out by private companies were controversial even then.

By the early 1870s there were a number of private investigators working in London and advertising in *The Times*. These included Arthur Cleveland Montagu and Co., Legal and Confidential Agents, 11 Old Broad Street, who could be 'consulted daily on home and foreign cases', and Wendel Scherer of 11 Blomfield Terrace, Paddington, who with '24 years' English and Foreign experience, can be daily consulted in all cases of importance'. Charles Frederick Field's inquiry office had now moved from 20 Devereux Court to 33 Essex Street, Strand, and was now operated by C. Nicholls.

On 27 September 1874, Charles Frederick Field died. His wife and at least one of his siblings had predeceased him, and in his will he divided his estate between his nieces and his friends. The following obituary appeared in the *Cornwall Chronicle* on Wednesday, 16 December 1874:

Passing from births to deaths, the month has seen the last of a very interesting character, whose antecedents and connections with a great man lately gone from amongst us are of some public interest. Mr Charles Field, the immortal "Inspector Bucket," of Bleak House, died in London the day after the despatch of my last letter. The famous detective was very intimate with Charles Dickens, to whom he was useful in giving information and by whom he was much liked and respected. The amusing sketch by 'Phiz,' in which Bucket is so well drawn nursing Mrs Bagnet's children, one on each knee, will no doubt be fresh in every reader's recollection, together with the professional skill shown by the inspector when, after making himself agreeable and partaking of the Bagnet hospitality, he coolly follows George Rouncewell out of the house and arrests him for the murder of Tulkinghorn. To recount all Field's exploits would require a large book, but perhaps the best-known or them was the clever war in which he managed to sift the case of Dr Smyth, who in 1853, claimed to be the son of Sir Hugh Smyth, of Ashton Court, near Bristol. Field went to the residence of the claimant's sister in a very quaint disguise, and soon ascertained to a certainty that the man was an impostor, and that his name was Tom Peorig. The inspector is described by Mr Sala [George Augustus Sala], who had frequently met him at Charles Dickens's, as "a very worthy soul, straightforward and outspoken, and full of humorous anecdote." He was buried in Brompton cemetery on the 8th.

In 1888 a biographical article about Pollaky appeared in the press entitled 'Mr Pollaky'. It came from a book published the previous year called *A Novelist's Note Book* by David Christie Murray. The article was a shortened version of one which had appeared as early as 1875 in the *Queensland Times*, and it is the more complete, earlier version which will be discussed here.

During the course of the interview Pollaky gave to Murray, he paid tribute to his old employer, mentor and friend Charles, Frederick Field.

Queensland Times – Tuesday, 6 April 1875
MR POLLAKY

I think it not improbable that Mr Ignatius Pollaky is the holder of more secrets than ever burdened the secret breast of Mr Tulkinghorn. He is prince of detectives and king of spies. He knows terrible stories about all manner of people. [...] But Mr Pollaky has no aspect of secrecy. [...] You would take him for the most open, the most confiding, the frankest of men. [...] He has the Bismarckian art of telling you nothing while telling you everything.

That the author writes as if in awe of the man shows not that this was necessarily his own belief, but that, perhaps, he knew what the public wanted to hear and what would make good copy.

Pollaky could not have objected to the rather overblown description awarded him, it is, after all, the image that he himself had tried to cultivate for many years.

Firstly, Murray goes on to describe a little of Pollaky's home at 13 Paddington Green. The house was demolished in 2010, so we can only know how the house looked from Murray's 1875 description, together with the 1884 notice of sale and the very few images that exist: all photographs were taken after 1950:

> His very house stands rather higher than its brethren in Paddington Green, and seems to lift its dominant shoulders as if it disdained to be or to hold a secret.
>
> In Mr Pollaky's entrance-hall is an ancient picture on the possession of which he prides himself. It represents the banishment of Adam and Eve from the garden of Paradise. [...]
>
> The great private detective is at home and will see me. A moment after having ascertained this I discover that my informant is the great detective himself.

Taking this at face value, it seems that 'the great detective' must have had a sense of humour:

> He is brisk in manner, and a little brusque, and very slightly foreign. He speaks capital English, and is not unwilling to let one discover that.

This is surely the best description of the man that we have. And we at last find out about the quality of his spoken English – 'capital' and 'slightly foreign':

> He receives me [...] with some show of disfavour, because he wishes that I should see that he does not care to have his business advertised.

Maybe he did, and maybe he didn't. Perhaps he felt no need for advertisement, after all he was well enough known as it was. And busy, too. Perhaps it wasn't just false modesty, but a natural shyness that he possessed, despite his need for a public face:

> When he places his visitor on a chair facing the light, his own face is in complete darkness. That, says Mr Pollaky lightly [...] is a mere accident of the construction of the room.

In the next paragraphs, Murray quotes Pollaky on Pollaky at length, and we gain more than a glimpse of his personality:

I have been pitched into a great deal, [...] I do not like it. Who does? But I do not care either. I have been called unpleasant names. Well, I admit my profession is not a nice one. But I console myself, I am a necessity. I would rather have been Mr Disraeli or the Bishop of London than a private detective [...] The very essence of my system is secrecy. My left hand does not know my right hand. I have no clerk about me, no writer. My men do not know each other. I do not suppose myself to know them. They do not come here. They are each known to me as number so-and-so. No. I employ no men from the detective force. They would not suit my work. [...] my men are small, insignificant, unnoticeable fellows; fellows who will walk with you, and about you, and up you, and down you, and you will not know that they are there.

We have already discovered that he employed men to work for him, but his insistence that so much secrecy was kept between them seems quite extraordinary. It seems as if we are moving in the kind of territory we associate with James Bond. And yet, we know that these are only fleeting glimpses of the agents he employed, and that, aside from his surveillance of the Confederates, almost everything we know about his cases comes from newspaper reports. He seems to have attempted to be elusive, and yet in the public eye at one and the same time; a contradiction: a man of mystery who tried to keep out of the limelight while at the same time struggling for recognition and publicity.

The interview continues:

Mr Pollaky relishes this, and lights a cigar in brisk enjoyment of it. 'I see queer things: I know queer things about eminent people. Men would laugh if they knew all I could tell them. But then I do not tell. It is my especial business not to tell. Of course people have attempted to bribe me. I have had a big bribe of jewels offered me in this room. But I am not to be bought. My clients know that, or they would not trust me.'

Pollaky indicates a cabinet of indexed drawers to Murray, and states that by using the information held within he could make many thousands of pounds. Murray wrote that when Pollaky speaks warmly, 'he loses his foreign manner'. Murray comments on this. 'A perfect English accent might act, at a pinch, as a fairly good disguise for a foreigner who was known always to speak in his own person in a very, very slightly foreign way.'

They go on to discuss Pollaky's work for the Divorce Court. Neither he nor his men ever appeared in court, as he knew their evidence would be 'regarded with suspicion', as it would be supposed to be in his own interest to establish cases. He then begins to talk about specific cases, though mentioning no names, of course.

A gentleman, 'high in the legal profession', asked him to watch his wife as he suspected her of being unfaithful. Pollaky's men watched her, and it was proved that any suspicions were unfounded. But then the lady visited Pollaky and asked him to watch her husband. The husband was guilty only of having set Pollaky to watch his wife. Both confessed to each other what they had done, and they forgave each other.

He was at pains to point out that he was not always out to establish cases where they did not exist. The next case mentioned had a different ending though. Set by an elderly nobleman to watch his young wife while he is away, what does Pollaky discover upon having her watched by his men?

> My lady walked out and took up a cab near the square. She drove to Knightsbridge Barracks, and there a swell with a blonde moustache stepped in. They went to the Star and Garter at Richmond. Nice little dinner. Came home to the lady's house together. Swell left the house in the morning.

Pollaky in this remarkable interview continues by discussing his early career in 'that open-handed free-spoken way of his':

> I am not the originator of this style of business in England [...] George Frederick Field – the chief of the detective force at Scotland-yard started it. He is dead now. His portrait is behind you.

The portrait referred to was a photograph of Field. That Pollaky had it on display shows, perhaps, that they remained on good terms even after they became rivals for business:

> George Frederick Field and I [...] worked together for a long time. He was a very clever man, and knew his business well. In those days I was going everywhere, and knew every nook and corner in the empire. I was a private soldier then, and not a general. I am a general now, and I do my spiriting from this desk. For myself, I never go out now. All my work is done through my men.

In 1875 Pollaky was 47; that he felt his days of doing the donkey work were past, and that he was willing and able to pay to let others do the staking-out that he evidently found so enervating, is an indication of how tedious this work was. Years of being the one who had to do the following, the waiting, and making of inquiries, combined with a growing feeling of insecurity, shown by the interesting sentence, 'For myself, I never go out now', already seem to be making his work more of a burden than a vocation. His next statement makes us realise how disillusioned he is with mankind in general, and the English in particular:

You are right, I have contracted a low opinion of human virtue, especially in England. It is the fashion here to talk of the immorality of the French. Pooh! I know France well. I know Europe well. There is no nation as immoral as England. I had a clergyman here not long ago. If I gave you his name you would be surprised. He wanted to reform a girl, having already formed her for his own purposes. If you were to hear that man preach, you would say, 'How holy this man is!' I know better.

Sex scandals and the church continue to come to light even today. These ways of behaviour were nothing new, even then; nowadays we would call this grooming.

The interview concludes with Pollaky showing photographs of his foreign agents – rather belying the previous statement that his men are unknown even to him. All but one are, 'foreign-looking men in uniform'. Pollaky says of them that they are generally army men:

I have people everywhere. I have cabmen in my employ. I have omnibus conductors. I have men in the clubs. I have waiters. I have people everywhere in England and abroad.

One of his agents is a sweet-looking girl of about 20 years. Murray looks at her portrait which is:

… very delicate and refined. It is one of those feminine faces which at once appeals to and touches the manly heart. 'One of the finest little adventuresses now in Europe,' says Mr Pollaky.

As we have proceeded through Pollaky's life, correspondence and cases, one aspect is present by implication and occasionally by name, but never properly dealt with in one place. Who were Pollaky's agents? There are mentions during the Confederate correspondence of the surveillance he established, but only three of his agents are mentioned by name in that corresondence.

Ed Brennan, G. Grub and James I. Thomson all supplied him with information, and the letters they wrote still exist. Grub on 7 October 1861 had watched the postman deliver letters to 58 Jermyn Street, and noted the various recipients, and the places of origin of each letter, and the comings and goings of visitors to that address; Brennan, on 10 October had discovered the whereabouts of the *Fingal* in Greenock, Scotland; Thomson on 15 October had written to Pollaky at 20 Devereux Court from 19 George Street, Euston Square (not to be confused with George Street, Mansion House where Pollaky later had an office), detailing his watching of a number of warehouses, and also the fee (4 shillings a day including expenses) that he required for his services.

In a letter to Sir Richard Mayne from early 1862, Pollaky mentions his office clerk. But a clerk is not an agent, employee though he may be.

On 29 November 1867, Pollaky advertised in *The Times* that, 'Subpœnas on Mr W. Bates, an officer of this establishment who has been absent on a special mission to India can now be duly served, he having returned on the 25th inst.' and in February 1869, the same 'private detective' William Bates from Pollaky's private inquiry office gave testimony in a court case in Worcester, as reported in the *Worcestershire Chronicle*.

On 11 December 1870, *Lloyd's Weekly London Newspaper* reported on a divorce case – *Jex-Blake* v. *Jex-Blake*. Mrs Jex-Blake asked for a divorce on the grounds that her husband was both unfaithful and cruel, and that he had transmitted to her 'a loathsome disease'. During the course of this case, at the end of which Mrs Jex-Blake was granted her divorce, evidence was given of the defendant's adultery by William Sherrers, described as 'foreign agent at Mr Pollaky's inquiry office'.

On 23 January 1873, the *Western Mail* reported that one Thomas Carter, lace maker and trade unionist, appeared at the Nottingham police court charged with using threatening and abusive language to a non-unionist co-worker. 'The only witness for the complainant was Charles Worlege, a detective, from Pollaky's Private Detective Office, who had been employed at Mr Booth's lace factory as a labourer, but virtually as a spy, to associate with and ascertain the doings of the workmen when they were expected to go on strike'. The magistrate in this case refused to accept the evidence of, 'such a witness'.

What can we make of Pollaky's boast that he had agents, 'everywhere in England and abroad'? Did his network really stretch that far? If so, should there not be further hints at least in the correspondence of others?

An example of the slipperiness of Pollaky's agents can be found in a case which came to trial at the Old Bailey on 6 August 1881. Though the case itself seems to be of little importance to Pollaky's business, it does include some interesting details. Testimony was given by one Henry Burrage, a commission agent of Hanwell, aged 34. Burrage, whose evidence amounted to his having pretended to be a fence, while in reality communicating the fact of stolen goods to the police, included the following information:

> My name is Matthew Henry Burridge Burnside, and I have many other names; I might change my name before I get home tonight – to give you the whole of my names I hope you have got a double sheet of foolscap paper – I have been in the House of Detention, the same as some of your clients have – I was innocent –

Under cross-examination he added:

I have passed by the names of Smith, Brown, Bailey, Blake, Jones, and it is impossible to say how many more – Purdon is one – I do not remember Perry – I have not received money from any source during the last four months – I had money at home, and my credit was good – I acted as agent for Mr Cowley between September and April last, under the name of Purdon, and was acting at the same time as agent for Mr Lacey under the name of Burnside – I received money on behalf of Mr Cowley, and have paid him some, and I should not reckon there is 1l. between us – I received 24s. from Matthews for Mr Cowley; I have not paid him the whole of it; there is a difference between us, and I have not paid it. I also received money on behalf of Mr Macey, and have not paid in all the amount – as late as April last I received money from Mr Coupal, and have not paid it, and do not intend to – it was about 10 guineas – I was in the employ of Pollaky Brothers many years ago in the name of Burnside – I did not abscond with 200l.; I don't know how much it was, it is 17 years ago – I don't know whether my friends paid it, and I think the less Mr Pollaky says about it the better –

In this last case there are details of some of the aliases used by one of Pollaky's agents. He is, though, traceable, as he appears in census forms in 1871 and 1881. Matthew Henry Burnside was living in 1881 with his wife Annie and their six children at 14 Half Acre, Hanwell. His occupation is listed as 'Ships Clerk'. Ten years earlier, he was living with his wife and son in Lambeth, and described as a 'Ship's Cook (out of employ)'.

The list of known agents is as follows: Ed Brennan, G. Grub, James I. Thomson, William Bates, William Sherrers, Charles Worlege, Matthew Henry [Burridge or Burrage] Burnside. Aside from the last named, we shall probably never know who these agents were, nor, when they gave a name, whether that name was genuine, and there is little doubt that the spellings of at least two of the surnames (Sherrers and Worlege) as given in newspaper reports are wrong.

Pollaky had spent a considerable amount of time in the second half of the 1850s attempting to make himself indispensable to certain important political figures: Lords Derby, Palmerston and Lytton. That in 1861 he accepted a commission from Sanford to spy on Confederate movements in Great Britain might be seen as something of a come-down, for had his previous efforts been successful, he would have been receiving requests for his services from the British government. After Sanford, he turned to the Metropolitan Police, but there was no persuading Sir Richard Mayne of his usefulness. Pushing himself before the public Pollaky became something of a paradox – a private detective who wished for publicity while keeping facts of his cases secret; a man who craved acceptance, but whose methods for gaining the good opinion of those whose acquaintance he valued were inevitably doomed to failure. An outsider at a time when good pedigree was considered vital, it is, perhaps, hardly surprising that he was mocked and derided in certain quarters.

⌒

Number 13 Paddington Green had been in uninterrupted occupation by the Pollakys since 1872, though Pollaky had his office there from 1863. On 10 December 1881 the Reverend Dr William Stainer (1828–98), brother of composer John Stainer, advertised his need to acquire a fourth premises to house another of his Homes for Deaf Children, specifying the Edgware Road district. A few months later, Pollaky had decided to retire, and 13 Paddington Green was acquired for the purpose. Pollaky moved his family to Brighton in the middle of 1882, his last advertisement in *The Times* as a private investigator appeared on Friday 19 May that year. Stainer rented the house at Paddington Green from him, and a new home for deaf children opened with about twenty boarders aged 5 to 9, with four live-in members of staff. By the beginning of January 1883 Stainer already owed £531 in back rent. Afraid that his debt would increase still further, and relying on charitable donations to which he himself contributed, Stainer began advertising in *The Times* in November 1883 for, 'CONTRIBUTIONS towards the expense of fitting up the fourth home recently opened on Paddington-green'. Pollaky, not receiving any rent, put the house up for sale in January 1884. Money for Stainer's home must have been forthcoming, for in 1885 he was still there having managed to acquire the freehold of the property, presumably mortgaged. He now named it 'Stainer House', and in 1892 announced that he hoped to secure the premises as a permanent place for a college for teachers of the deaf. The Stainer Homes did not long survive William Stainer's death in 1898 as they were poorly managed, and were condemned by a School Board report in May that year. This resulted in the children being moved out, and by 1901, the home at Paddington Green had closed, the sole occupant being a night watchman named Samuel Smith. In 1911 the house appears in the census as No. 12a Paddington Green and has a number of households living within, though the premises seem to be owned by J.P. Barradell & Co., wine coopers and bottle merchants who had acquired most of the houses in that row.

It is worth comparing the description, given earlier, of Pollaky at home with the description of the house in the advertisement for its sale which appeared in *The Times* on 14 January 1884:

No. 13, PADDINGTON-GREEN (postal district, W.). – To be SOLD. by Private Contract, this commanding and valuable FREEHOLD HOUSE, southern aspect, standing in open and healthy position, facing Paddington-green, close to two Metropolitan Railway Stations; omnibuses passing the

Green every few minutes to City and the Zoological-garden; also within easy walking distance of Hyde-park and Kensington-gardens. This house (with front garden about 92 feet, planted with 12 almond trees, and large back garden about 102 feet, protected by good brick wall; wire fenced about 12 feet high; also summer-house with cemented floor) contains 19 good rooms, including bath room with hot and cold water service, and three water-closets; lofty drawing room, costly decorated with arched statuary marble chimney-piece of exquisite workmanship, three large French windows (plate-glass), opening on to balcony provided with permanent fire escape; dining room leading by iron steps into back garden. Would be a suitable residence for a medical practitioner, solicitor, school, or private hotel. The sanitary arrangements are of the most approved system. The house has been in uninterrupted occupation of the owner since 1872. Price of house and freehold, £2,500, part of which could remain on mortgage at four per cent, and fixtures and planned furniture at valuation. Apply to the owner, Mr Pollaky, 13 Paddington-green, W.

Given the facts of the following reports, Paddington was not the loveliest of areas even in Pollaky's day. On 3 July 1865, a question was asked in the House of Commons regarding the, 'nuisance to health arising from the foul state of the Grand Junction Canal Basin, and of the wharves adjoining, in the parish of Paddington'. A feeling for the area around Paddington of the period may be gained from the following information taken from contemporary accounts made by or on behalf of the Paddington Vestry, which was responsible for carrying out public works and agreeing local planning permissions.

The Paddington Sanitary Report for the year 1870–71 by Dr William Hardwicke stated that Paddington ranked as 'thickly-populated', (the population in April 1871 was 96,784 – how he would have ranked London's East End one can only imagine!) He felt that, even with over 7,000 horses in the area and the demands made on available air, there would not be any danger to public health, provided that 'the excreta of so many horses [which] adds also to the sources by which atmospheric air is often tainted', was 'promptly removed'. There had been 386 deaths that year from infectious diseases, one third of which had been due to scarlet fever, which had been epidemic in London for nearly two years. Pauline Pollaky had been a victim of this epidemic. Among other diseases causing deaths that year he lists diarrhoea, which the following year would be the cause of death of baby William Pollaky.

Hardwicke also highlights other concerns:

Poultry keeping increases to a great extent in London, and frequent complaints are made to me that fowls should be done away with as a nuisance. It ought to be more generally known that I cannot proceed against the owners of domestic animals for the noises they make. It exceeds my province to interfere with fowls, pigeons, and dogs if kept in a cleanly state. Cock-crowing at 1 a.m., the barking of dogs, the cooing of pigeons near your chamber window, or any other nuisance arising from noise, by which the sleep of nervous people is disturbed, is a serious annoyance, and probably ought, as in the manner of street music, to be under control by law: but I cannot treat them as Sanitary nuisances.

Under the heading, 'Urinals and Urinal nuisances' he writes, 'it should be obligatory upon the publican whose licences were renewed that an efficient urinal should be provided', pointing out at the same time that there were only five public urinals in the parish: 'at least ten more are required'. He did make a point of stating, 'that W.C. accommodation for females as well as males [...] could easily be provided'.

Hardwicke felt that many houses in the area were unfit for human habitation. While these do not include those in the immediate vicinity of Paddington Green, these were just round the corner.

In another report on the health of Paddington published in May 1870 Dr Hardwicke mentions that the rich districts as well as the poor had been affected by the scarlatina epidemic, and quotes Horace: '*Pallida mors aequo pulsat pede pauperum tabernas regumque turres*'. ('Pale Death, with impartial step, knocks at the cottages of the poor and the palaces of kings.') In his health report of July, Dr Hardwicke includes a register of complaints made of unsanitary conditions in the area, including: defects of drainage, dirty premises, water closets and urinals, frying of fish, bad meat, overcrowding, bad ventilation, smoke, dirty and noisy animals, manure, garbage and dung, and decaying and putrid substances.

By 1956 the house was not looking quite as charming as the sale notice describes it. Nos 11–13 were all very dilapidated. They were demolished in 2010 despite the findings of the *Paddington Green Conservation Area Audit of 2003* which stated that 'the east side of Paddington Green boasts a fine collection of Regency and Victorian buildings which form an important backdrop to the green'. By 2010, Nos 11–12 had been rebuilt. The internal walls on the ground floor of No. 13 had been demolished and the front bricked up. Rooms on other floors had been subdivided. Internal photographs show the house to have been in a very sorry state.

Dickens, Lewis Carroll, W.S. Gilbert, and Others

12

What was it that made the press, novelists and playwrights write about Pollaky and not so much about other private detectives? True, Field and Whicher had both been immortalised in one form or another by Dickens and Collins, but that was as policemen, not private investigators. That Pollaky's advertisements were so strangely wonderful as to excite comment is beyond doubt. That the fact of him being foreign, and from a less well-known part of Europe may have lent an exotic and almost mystic touch to the general perception of the man, though he himself was really quite ordinary underneath.

In 1868, the Theatre Royal, Holborn, (which was destroyed by a fire in 1880) included in its advertisements for that season's productions, 'a New and Original Burlesque Extravaganza founded on a famous opera, and entitled *Lucretia Borgia, M.D.*' The writer was H.J. Byron and the music was composed by J.T. Haines. (The opera it burlesqued was by Donizetti.) The characters included one Rustighello, described as 'the "Pollaky" of the period'. This is just one example of the use of his name without any sobriquet preceding it. Surely Gilbert was the first to make use of the term 'Paddington Pollaky' in what would become, among fans of the Savoy Operas, almost the only way that Pollaky's name would be kept alive during the twentieth century: even his obituary in *The Times* used PADDINGTON POLLAKY as its title.

In this brief extract from *Lucretia Borgia MD*, the Dook (Duke) reads Rustigello's latest circular:

> The Dook: *(reads)* To jealous wives,
> Suspicious husbands, and the world at large.
> Inspector Rustigello's reg'lar charge
> Is his expences, and a small per centage;
> Heart-broken parties will see the advantage
> Of trying one who's secret, sharp, and steady.
> What's this! 'N.B. – Divorces always ready.'

Henry James Byron (1835–84) was a predecessor of W.S. Gilbert in the burlesque-creating line, and gave Gilbert an early chance by collaborating with him in 1867 on a version of *Robinson Crusoe*. His writing skills do not, however, bear comparison with Gilbert's, as may be deduced from the above quotation.

As early as 1863, Pollaky was well known enough to be featured as a subject in an essay by an important author. On 20 June that year there appeared in Charles Dickens's weekly journal, *All The Year Round*, an article in the series entitled 'Small-Beer Chronicles'. (It can be found in Appendix 1.) Dickens writes in no very flattering terms of Pollaky and what he later describes in the article as the 'Pollaky System'. He wonders if the men he now sees '[...] standing about at the corners of streets [...] generally seedy in their attire, and in the habit of sucking small pieces of straw or chewing the stalks of leaves to while away the time – are [...] the agents of Pollaky and Co.'

He wonders what they are looking out for there and goes on to denigrate the petty matters that Pollaky and private detective agencies in general must be investigating, and gives a number of amusing scenarios which have a ring of possibility about them.

The fact that Pollaky's name was the one chosen to lead this article, and not another's might be laid to a number of factors. Pollaky had the most memorable name, Pollaky was already known for his extraordinary advertisements and coded messages, Pollaky was a foreigner, and Dickens was not known for being shy in making digs at foreigners – think of *American Notes*, *Martin Chuzzlewit*, and of the characterisation of Fagin in *Oliver Twist*. To his gallery of unusual characters we might add among other lesser known people written about by Charles Dickens not only Joseph Grimaldi, the actor and clown whose memoirs Dickens wrote, but also Ignatius Pollaky; their names seem to have as much to recommend them as Mr Micawber, Miss Haversham, Mr Bumble, and Jarndyce and Jarndyce. Finally, although Field's name is also mentioned in the article, it is Pollaky who gets the brunt of the criticism – after all, Field was a friend, and Dickens had already written about him favourably. Dickens mentions Charles Frederick Field as another private investigator in this piece, but only in passing.

In 1851, as mentioned in Chapter 3, Dickens had written a piece entitled 'On Duty with Inspector Field', which appeared in his weekly journal *Household Words*. It appeared in the edition of Saturday, June 14. Charles Frederick Field was still a member of the Metropolitan Police, and Dickens describes in this article in some detail the acute powers of observation of his subject:

> Inspector Field is, to-night, the guardian genius of the British Museum. He is bringing his shrewd eye to bear on every corner of its solitary galleries, before he reports 'all right'. Suspicious of the Elgin marbles, and not to be done by cat-faced Egyptian giants with their hands upon their knees, Inspector Field,

sagacious, vigilant, lamp in hand, throwing monstrous shadows on the walls and ceilings, passes through the spacious rooms. If a mummy trembled in an atom of its dusty covering, Inspector Field would say, 'Come out of that, Tom Green. I know you!'

Such a contrast there is between Dickens's glowing account of Inspector Field and his methods, and his account of Pollaky and his, that one cannot help but see a partiality in Dickens's eyes for the former gentleman; and though by the time he wrote of Pollaky, Field was lumped in with private investigators, it is Pollaky's bureau which takes the criticism, not that of his former employer. Had Pollaky's departure caused some rancour? Did Dickens know of this and taken sides with a friend? Dickens's previous description of Field in 'A Detective Police Party' (1850) was as, 'a middle-aged man of a portly presence, with a large, moist, knowing eye, a husky voice, and a habit of emphasizing his conversation by the aid of a corpulent fore-finger, which is constantly in juxtaposition with his eyes or nose'. And, of course, Field as mentioned before is generally accepted as having been Dickens's model for Inspector Bucket in *Bleak House*.

It has been said that all publicity is good. Pollaky, presumably, would not have been displeased by being written about by the most famous author in the world, and, critical though the article is (in a gentle way, mind you,) the piece does imply a thoroughness about the 'Pollaky System' which would not have done him any harm.

On 25 January 1866, Charles Lutwidge Dodgson, better known to most as Lewis Carroll, wrote a letter to dramatist Tom Taylor, later to become editor of *Punch*. Taylor, whose play *Our American Cousin* was being watched by Abraham Lincoln when Lincoln was assassinated in 1865, had introduced his colleague, *Punch* artist John Tenniel, to Dodgson. Tenniel went on to illustrate *Alice's Adventures in Wonderland* (1865) and *Through the Looking-Glass, and What Alice Found There* (1871). Interestingly Pollaky was Tenniel's neighbour as mentioned in Chapter 7; during that time Tenniel illustrated both books. Dodgson's letter to Tom Taylor is a discussion of a synopsis of a play which in the event was never written, but he does make the following suggestion: 'As a comic element for the piece, it occurs to me you might make a good deal of fun of a "Private Enquiry Office", à la Pollaky'.

Pollaky makes a more interesting appearance in another of Dodgson's letters some three years later, dated Saturday (possibly 22 May 1869). This letter purports to be from actress Kate (Terry) Lewis (grandmother of actor John Gielgud), but was in fact penned by Dodgson himself and sent to 17-year-old Lilia MacDonald, (daughter of his friend George MacDonald, author of *The Princess and the Goblin*). He had taken Lilia to meet Kate Lewis, but the actress had been caught in the rain when out, and had not yet managed to get home. Lewis sent a letter of apology, and Dodgson substituted the letter he had fabricated in order to tease his friend's daughter. The letter is particularly interesting in that it contains a mini-story about Pollaky by Lewis Carroll:

Moray Lodge [Campden Hill Road, London]
Saturday [22 May 1869]

My Dear Dodgson,
I think I had better tell you candidly my reasons for being absent when you called with Miss Lily MacDonald. Before making her acquaintance, I felt it right to make a few enquiries, in order to be sure whether or not it would be desirable to meet her. With this object, I put the matter into the hands of an experienced detective officer, Inspector Pollaky, who kindly undertook to make out all about her 'in less than no time', as he forcibly expressed it. I grieve to tell you that he has discovered her to be *mean, vindictive,* and *barbarous* to a degree you will hardly credit.

But I will give you the painful particulars, as Mr Pollaky has just been here: his head and shoulders were covered with earth, and he was altogether so shaken and confused that I had some little difficulty in making out his story, which was as follows:

It appears that he got into the garden behind the "Retreat" (your friend's house) disguised as a clothes-horse (I asked him how this was done, but could not understand his explanation, beyond the fact that he had a blue apron over his head). He then proceeded to make observations through the dining-room window, where Miss L.M.D. was superintending the meal of the younger children. He declares that after watching a minute or two, he saw her seize an unoffending chicken, plunge a fork into the poor thing, and with a sharp knife cut off its wings and legs! He was so horrified at this piece of barbarity that he fainted, and fell headlong into a flower-bed, where he was found, half buried, by Mr M.D., who however let him go, on his explaining that he was trying to find his way to the Underground Railway. He then hastened to me with the dreadful news. I asked him if he was sure the chicken was alive, to which he replied, with tears in his eyes "If it hadn't been, do you think I should have fell that sudden?" which convinced me.

I trust that you will take warning by this, and have no more to do with such a wretch (it is strong language, but no stronger than she deserves), in which case you will be grateful to me for having shown you her true character. Believe me
Sincerely yours,
Kate Lewis

(Reprinted by kind permission of United Agents on behalf of Morton Cohen, The Trustees of the C.L. Dodgson Estate and Scirard Lancelyn Green.)

Both letters appear in *The Letters of Lewis Carroll Volume 1* by Morton M. Cohen (Macmillan, London 1979), the first is part of the Henry W. and Albert Berg Collection, New York Public Library, and the second is held by the Beinecke Rare Book and Manuscript Library, Yale University, where it is part of the George MacDonald Collection.

From *The Triumph of Baby* by George Augustus Sala
In *Belgravia, A London Magazine* – June 1871

I am in the habit of smoking over the second column of the *Times*. That section, as you are aware, used to be called the 'Agony Column' […] descriptions of stolen dogs have long since supplanted 'Agony' in the second column. […] They have even elbowed out the occult notifications in which Mr Pollaky, erst of Paddington-green, instils vague ideas into the public mind of his dealings with foreign potentates, and his readiness to make "private inquiries" in the interests of wronged husbands and outraged wives. I should like to talk with this wondrous Pollaky. What an immense deal he must know about people! Perhaps he is privately aware of something about me.

On 28 January 1874 a picture of Pollaky appeared in *Figaro's London Sketch Book of Celebrities* (see plate No.1). Drawn by French artist Jean Faustin Betbeder (1847–1914), whose most famous illustration for the series was of Charles Darwin. The fact of Pollaky's inclusion is a measure of how well known he already was. The motto underneath the picture reads, 'Pollaky. A snapper up of unconsidered trifles. *Winter's Tale, act 4 sc. 2.*' (It actually comes from act 4 scene 3.) Pollaky, dressed in evening clothes, is seen carrying some documents in his left hand while listening at a keyhole. The shadow of a bearded policeman with truncheon is seen emanating from his highly-polished dainty shoes. What that shadow really represents is open to speculation. The picture is signed 'Faustin'. This series of chromo-lithographs was published by the *London Figaro* in conjunction with *The London Sketch Book*, however the Pollaky image seems only to have appeared with the *Figaro* and not with *The London Sketch Book*. (Most of the images appeared in both.) From May to October 1875 *The London Sketch Book* ran an advertisement stating:

A few copies of almost the entire series of Chromographs, in four colors, which have recently appeared in connection with the FIGARO and the LONDON SKETCH BOOK, may be obtained on application to the publisher.

The image of Pollaky is not included in the list.

In June 1875, the same journal ran another advertisement:

The Figaro volumes for 1874 containing all the Chromographs and Photographs issued with the paper during the year 1874 are now ready. As only a limited number is published, to prevent disappointment orders should be given at once.

This volume is now extremely rare. The British Newspaper Library has one. Aside from that, only the Billy Ireland Cartoon Library & Museum at the Ohio State University seems to have a readily available copy of Faustin Betbeder's Pollaky cartoon in its archive. Aside from Darwin and Pollaky, other personalities in the series included Queen Victoria, Disraeli, the Tichborne Claimant, Gladstone, the Prince of Wales, Henry Irving, Richard D'Oyly Carte, and Alfred Lord Tennyson.

The text which goes with the image was as follows:

THE LONDON FIGARO
JAMES MORTIMER, EDITOR AND SOLE PROPRIETOR
LONDON: WEDNESDAY. JAN. 28, 1874

HE SEES AND HEARS THROUGH BRICK WALLS

A GREAT detective, like a true poet, is born, not made. When the battle has been fought and won, everyone feels confident that, with such a clue, he could have run down the game as certainly and as speedily as the eminent detective. That is very doubtful; for it needs tact and skill to walk in the dark, even when you have a clue. If you swerve a little to the left or to the right, the thin thread is broken, and the clue is clean gone. We admit, however, that any man of fair ability may learn how to course the hare if he is put on the scent. But the prime difficulty is discovering the clue. That, we say, is an art that no man can acquire. The gifted detective rejects the apparent clues that would be adopted by the non-detective mind, and he sees and seizes upon a clue that the non-detective would pooh-pooh if it were pointed out to him. This is illustrated by what people call the blundering of the police. There is no reason to doubt the zeal and general ability of the members of the force who are selected for detective work, but they are not born detectives, and, not being able to perceive the true clue to the solution of the problem, their time and energy are wasted.

Mr Pollaky is a very distinguished detective. Curious stories are told of his successes. He has elucidated mysteries when those who employed his agency could not, as they thought, give any clue whatever. Success is often achieved by the aid of an elaborate network of agencies; but it is frequently and entirely due to the personal prescience of Mr Pollaky. He is indeed a formidable foe to criminals of all sorts.

The art of detection is not fairly appreciated. No one does more for the protection of society than the gifted and skilled detective. It is not the fear of punishment, but the fear of detection that mainly checks the criminal and wicked desires. Those who commit crimes or offences against morality, do so in the hope of not being found out; and it follows that the more certain the detection, the less crime and wickedness.

Willmer A. Hoerr in an article entitled, 'The Case of the Archetypical Agent', published in the *Baker Street Journal* (Vol. 18, No. 1, March 1968) says of the *London Figaro*'s article, 'Belying the snoopiness implied in the drawing, and more in line with the prestigious association with Shakespeare, an inside page carries a tribute that should delight all Sherlockians, especially since it was probably written by the editor, one James Mortimer!'

In December 1874, an article about Pollaky appeared in a short-lived journal called *The World: a Journal for Men and Women (No. 23)*. The issue was advertised in the *Pall Mall Gazette*, but this author has not found a copy of that article.

In 1876 *Benjamin D His Little Dinner* by an anonymous author was published. This magazine ran to 114 pages including the covers, and largely made fun of Prime Minister Benjamin Disraeli. Two images from that publication appear here – firstly a caricature of Pollaky, and secondly the back cover of the book.

In the first image, which appears together with a poem entitled 'The Lord of Intrigue', Pollaky is seen sitting at his desk wearing a loud check suit, surrounded by advertisements for rewards for the discovery of various missing young ladies. The picture appears not to be so well drawn as that produced by Faustin Betbeder, but though there are some similarities such as hairline and moustache, for example, one might wonder which is the more like the real man. Should we imagine him to be like the dapper handsome fellow of the picture by Betbeder in 1874, or could he have been more like the rather more stolid man in the check suit as pictured by 'Whew'. The images were drawn only two years apart.

Finally, can we be certain that either Betbeder or 'Whew' really knew what Pollaky looked like? No photographs of him from that time have yet been identified. This does not mean that there are none. Hopefully someone will, on reading this, come forward with more information:

From *Benjamin D His Little Dinner* (by an anonymous author) 1876
Published by Weldon & Co., Wine Office Court, Fleet Street, London
Advertised as Weldon & Co.'s Annual – Price One Shilling
One of a series of anonymous publications, satirising contemporary personalities.

'Heard at the club last night,' says Sir Verdant, as soon as Hard Hunt has finished his story, 'that our mutual friend the confidential adviser of deceived husbands and neglected and abandoned wives, the great genius of intrigue and the pet confidante and acknowledged detective-general of the aristocracy, has got his hands fearfully full just now.'

'I'm awfully sorry to hear it,' says Cross. 'If the aristocracy of this world isn't speeding to perdition with the haste of an express, then I'm not the Home Secretary and Benjamin isn't Prime Minister. Now it's a ballet-girl, now it's a row about a yacht race, now a dispute about the precedence of three princesses, now a titled lady left to die in an obscure lodging-house – it's fearful, it really is.'

'Talking about the great detective-general of the aristocracy,' says Icano'er Power, 'I've got an MS. poem of Swinburne's about me in my pocket, called "The Lord of Intrigue". I haven't read it yet. Shall I read it to you?'

Having nothing else to do, and feeling ourselves at the same time growing very languid under the influence of the smoky clouds which fill the room from our Havanas, and the fumes which ascend into our brains from rather free libations of '34, we acquiesce with a general feeling of great helplessness.

The Lord of Intrigue

Pollaky sat in his oaken chair.
Carte de visite and letter lay there,
Princely coronet, lordly crest.
Many a mystery, many a quest,
With missive and *billet* of lesser degree,
In sooth an extraordinary company;
And they seemed to ask, oh, unravel me;
Never, I ween,
Was a subtler seen,
Concerned in divorce, or elopement, or league.
Than love's autocrat, Pollaky, lord of intrigue.
In and out
Through the motley rout,
The Lord of Intrigue goes hunting about,
Here and there.
Like a dog in a fair,

Through flights and divorces,
Elopements and curses.
Through a lady's love and a husband's grudge,
Proud as a Cardinal, sharp as a Judge;
And he smiles in the face
Of the scrawl of his Grace,
With a satisfied look, as if he would say,
"Oh, the duchess must fall in our trap to-day."
While his clients with awe
As such schemes they saw.
Said, "Pollaky's sharper than Hades, you know."
Never, I ween,
Was a subtler seen,
Concerned in divorce, or elopement, or league.
Than love's autocrat, Pollaky, lord of intrigue.

'I hear it rumoured,' says Sir Verdant, 'that Sir James Hannen's Court promises to be the scene this season of an unusually plentiful crop of *causes celebres*. A lot of exceedingly ugly rumours, I hear, are going the round of the clubs with, of course, the usual club exaggerations. The army, I understand, true to its ancient traditions, figures very prominently, and I also hear something far from savoury about a remarkably clever man in Her Majesty's navy. But, *nous verrons*, eh, Benjamin?'

There is no poem by Swinburne called 'The Lord of Intrigue', which is apparently a parody of the poem 'The Execution', one of the *Ingoldsby Legends* by Richard Harris Barham (1788–1845).

～

Pollaky had become a well-known figure whose name even featured in the correspondence of the most unexpected people. On 28 November 1882, Friedrich Engels, co-author with Karl Marx of the *Communist Manifesto* wrote to Eduard Bernstein, who was in Zurich, a letter with the following curious passage:

Wenn Sie das Resume der Broschüre benutzen wollen, so ist das mir ganz recht. Die Schlußnote erfolgt jetzt bald. Die Schmidt-Affäre ist sehr schön. Der Pollaky hat seit längerer Zeit ein Privatpolizeibüro in London: Im Adreßbuch steht unter Inquiry Officer (es sind ihrer 18 aufgezählt) Pollaky, Ignatius Paul, 13 Paddington Green, W. (gar nicht weit von mir), Correspondent to 'Foreign Police Gazette'.

Translated into English:

> If you want to use the Resume of the Brochure, that's all right by me. The final touch will follow soon. The Schmidt Affair is very good. Pollaky has long had a Private Police Office in London: In the address book he is listed under Inquiry Officer (there are 18 listed) Pollaky, Ignatius Paul, 13 Paddington Green, W. (not far from me), correspondent to 'Foreign Police Gazette'.

More mysteries – what was the paper that Pollaky was at that time apparently correspondent for, what was Engel's interest in him? A clue to the latter may be contained within the paragraph. It seems that the 'Schmidt Affair' referred to by Engels involved the unmasking of a German police spy in Zurich called Johann Karl Friedrich Elias Schmidt, one of a number who had tried to infiltrate the doings of those who were developing the Communist idea. Schmidt had pretended to be a merchant who had found it necessary to leave Dresden in a hurry on account of some shady dealings. On arrival in Zurich he had, according to Marxist politician August Bebel, recommended the founding of a 'fund for assassinations'. This seems to have been the cause of some amusement, when, in 1898, Bebel mentioned this in a speech he made in Berlin, but perhaps for Pollaky there were more serious ramifications. For it seems that these police spies were agents of the Prussians, and surely Engel's mention of Pollaky immediately after referring (possibly in joking fashion) to the Schmidt Affair implies that Pollaky himself had some involvement. Further investigation uncovered the original brochure referred to by Engels. A pamphlet of sixty-four pages published at the end of 1882 which names Schmidt and other German police agents. The booklet includes thirty-four letters written to Schmidt. The final two are from Pollaky, written in German (and printed, as is the entire document, in Gothic font). This socialist brochure was banned in Germany after its publication. Pollaky's letters read as follows:

Letter 1

London, 14./10. 82

13 Paddington Green W.

privé !

Geehrter Herr!

Ich danke Ihnen für Ihre sehr geschätzte Zuschrift vom 8.c.

Noch vor 3 Monaten wäre mir Ihre Offerte sehr willkommen gewesen, doch heute ist die Nothwendigkeit hiezu nicht mehr vorhanden – und von wenigerem Interesse für hiesigen Bedarf. – Ich selbst bin der Unsicht, daß der

Kram kaum die Mühe lohnt – und an maßgebender Stelle scheint man keine Geldopfer machen zu wollen! wohl deshalb, weil man aus Erfahrung gelernt – daß wenig dabei erlangt ist – und daß Uebel fort besteht* – ich sage Ihnen dies natürlich nicht, um Sie abzulenken, mir interessante Mittheilungen zu machen, sondern um Ihnen den Standpunkt klar zu machen.

Herr Krim-Rath J.W. hat mir Sie als einen recht ehrenhaften Agenten empfohlen und will ich Ihnen gleich im Vorhinein reinen Wein einschenken.

Sollten Sie mir jedoch etwas wirklich wichtiges, noch nicht Bekanntes mittheilen, so bin ich gerne bereit, Ihnen für solche Mittheilungen ansehnliches Honorar zu zahlen, doch nur unter der Bedingung, daß die mir gemachten Mittheilungen nicht andern Orts schon feilgeboten worden find.

Das ist das 'sine qua non'. Jedenfalls ist es mir lieb, daß ich Ihre Adresse für eventuelle Fälle besitze, es dürften einige Aufträge folgen der Zeit, wer weiß? Ihr ergebener Pollaky.

Translation of the above:

London, 14./10. 82
13 Paddington Green W.

privé !

Dear Sir!

I thank you for your valued letter of the 8.c. [8 October]

Only 3 months before your offer would have been very welcome to me, but today the necessity no longer exists – and of less interest for our needs. – I myself am the unseen, the affair is hardly worth the trouble – and it seems that those in charge do not want to make any sacrifice of money! probably because someone learned from experience – that little is gained thereby – and that evil persists* – I do not say this, of course, to distract you, to make communications interesting, but to help make the point clear.

Criminal Investigator Mr J.W. has recommended you to me as a very honourable agent and I will tell you the plain truth from the start.

Should you have however something really important for me, not yet known, then I am willing to pay you a handsome fee for such information, but only under the condition that the information is given to me and has not already been offered for sale somewhere else.

This is the 'sine qua non'. Anyway, it's good for me that I have your address for any future cases that, it should be that some orders may follow over time, who knows?

Yours sincerely Pollaky.

Editor's note published below the first letter:

* Dies Geständnis aus polizei Munde ist kostbar. Allerdings ist der geriebene Pollaky nicht bereaukratischer Polizist, sondern Detektive, auf eigene Rechnung. Und er versteht zu rechnen. [This acknowledgement of police views is valuable. However, the wily Pollaky is not a bureaucratic policeman, but a private detective. And he understands what is expected.]

Letter 2

London, 20./10. 82

Geehrte Herr!

Ihre gefl. [geffälig] Zuschrift vom 17. ds. mit Bericht über Sozialisten dort richtig erhalten – der Inhalt Ihres Berichtes ist wohl im Allgemeinen sehr interessant, doch entbehrt solcher einen positiven Wert und ist man nicht geneigt, auf diesen Kram (recte borstige Umtriebe) auch nur das Geringste zu verwenden.

Le jeu ne vaut pas la chandelle!!

Mir thut es Ihrethalben leib – doch will ich Sie gleich von dem richtigen Standpunkt in Kenntnis gesetzt sehen.

Also Sand darüber!

Ich bin nicht mehr Katholisch als der Papst. Sie verstehen dies? Ich hoffe jedoch daß in Zukunft sich eine Gelegenheit darbieten wird, wenn ich von Ihren Diensten Gebrauch zu machen nicht versäumen würde.

Ihr ergebenster Pollaky.*

Translation of the above:

Dear Sir!

Your kind letter of 17 ds. with report on the Socialists arrived safely – the content of your report is probably in general very interesting, but lacks such a positive value and one is not inclined to use this stuff (properly called 'bristly plotting') even the slightest.

Le jeu ne vaut pas la chandelle! [The game is not worth the candle!] I do it for its own sake – but I would like you to have the correct viewpoint of the information.

So put sand over! [Forget it?]

I am no more Catholic than the Pope. You understand this? But I hope that in the future, there will be an occasion when I can make use of your services.

Yours faithfully Pollaky.*

Editor's note published below the second letter:

> * Es ist dies der Geheimpolizist, an welchen Schmidt durch Weller in Dresden
> gewiesen und empfohlen ist. [This is the secret policeman who was rejected
> and recommended by Schmidt through Weller in Dresden.]

So it would seem that Pollaky was approached by the German authorities to
spy on their behalf against the Socialists, just as he had been approached a little
over twenty-one years earlier by the United States to spy on the Confederates.
Whether he actively kept an eye on the Socialists or not is impossible to say.
From the tone of his letters, it would appear that he did not take this task on
with the same enthusiasm and energy that had filled his days all those years ago.
Nevertheless, his letters appear in the brochure, and he cannot have been pleased
to discover this, if indeed he did find out. Pollaky always had his ear to the ground
so it would seem unusual if he were unaware of this publication.

The Socialists, if they believed that Pollaky had some involvement with the
activities of the German police, might not have been pleased. Pollaky may
have thought that there was a good chance that they might resent his implied
interference. Could this have influenced his decision to take early retirement?
Might this be the reason that he is known to have kept a revolver nearby after he
was retired?

In a letter to *The Times* dated 22 April 1911, Pollaky wrote that he had been
the London Correspondent of the *International Criminal Police Gazette* for more
than a quarter of a century. On 10 May 1914, he wrote a letter to *The Times*
recommending that cooperation between individual police forces of various
countries would be more effective than an 'International Bureau'. This letter,
published two days later, is signed 'RITTER VON POLLAKY, formerly the
London Correspondent for the Internationales Criminal-Polizeiblatt'. It would be
convenient to assume that this refers to the paper known in French as the, *Moniteur
International de Police Criminelle* and in English as *The International Criminal Police
Times*. Based in Frankfurt-am-Main in Germany this was a trilingual paper with
text in French, German, and English with photographs of wanted men and women
and descriptions of their crimes. It celebrated the twentieth anniversary of its
founding in January 1906 and was founded in 1886 by Polizeirat [Superintendent]
Travers. (Copies of it are now fairly rare.) However, though the 1882 Post Office
Directory lists Pollaky as, 'Correspondent to the Foreign Police Gazette', the
Internationales Criminal-Polizeiblatt had not at that time been founded. As early
as 1859 he had declared on the death certificate of his first wife that he was a
'Newspaper Correspondent', but this refers to the *Morning Post*. There is also no
evidence that he wrote for the American *National Police Gazette*, founded in 1845,
a tabloid which eventually became a fairly racy sports orientated paper. And so the

mystery remains; what was the newspaper Pollaky wrote for? Surely not the *Police Gazette* of London, for that was not an international paper.

He did, though, write articles for international journals. In December 1898, the monthly journal *Kosmodike* — Periodical for International Law Matters (to give its English subtitle) which was published in Germany for only three years (1898–1900), and boasted articles in French, German, and English, printed a piece in German entitled *Die Londoner Polizei [The London Police]* by Criminalrath Ritter Pollaky. He had been retired for over sixteen years, and much had changed in the Police force in that time. He expressed his admiration for the London Metropolitan Police and Assistant Commissioner Sir Robert Anderson, showing particular appreciation for the handling of terrorism and criminals by the former, and the astuteness of the latter, but still seemed not to think too much of the other London force the 'so-called' City Police. After referring to new treaties of extradition between European countries, he finished with a paean to the London policeman which translates as follows: 'The London constable remains in his nature a pattern of civilisation and human love, as it is found nowhere else.'

In any case, there can be no doubt that he felt fully entitled to call himself, 'Ritter von Pollaky'; he had, after all, received his Ritterkreuz (2nd Class) in 1871.

Aside from the exotic and mystic aura that surrounded him, it would seem that his name certainly lent itself to humour – witness W.S. Gilbert's use of it more than once (see Appendix 2), as well as the fun made of him by the *Tomahawk* and *Fun*. For a pleasingly humorous effect, try repeating 'Paddington Pollaky' over and over again at a moderate tempo. From 1861, Gilbert had written poems for *Fun*.

In 1881, Pollaky found a kind of immortality when Gilbert used his name in a lyric for his new comic opera, with music by Sir Arthur Sullivan: *Patience, or Bunthorne's Bride*. First performed at the Opera Comique Theatre (now demolished) on 23 April, it transferred to the newly built Savoy Theatre in the Strand on 10 October the same year. Before its first performance there, Richard D'Oyly Carte, owner of the theatre and the third part of the triumvirate with Gilbert and Sullivan, famously appeared before the audience and broke a glowing lightbulb to prove the safety of a new technology: the Savoy Theatre was the first public building in the world to be lit by electricity.

Among the characters in *Patience* is Colonel Calverley of the Dragoon Guards, whose first song describes the attributes necessary to make a heavy dragoon. These include: 'The keen penetration of Paddington Pollaky.'

We might ask whether the nickname, 'Paddington Pollaky' was used by Gilbert in a way that was already in use, or whether Gilbert, with his usual facility for rhyme and metre actually coined the phrase himself. I haven't found it used earlier than 1881, the year Gilbert used it in *Patience*. And this may be the place to mention that Pollaky's newly coined sobriquet, was its first famous use. Not until 1958 would 'Paddington' again become a popular sobriquet, and that for the fictional *Paddington Bear* created by Michael Bond. In 1939, though, the Laurel and Hardy film *A Chump at Oxford* was released. Stan and Ollie go to study at Oxford University. Stan gets a bump on the head and realises that he is in fact Lord Paddington, a brilliant scholar who had gone missing from the university some years before. So brilliant is he that he agrees to help Einstein with a problem he is having with his *Theory of Relativity*.

Gilbert had used Pollaky's name twice before. His first recorded uses of Pollaky's name were in his plays *No Cards* and *An Old Score*, both from 1869; the relevant texts are given, together with the full text of Colonel Calverley's song, in Appendix 4. As a theatre-goer, and as a keen reader of newspapers where these pieces were reviewed, was Pollaky aware of these mentions of his name? He cannot have been unaware of this last mention, for with it came a certain amount of notoriety. *Patience* has outlasted Pollaky's name in fame. His name has been sung and heard at every performance of this piece, and there have been very many of those.

By 1881, Pollaky was 53, and retirement in Brighton with Mary Ann was not far away. Might the new notoriety given him by W.S. Gilbert's use of his name in *Patience* have irritated him enough to have been one factor in his decision to end his practice as a private investigator? As seen from earlier newspaper items, he was sometimes gently mocked, but now his name was a byword for something humorous. Every one of his obituaries mentioned his name in association with Gilbert's lyric. One wonders whether Pollaky as a theatre goer ever saw a performance of *Patience*. It was not the last time that Gilbert used real personalities in his lyrics. Famously, Captain Shaw of the Metropolitan Fire Brigade was present at the first night of *Iolanthe* at the Savoy Theatre when Alice Barnett, as the Queen of the Fairies, opened her arms out to the audience as she sang in her song the lines:

> Oh, Captain Shaw!
> Type of true love kept under!
> Could thy brigade
> With cold cascade
> Quench my great love, I wonder!

Had Pollaky heard Richard Temple (the creator of the role of Colonel Calverley) sing about him in their previous production?

Pollaky is mentioned in passing in a number of novels including *The French Lieutenant's Woman* (John Fowles, 1969), and *Rupert Godwin* (Mary Elizabeth Braddon, 1867). Perhaps the most unusual reference to him is to be found in *A Sherlock Holmes Companion* edited by Peter Haining. First published by W. H. Allen in 1980, page 207 (page 264 of the revised edition, Warner Books, 1994) is the conclusion of a short chapter entitled 'Holmes Beyond the Grave'. This chapter describes a séance which seemingly took place on 7 July 1955 in America, in which the spirit of Arthur Conan Doyle was apparently interviewed. On being asked if Paddington Pollaky had helped with the Sherlock Holmes stories, the shade of Doyle is supposed to have answered, 'He was there'. The séance was, according to Haining's introduction, reported in the *Baltimore Sun*. Haining goes on to say that certain persons were, 'attempting to prove that Holmes was modelled on Pollaky'. In April 1955 an American journal called, *The Victorian Newsletter* announced on its last page that one B.D. Emmart was 'working on a biography of Pollaky, most famous of Victorian Private Detectives'. One might wonder if this (never published) work, the intended product of Lecturer in Journalism, Barney D. Emmart (1923–89), who lived in Baltimore, had something to do with the séance.

One might wonder if Pollaky influenced Agatha Christie when she created Poirot. Now here there are more similarities; the lavish moustache, the foreign origin, the characterful speech – good but not quite English. Here again, problems arise. Firstly, Poirot as originally devised was quite old, certainly a lot older than usually portrayed in film and television adaptations, whereas Pollaky retired from the business of private investigation at the age of 54. Since Pollaky was no longer well known by the time Poirot was created, one must ask not only if Agatha Christie knew of him, but also whether she could possibly have known what Pollaky looked like as images of him were very rare. She certainly does not seem to have mentioned him in any of her writings.

Retirement

13

ollaky retired abruptly, it would seem, in 1882 and moved with Mary Ann and their family to Brighton. Their surviving children were approaching adulthood. Minna was 18, Francis was 16, Rose was 14 and Mabel was 12. Mrs Pollaky was now 41, and Pollaky himself was 54. That year he had found it necessary to place the following advertisement on the front page of *The Times*:

The Times – 6 March 1882
POLLAKY'S PRIVATE INQUIRY OFFICE (established 1862). – The rumour that I am dead is not true. – Pollaky, Paddington-green, W.

This is one of the more unusual of Pollaky's advertisements; one wonders why it was necessary, and how this rumour could have started; there seems to be no mention of it prior to this anywhere else. It predates the more famous quote of Mark Twain from the 2 June 1897 New York Journal (seventeen years later): 'The report of my death was an exaggeration. (Not: 'The reports of my death are greatly exaggerated'.) But his days as a private investigator were almost over for good.

Pollaky's last advertisements:

The Times – 18 May 1882
POLLAKY'S PRIVATE INQUIRY OFFICE. Established reputation in England and with the Foreign Detective Police – 13, Paddington-green, W."

The Times – 19 May 1882
POSTCARD ! (Richmond). – Call on Mr Pollaky, The Green, Paddington, where on proving your identity, you will receive the reward.

In July, he and Mary Ann some spent time holidaying in the Isle of Wight, arriving at the Esplanade Hotel in Ryde on the 14th or 15th. For the first week of their stay weather was pleasant, though there were passing showers, but if they stayed on after that they would have enjoyed some glorious sunshine, as well as the chance of seeing the 'singular sight as was presented by the large plank exhibited during the week by the coastguards. It was covered with thousands of large goose barnacles which moved themselves about like so many large leeches' (*Isle of Wight Observer* 29 July 1882). This was evidently deemed to be one of the highlights of the month, and appeared on page 5 of the newspaper (the first page of news was page 4, and even that was mostly advertisements).

Their new address in Brighton was Miramar, 33 Stanford Road, Preston Park, Brighton, Sussex. The house, built in the early 1880s, still stands at the time of writing.

Pollaky had destroyed all his personal records of his investigations, but, still receiving inquiries for his services, placed the following advertisement in *The Times*:

The Times – Saturday, 26 April 1884

ANNOUNCEMENT. – Mr POLLAKY finds it necessary to state publicly that he has RETIRED from BUSINESS: that all records and correspondence with former clients have been destroyed; and any person claiming to be his successor would do so fraudulently. – April 25th, 1884

As a result of this advertisement, the following item appeared two days later:

Manchester Evening News – Monday, 28 April 1884

A notable figure has just disappeared from London life. This is Mr Pollaky, who has for upwards of 25 years conducted a private inquiry office at Paddington Green. [...] Mr Pollaky will now be able to devote his leisure to the cultivation of roses or the study of music, which are supposed to possess a peculiar fascination for the detective mind.

Of course, the paragraph in the *Manchester Evening News* is not entirely correct, as Pollaky had not been at Paddington Green for as long as twenty-five years. But the most interesting suggestion is in the last sentence. Was it Pollaky, though, who was supposed to have a fascination for cultivating roses and studying music, or were these supposed to interest detectives in general? His house in Paddington Green had large gardens in front and behind. The front garden had twelve almond trees, but these are the only plants recorded as being there.

The fact of his retirement did not prevent others from taking advantage of his name; despite his having clearly advertised in 1884 that he was no longer active, there were instances of impersonation, if not of the man himself, then certainly of his representatives, as the following letter shows:

British Medical Journal, 18 April 1885

A CONSULTING-ROOM THIEF.

Sir, – About 5 o'clock on Thursday afternoon, April 2nd, a broad shouldered man, from 40 to 50 years of age, with fair sandy whiskers, called at my house under the pretence of seeking information about a Mrs Ward, and representing himself as an agent of Messrs Pollaky. He was permitted, in my absence, to go into the consulting-room to write a letter to me. He availed himself of the opportunity to steal a large brass syringe lying on my table, although my servant never left him alone for a moment. My servant gathered he had paid visits to other medical men near, which, on further inquiry, I found to be the case; but, happily, in each instance, his predatory instincts were defeated.

I gave full information to the police, who discovered my syringe the next morning at a pawnbroker's about a mile distant. At the same time, he pawned a square marble clock, evidently the result of his day's labour.

I have reason to hope, from certain circumstances, that his career will not be a long one; but, in the meantime, I am desirous of warning my professional brethren, so that they may be on their guard against such a character. He wears a dark Chesterfield great coat, with billycock hat, and light trousers; and the tale he tells is generally a little involved and rather incoherent. – Yours faithfully, J. ROCHE LYNCH. 8, Boyne Terrace, Holland Park, W.

Meanwhile, Pollaky enjoyed his retirement. Signs of his continued activity, vague though some of them are, can nevertheless be seen in letters and newspapers. He had been quite methodical not only professionally, but also in his private life. By selling the house in Paddington Green, and moving to Brighton, he would have realised a fair amount of equity, as property prices, then as now, would have been far lower away from London. Furthermore, he had invested a good amount of the money he saved in railways, in particular the Entre Rios Central Railway in Argentina. In August 1891, he attended a shareholders' meeting in London and seconded one of the chairman's proposals.

According to Henry Mackinnon Walbrook in his book *The Gilbert and Sullivan Opera: A History and a Comment 1922*:

The 'Paddington Pollaky' alluded to by the Colonel [in *Patience*] was a celebrated detective of the day, a man of international reputation who, after his retirement lived at Brighton and was for some years an almost daily habitué of the public chess-room in the Royal Pavilion. He died during the Great War.

The distance from the Royal Pavilion to his new house was a good mile and a quarter, and must have taken at least half an hour each way if he walked. He may, though, have used the horse-drawn buses which passed not too far from his house.

The Public Room at the Royal Pavilion was opened in 1873 (or 1874 according to the *Southern Weekly News* of 12 October 1889.) It still existed in 1921, three years after Pollaky's death. Walbrook's passage on Pollaky in his book is the only reference currently found of Pollaky having played chess there (or anywhere at all) and yet we should not be surprised that chess might provide him with the intellectual stimulus needed by a retired private detective.

Discover the Royal Pavilion, published by Royal Pavilion Museum, says of the Banqueting Room Gallery:

> The decoration in this room is toned down not only to contrast with the Banqueting Room, but also to create a calm, relaxing atmosphere. Guests would withdraw to this room after eating. Ladies would retire first, leaving the gentlemen to their port and cigars. Games such as cards, backgammon and chess would be played here. Palm trees, made of cast iron, covered in carved wood, support the upper floor.

On Friday, 24 April 1846, the *Monthly Times of London* had reported on a chess match that had begun in September 1842 between the Paris Chess Club and the Pesth Chess Club of Hungary. The Hungarian club had sent a challenge to play a match by correspondence. Their players included one called Pollaky. The match finished in April 1846 (hence the report). The Hungarian team won, largely, according to the report, due to the 'fine play of Szen and Lowenthal'. Johann Jacob Löwenthal (1810–76) was a Hungarian chess player expelled from Hungary in 1849 after the unsuccessful revolution. Although he initially went to America, in 1851 he went to England to take part in the London Chess Tournament and remained there till his death. József Szén (1805–57), founder of the Pesth Chess Club and chess teacher of Löwenthal, on the other hand, remained in Hungary, although he too was in London in 1851 to play chess in the London Chess Tournament. From 1872 to 1876, Löwenthal wrote the chess column for the *London Figaro*, that same journal in whose supplement in 1874 appeared Betbeder's caricature of Ignatius Paul Pollaky.

From this information, vague though it is, as if clutching at straws, we see the name Pollaky associated with the game of chess as early as 1842–46. However this was not Ignatius Pollaky, but one Br. Pollaky who was reported as being a member of the Hungarian team in *Le Palamède* of 15 July 1842 (a periodical about chess published in Paris). Was he a relation? It is the first mention of the name Pollaky connected with the world of chess, and with that we must be satisfied.

Live-in servants came and went, judging by the census forms. In 1891, Sussex-born Mary Ede, 23, was their domestic servant, in 1901 it was 21-year-old Louise Sayer, also from Sussex, and in 1911, Gertrude Cooper, 20, from Herefordshire. Doubtless there were others, though it is to be hoped that none were as notorious for their behaviour as child stealer Elizabeth Barry, their cook for a short time in 1869. The 1911 census form states that the Pollakys had seven children born alive. It is apparent that after forty-nine years, they were still unable to come to terms with the stillbirth of their first child.

Next door, at No. 31 Stanford Avenue, lived the Treacher family who had moved there in 1889. Thomas Treacher initially worked for his father, Harry, as a bookseller's assistant, eventually taking over the shop, H. and C. Treacher, 1 North Street, Brighton, on the death of his father in 1891. (His uncle Charles, co-founder of the business, had died twenty years earlier.) Thomas Treacher described himself as a 'Fancy Stationer and Bookseller'. The business also published a number of books and was a subscription library. Thomas and Minnie Treacher would eventually have six children, all living at home, together with a cook, and a nurse to look after the youngest children. (Thomas's brother Arthur was a solicitor in Brighton; Arthur's son would grow up to be the Hollywood actor Arthur Treacher, player of a number of supporting roles.) In 1914 Thomas Treacher would act as one of the referees for Pollaky's application for British citizenship, stating that he had known Pollaky for twenty-five years and had always known him to be of good character. Although the Treachers were somewhat younger than Mr and Mrs Pollaky, a friendly relationship evidently existed between Ignatius and Mary Ann, and Thomas Treacher and his wife Minnie.

Neighbours on the other side at No. 35 did not stay as long as the Treachers. In 1901 the house was lived in by Richard Gamble, commercial lawyer, and his wife Annie. In 1911 the house was occupied by retired Lieutenant Colonel Alfred Ashmead, who had served in the cavalry in Canada, and his Canadian wife Martha. They had married in England in 1887, and gone out to Canada in about 1890.

Never one to remain inactive for long, Pollaky continued to write letters to newspapers after his retirement. He felt that his long experience in crime detection and matters concerned with nationality made him an expert whose opinions should carry weight. His letters are often quite opinionated and some disagreed with his conclusions. Most are signed 'Ritter von Pollaky' (making use of his German knighthood) or 'Criminalrath' (modern spelling 'Kriminalrat') – meaning a kind of German police investigator, and sometimes 'Ritter von Pollaky, Criminalrath'. As early as 19 April 1881, the German language newspaper *Der Deutsche Correspondent* of Baltimore, US, referred to Pollaky as 'Criminalrath Pollaky'. Several of his letters were published in *The Times*. The following letter to the *Daily Mail* of Tuesday 28 July 1896, is a rare example of Pollaky attempting to be humorous:

To the Editor of the Daily Mail.
Your Leader headed 'Husband and Holidays' reminds me of an episode which came under my personal experience in a friend's house. The husband, overworked, fell ill, and a physician was called in. He saw the patient, and the

wife anxiously awaited his verdict, which was to the effect that the patient must have a change and travel. 'Where shall we go to?' asked the distressed wife. The doctor somewhat brusquely replied, 'I did not say you should travel with him, but he must travel.'
POLLAKY.

His letters offer an insight into the workings of the mind of a man who still felt, after all these years, the need for appreciation, and a need to be known by the public at large. In 1909, there were several letters to *The Times* discussing the merits of the method for classifying fingerprints devised by Francis Galton, famous for his now largely discredited theory of Eugenics. 'Ritter von Pollaky wrote a letter published on 7 January 1909 pointing out that 'my countryman, the Austrian professor, Dr. Purjonje, in the year 1823, lectured on finger-prints at the University at Breslau.' This refers to the lectures given by John Evangelist Purkinji, professor of anatomy. His lecture discussed fingerprint patterns but did not mention the use of fingerprints for identification. Pollaky continuing to dwell on this matter, and feeling that he had more to offer as an expert in detection, wrote again a few days later:

TO THE EDITOR OF THE TIMES.
Sir, – Last August the president of police of one of the most important towns on the Continent honoured me with a visit at Brighton; he came direct from London, where he devoted several weeks to a thorough study of the metropolitan police system both administrative and executive. The president's professional admiration and enthusiasm for Scotland Yard was great; for the finger prints (Sir Edward Henry's method of registration) it was still greater; for the universal courtesy of the constables in regulating the traffic it was greatest.
Yours faithfully,
RITTER VON POLLAKY.
Brighton, January 11.

Though Pollaky would leave us in the dark as to who this President of Police was he must have felt that mentioning his visit gave his opinions a weighty credibility that otherwise they might not have. In October 1910, the new Chief of the Berlin Police (Police President) Traugott von Jagow, together with the Chief of the Charlottenburg Police, Günther von Hertzberg, and the Chief of Police of Dresden, visited London in order to study the English police system. They were particularly interested in traffic control and administration of police stations, and were given full assistance by Scotland Yard. During their visit, they attended part of the proceedings of the Crippen murder trial, so visits of foreign police were not unknown at that time. And after all his problems with one particular commissioner of police in days of yore, Pollaky's approval of Commissioner of the Metropolitan Police, Sir Edward Henry, and his methods may show a softening in his attitude.

Most of Pollaky's 'Ritter' letters to *The Times* are about the naturalisation of aliens:

The Times – Saturday, 7 January 1911
TO THE EDITOR OF THE TIMES.
Sir, – THE ALIENS ACT VERSUS ANARCHISM
An Englishman travelling on the Continent has [...] to submit to certain police regulations.

Pollaky lists some of the documents necessary to carry or to complete: passport, hotel register (which the proprietor copies for the police), and a permit stamped on his passport if he intends to settle in that country:

I never heard of any Englishman travelling abroad complain of these purely administrative police measures. Why should a foreigner coming to England and remaining here object to certain similar rules and regulations?

The terrible and horrifying events in the City surely call for more drastic measures in the supervision of aliens.

The terrible and horrifying events he refers to are the Houndsditch Murders of 16 December 1910 and the Siege of Sidney Street of 3 January 1911 which followed as a direct consequence. These events involved a group of international anarchists who attempted to rob a jeweller's shop killing a number of policemen in their bungled attempt. In the background lurked the mysterious figure of a man known at the time as 'Peter the Painter', whose true identity has been the subject of much speculation. These complex events have never been fully explained, but one of those involved, Jacob Peters, later became a senior figure in the Soviet government and may have been killed during one of Stalin's purges:

The Times – Saturday, 22 April 1911
AN ALIEN ON THE ALIENS BILL.
TO THE EDITOR OF THE TIMES.
[...] I am an alien in possession of a revolver. Your readers need, however, not feel nervous. I am in my 84th year, and the revolver was bought by me in the year of our Lord 1867 when I was sworn in a special constable in the X Division of the Metropolitan Police [...] I kept this revolver 44 years without using it once. My unbroken domicile in my ever-beloved adopted

country has lasted 60 years, and during 50 years I paid rates and taxes like a true Briton, only I did not grumble as Englishmen do, but I still remained an alien. The very sound 'stinks in the nostrils of heaven' [...] My children grandchildren and great grandchildren, born, every one of them in England and British Colonies, will be called upon to fight for England, but I, their ancestor, would still be 'an alien'. May I venture to ask why I should be called upon to forswear my allegiance to my venerable and dearly-loved old Emperor Francis Joseph of Austria and Hungary, simply to get rid of the stigma as now understood and attached to the word 'alien' by the general public? As the London correspondent for more than a quarter of a century of the International Criminal Police Gazette, I think I may in all modesty claim to be an expert able to give an opinion that the new Aliens Act will in the shortest possible time clear this country of undesirable foreigners [...]

I remain, sir your obedient servant,

RITTER VON POLLAKY, Criminatrath

Brighton, April 20.

The Times – Saturday, 15 July 1911

An alien desirous of becoming naturalized in England should first of all petition the Government of his own country for sanction to be released from his native *Staatsangehörigkeit* [Affiliation]. [...] All doubts and disagreeable complications now frequently arising respecting the legal status of a naturalized alien returning to his native country would henceforth be avoided.

Your obedient servant.

RITTER VON POLLAKY, Criminal-Rath

Pollaky's suggestions were not met with universal approval. An editorial in the *Jewish Chronicle* of 21 July 1911 stated that, 'It need hardly be pointed out that the greatest difficulties would be experienced by Russian Jews in carrying out Ritter von Pollaky's suggestion.'

The Times – Tuesday, 12 May 1914

TOURING CRIMINALS

TO THE EDITOR OF THE TIMES

Sir, – Whoever the writer of the article in The Times of May 9 may be, he certainly shows himself a most tactful master of the craft; and I should say that whatever he does not know on the subject of the proposed 'International Police Bureau and Police Congresses' is indeed not worth knowing.

I fully appreciate his recommendation that 'if the ... [Pollaky's ellipsis] international criminal is to be kept in hand it will be by a freer interchange of information between the individual forces, than by the expensive and ineffective method of establishing an International Bureau.'

I remain, your obedient servant,

RITTER VON POLLAKY, formerly the London Correspondent of the official Internationales Criminal-Polizeiblatt.

After this last letter, Pollaky's name is rarely seen in *The Times*. On 4 June, his name appears in a list of charitable donations, where he is shown to have contributed 10*s* 6*d* each to staff of the South Shields Education Office and this seems to be the last time his name would appear there until his obituary in 1918.

In 1921 Major Fitzroy Gardner, OBE (1855–1931) included in a volume of memoirs entitled *Days and Ways of an Old Bohemian* (pages 235–36) the following account of his acquaintance with Pollaky:

My first acquaintance with detective work was, when I was twenty-four, under the tuition of the then best-known detective in the world – Ignatius Pollaky, a Pole, who acted in England for several foreign governments, and was often consulted by Scotland Yard. He spoke and wrote six languages fluently and knew intimately some of the most dangerous criminals of four countries. He had an office on Paddington Green; hence 'Pollaky of Paddington Green', a music-hall skit of the old popular ditty, 'Pretty Polly Perkins of Paddington Green'. I happened to make his acquaintance in connection with the abduction (by a man holding an important Government position) of one of my mother's servants, and, finding that I could speak German fluently and some French, he made use of me in a difficult matter in which foreigners were concerned. I gave my services enthusiastically, and have never forgotten the lessons which Pollaky taught me in our conversations. Thirty years later I was anxious to obtain certain information about dangerous Russian and Polish refugees in this country, and I paid a visit to Pollaky, who had retired from business and was living at Brighton. I had no idea that he had recently developed a form of insanity. He was obsessed with the idea that some of the men whose arrest he had effected in years gone by were trying to murder him; moreover, he had lost his memory, and not only did he not recognise me or my name, but, when he came to the door in answer to the bell, he threatened me with a revolver, and I returned to London without the desired information. Pollaky died about three years ago.

Gardner was wrong about Pollaky's nationality. The story about the abduction case is interesting, and typical of the kind of work Pollaky undertook, though why Gardner's help was needed for his language skills is a mystery since Pollaky spoke both those languages fluently himself. Of even more interest, is the description of his behaviour in his old age. Gardner was 24 in 1879. If his 'thirty years later' is correct, then this meeting happened in 1909 (when Pollaky was 81). Was his nervous behaviour and his need to protect himself with a revolver justified? Did he have, or had he had, enemies who were really to be feared? Might it have been the Socialists whom he felt might be dangerous? If, as is possible, Gardner was approximate as to the years, then it is possible that the interview with Pollaky was as late as 1911, and that the Russian and Polish refugees to whom he refers have some connection with the Siege of Sidney Street. We already know that Pollaky was quite exercised about this, and this may also explain his behaviour with the revolver.

In another memoir, *More Reminiscences of an Old Bohemian* (page 191), Gardner discusses the original case in more detail:

> A lady relative of mine had a remarkably pretty nurse for her baby, daughter of a highly respectable tradesman. One night the girl disappeared from the house, taking all her belongings with her, and my services were enlisted to trace her. At that time there were sensational stories in the newspapers about men decoying good-looking servant girls in London and taking them to houses of ill-fame on the Continent. With the aid of Ignatius Pollaky, the then famous international detective – that started my acquaintance with him – I traced her, not to any foreign country, but to a boarding-house near Westbourne Grove, where she was living with a man occupying a high position in the Civil Service. She was sent back to her people, and neither my relative or I ever heard of her again until some fifteen years later, when I discovered her, as wife of a man of considerable means and mixing in quite good society; incidentally she was hostess at a big function at which the late King, when Prince of Wales, was present.

As for the rest of the family, Rose Katherine Pollaky married in 1890 Luer John Charles Varrelmann, a clerk in the War Office. The sisters were still close. Minna Mary Ann, the oldest surviving sibling was certainly staying with her sister Rose and Luer on the night of the 1891 census. Minna remained unmarried. Rose died in 1924; Varrelmann remarried in 1932 to Evelyn Paskins. Rose and Luer had two children: Rose Margaretha Varrelmann born 1891, and Luer Frederick Cyril Varrelmann, born 1893. The Varrelmann family lived in Croydon, Surrey.

Mabel Mary Pollaky also married in 1890. She became Mrs Andrew Charles Chapman. Chapman was a grocer. A year later, they were living in Petersfield, Hampshire where they had two children, John, born 1896, and Lilian, born 1897. By 1901, they were living in Islington, London.

No expense had been spared on the education of Ignatius and Mary Ann's son Francis. He attended University College School, London from 1877 to 1880. At that time the school was within the premises of University College itself. After leaving school, Francis Hughes James Pollaky worked in Grantham as an apprentice to a chemist and druggist and eventually married Helena Johanna Spiers. They had a daughter Elizabeth Mary Ann, born October 1889 in England. At some point in the 1890s Francis Hughes James Pollaky, his wife, daughter and his sister Minna travelled to South Africa where his son Francis Cecil Pollaky was probably born. They may not have travelled together, as Elizabeth Mary Ann was certainly baptised in London in 1899. Both Minna and Francis Hughes James Pollaky died in 1899 in South Africa. Francis died of *phthisis asthenia* (tuberculosis) at Old Somerset Hospital, Cape Town. He had been working as a Law Agent in Darling District, Malmesbury, Cape Colony. Malmesbury is about 40 miles north of Cape Town.

His death was announced in *The Times*:

POLLAKY – On September 7 [1899], at midnight, at Cape Town, after much suffering, Francis Hughes James Pollaky, the dearly-loved and only surviving son of Ignatius Paul and Mary Ann Pollaky, in his 34th year.

His sister Minna Mary Ann Pollaky died of influenza and exhaustion on 3 October 1899 and is buried in Willowmore, South Africa some 330 miles east of Cape Town, where she had been working as a teacher. She never married. The Varrelmanns named their house 'Willowmore'.

Pollaky's granddaughter, Elizabeth Mary Ann Pollaky, married and divorced twice in South Africa. Pollaky's grandson, Francis Cecil Pollaky, born about 1893, became a doctor of medicine who qualified for practice in Dublin in 1937 as a Licentiate of Apothecaries Hall (LAH) and had a practice in London. He married cellist Kathleen Andrews in 1922; he is listed on the marriage register as 'Pollaky or Hughes'. On 4 May 1939, he changed his surname from Pollaky to Hamilton by deed poll. In 1949 he gave up his practice, as he was frustrated by all the form-filling he had to do when he thought he should be attending to his patients, and became a grocer in the village of Crawley Down, Sussex.

It is to be hoped that Ignatius and Mary Ann felt some comfort from the existence of grandchildren, some of who must have visited them in their late retirement, but the news of the deaths of Francis and Minna in 1899 must surely have left them devastated.

Naturalisation

14

As we move further into the twentieth century, the great events that were taking place must necessarily colour our view of life in England, even the life of a long-retired Hungarian private investigator, who on occasion exhibited confused behaviour. The year 1914 was notable for the start of World War One, and for the appalling life in the trenches for those serving in the armies of the nations involved. Pollaky was no longer the quick-minded, ever-ready-to-jump-at-a-chance detective of his youth and middle years. He was comfortably placed and had been retired from business for over thirty years.

But there was one thing that had still evaded him. One thing that he always harked back to, that plagued his mind and perhaps gave him sleepless nights when he thought of it – his treatment at the hands of the authorities over fifty years earlier.

And so, in 1914, he applied once more to become a British citizen. He was now 86 years old.

In his application he stressed that he had not been an Austro-Hungarian subject since 1879 as in that year a law was passed by both Houses of Parliament of the Dual Austro-Hungarian Monarchy stating that any Austro-Hungarian subject who remained out of his country for 10 years would lose his nationality:

> Having been absent for more than 63 years I am now absolutely denationalized by the above law – showing besides an unbroken domicile of sixty three years in England; sworn in a Special Constable serving during the Hyde Park Riots!

This time, his application received kinder consideration. The Chief Constable, Sir C. Matthews himself, hoped that the application would be given 'special treatment' as Pollaky was well known to him as an ex-secret inquiry agent.

Detective Inspector Forward wrote in his reference from the Police Station, Town Hall, Brighton on 27 August 1914:

> I beg to report that the Memorialist, Ignatius Paul Pollaky, of 33 Stanford Avenue, Brighton, states he was born at Pressburg (Pozsony), Hungary, on the

19th February 1828. His father, Joseph Pollaky, a private correspondent and musician, and his mother, Minna Pollaky, were both Hungarian subjects.

The Memorialist came to England in 1851, and for about 25 years resided in his own freehold house at 13 Paddington Green, W., during which time he was in the employ of Lloyd's Salvage Association.

He came to Brighton about 27 years ago, and has since resided in his own freehold house at 33 Stanford Avenue. Since he has been in Brighton he has been of independent means.

On the 2nd June 1861 he was married to Mary Ann Hughes, whose parents (now deceased) were British subjects. He now has two married daughters, aged 47 and 45 years respectively, whose husbands are British subjects, and are residing in England.

The Memorialist can read, write, and understand the English language perfectly. The signatures on the attached declarations are in his own handwriting.

He states his reasons for applying for a Certificate of Naturalization are:— that he has resided in England for 63 years, his wife is a British subject, his two daughters have married British subjects, and the whole of his money and interests are in this Country. He therefore has no desire to leave it, and wishes to enjoy the rights and privileges of a natural born British subject.

The Memorialist has been known to me personally for the past 20 years, and I have always known him to be a respectable citizen.

And so, on 17 September 1914, some fifty-two years after his original application, Ignatius Paul Pollaky became a British Citizen.

At the age of 87, on 14 May 1915, his name was included in *The Times* in a list of those naturalised British subjects of German or Austrian birth who expressed their condemnation of 'German military methods' while expressing their loyalty to Britain. This list was in response to a letter there from dramatist Arthur Wing Pinero which had appeared on 11 May following the sinking of the Lusitania by a German U-boat four days earlier asking for such a declaration to be made. Did Pollaky, therefore, consider himself to be Hungarian or Austrian by birth? It matters not, because first and foremost he was British.

One item in Detective Inspector Forward's reference is new information missing from reports that included Pollaky's name. The Lloyd's Salvage Association had been in existence since at least 1856, in the 1860s a number of attempted frauds took place against member companies, the earliest in 1862. In one of them a ship with a cargo of salt with a low value had been scuttled to secure a £14,600 of insurance money, the insurers having been told that the cargo consisted of valuable armaments.

George Lewis Jr conducted the prosecution. He was also also Pollaky's solicitor, and surely it is not too far a leap to suppose that it was Pollaky himself who had carried out the investigation on behalf of the Lloyds Salvage Association. The incident took place on 15 June 1866. The front page of *The Times* of 31 October that year carried an advertisement for information as to the whereabouts of one Thomas Berwick, shipowner. Entitled, 'ONE HUNDRED POUNDS REWARD', the advertisement included the following description of the wanted man:

> About 42 years of age, about 5ft. 8 high, fair smooth hair, without moustache or beard, and with thin whiskers; ruddy complexion, bloodshot eyes, and hard features; dresses in coloured clothes. Information to be furnished to Lloyd's Salvage Association; Messrs. Lewis and Lewis 10 Ely-place, Holborn, solicitors; and Inspector Hamilton, 26 Old Jewry, London.

Several men were caught and tried for this fraud. All those concerned in the business were sentenced to penal servitude for a long term – Berwick and his accomplice Lionel Holdsworth for twenty years each.

～

On 13 July1934 an article appeared in the *Nambour Chronicle and North Coast Advertiser* of Queensland, Australia. Entitled 'Pollaky – Detective of Genius. Sherlock Holmes in Real Life', it was written by Vaughan Drydon and had appeared earlier in the Melbourne *Argus*.

Drydon makes the same error as Fitzroy Gardner had in 1921 (see Chapter 13) in describing Pollaky as Polish, but finds other things to say about him which, though unsubstantiated by this author's research, may be true, and worth noting here for interest's sake:

> He was a man of no ordinary education, since he spoke six languages fluently. Those who knew him were amazed at the way in which he handled a case. His sagacity seemed superhuman. [...] He seemed to solve mysteries by a kind of instinct.

Drydon writes that the chiefs of Scotland Yard were, 'glad to consult this mysterious foreigner with the gift of tongues and the knowledge of the underworld'. As we have seen, this was not really true, though they seem to have made use of him when they felt there was no alternative. In Drydon's essay, we read that Pollaky grew rich, and saved 'every penny' so that he could retire:

The risks in his trade were great, and he went in fear of his life. His enemies in the underworld were many and desperate. Pollaky always went armed, and frequently he changed his bedroom. A revolver lay on his desk while clients consulted him. For years he knew neither peace of mind by day nor unbroken sleep at night.

A picture of a man can be built thus in our minds, but Drydon does not give his sources for these statements. They seem to be blown up from earlier interviews so as to give them extra colour. Pollaky we know kept a gun, but he himself wrote that he had never used it.

The essay continues with a story about Pollaky solving a disappearance of some jewels. A well-known lady (unnamed by Drydon) needed money to pay her gambling debts, and decided to pawn her tiara, after having it first copied so that her husband would not realise what she had done. The jeweller she took it to told her that the tiara was made of paste. Pollaky, on being given the case discovered that there had been no theft, but that the woman's husband had needed money, and with the same idea as his wife, had the tiara copied and sold the original.

Drydon finishes with a paragraph about Pollaky's skill at foiling blackmailers:

Pollaky had a diabolical skill in digging up their little secrets and inducing them to leave their prey alone. If all people who are blackmailed would seek advice this despicable form of crime would soon be all but stamped out.

⟾

Just as there are no details of his youth, there are no descriptions of his old age. Did he ever think of his childhood? Did it ever fill his dreams? His family and the friends of those days – did he think of them? The old times could never come back. He and Mary Ann would sit together in the evening: silent – nothing left to say to each other. He was no longer the man of action, quick-minded, able to find the solution to any problem in the blinking of an eye. Now, even his beloved chess was no comfort, and he was filled with foreboding.

Visits from grandchildren might distract him from the sickness of nostalgia. Mary Ann, ever practical, understood him better than any. Always cheerful when he was there to see her: never letting her despair show.

He looked back at his life trying to come to an understanding. 'This is who I am – this is who I was.'

And you who have read this book, do you know this man, with his failings as well as his strengths? Have you come now to feel the same affection for him as I?

15 Death

Ignatius Paul Pollaky died on 25 February 1918 aged 90 years in Brighton, almost nine months before the end of World War One. He and Mary Ann had lived in the house in Brighton for thirty-four years, the longest time that either had lived at a single address. The death certificate listed the causes of death as old age and cardiac failure. His daughter Mabel Chapman who was present was the informant. The announcement of his death in *The Times* three days later states his request that there should be no flowers at his funeral. The obituary printed there the same day was entitled '"Paddington Pollaky". A DETECTIVE MENTIONED IN SULLIVAN OPERA'. It summarised his work, saying, 'he acted through life on the principle of "*Audi, vide, tace*"' [listen, look, be silent] and went on to say of his later life, 'He was a well-known figure on the sea front at Brighton. He occasionally wore some half a dozen foreign decorations.' This is the only mention I have found of his wearing these medals, though we know he had at least one. Obituaries appeared in other newspapers as well, including the *Daily Mail* on 28 February, and the *Observer* on 3 March.

The March 1918 edition of the journal *Notes and Queries* has a short paragraph on Pollaky's *Times* obituary. The writer, Cecil Clarke, concludes with his own thought on Pollaky: 'He was certainly a remarkably astute investigator of crime'. The index to the collected journal for that year has the following entry: 'Pollaky (Ignatius Paul) Celebrated Detective'.

Pollaky's will has no surprises – he left his entire estate – gross value £9,887 10s 5d to his wife:

I Ignatius Paul Pollaky of 33 Stanford Avenue Brighton in the County of Sussex Gentleman – hereby revoke all former testamentary dispositions made by me and declare this to be my last Will I give all my estate both real and personal unto my dear wife Mary Ann Pollaky absolutely and I appoint her sole Executrix of this my Will In witness whereof I have hereunto set my hand this Fourteenth day of August One thousand nine hundred and sixteen.

After her husband's death, Mary Ann moved back to London and lived at 16 Kempshott Road, Wandsworth. Who can say how their relationship had been towards the end of her husband's life. He had been in a somewhat confused state of mind for some time if Fitzroy Gardner is to be believed (see Chapter 13). And yet some years after that meeting, Pollaky was single-minded enough to make a lucid application for British citizenship. This was so important to him, that one must surely hope that Mary Ann was supportive of his great need for security and attachment.

Mary Ann was now living at an address approximately half way between her two daughters, though about 10 miles from either one. Nevertheless, visits to her family must have been made much easier than they otherwise would have been had she remained in Brighton. Though she had lived there for thirty-four years, perhaps it had been her husband's wish that they went there to live and not her own. She died in 1923 aged 82 and was buried with her husband.

The inscription on the gravestone reads:

IN LOVING MEMORY OF

MY DEAR HUSBAND

IGNATIUS PAUL POLLAKY

WHO PASSED AWAY FEBY 25TH 1918. AGED 90 YEARS

ALSO OUR CHILDREN

LILY. DIED JULY 25TH 1862.

PAULINE. (LENA)

DIED FEBY 27TH 1871. IN HER 8TH YEAR.

WILLIAM ERNEST.

DIED JULY 18TH 1872. AGED 5 MONTHS.

FRANCIS HUGHES JAMES.

DIED SEPT 7TH 1899. AGED 33 YEARS.

INTERRED IN MAITLAND PARK CEMETERY. CAPE TOWN.

MINNA MARY ANN.

WHO DIED AT WILLOWMORE. S.AFRICA.OCT 3RD 1899

AGED 35 YEARS.

"UNTIL THE DAY BREAK."

ALSO MARY ANN.

WIDOW OF THE ABOVE I.P.POLLAKY

AND DEARLY LOVED MOTHER OF

ROSE CATHERINE VARRELMANN

AND MABEL MARY CHAPMAN.

WHO ENTERED INTO REST NOVEMBER 18TH 1923. AGED 82.

'ON THAT HAPPY EASTER MORNING.'

'Until the day break' is a quotation from the Song of Solomon 4:6. 'On that happy Easter morning' is a line from a hymn entitled, 'On the Resurrection Morning' words by Sabine Baring-Gold. The full verse is:

> On that happy Easter morning
> All the graves their dead restore.
> Father, mother, sister, brother,
> Meet once more.

This gravestone tells a touching story – a mini biography of its own. First born child, Lily, was stillborn. The next four children all pre-deceased their parents, one as a baby, one as a young child and two as adults while in South Africa. Father died next, and finally the mother, leaving behind two married daughters. Minna Mary Ann and Francis Hughes James are both interred in South Africa. Her grave is in very poor condition.

Kensal Green Cemetery is an interesting place with a number of famous and well-known residents, including authors – Thackeray, Trollope, Wilkie Collins; poets – Leigh Hunt; composers – Balfe, Benedict, Wallace (the three who each wrote an opera which together became known as the 'English Ring' – *The Bohemian Girl, The Lily of Kilarney* and *Maritana*); and many others.

The Pollaky stone lies in a comparatively unassuming spot, evidently not cared for for some time.

Appendices

Many of the exploits of Ignatius Pollaky are, unfortunately, still relevant today. Child abduction and abuse, sex trafficking, and police corruption are just three of the issues of the day that he tried to work against. That those matters and others are still reported in the press today is a sad reflection on society at large.

Meanwhile, the following appendices offers some lighter things connected with Pollaky. The first item was one of a number published in 1863 under the heading 'Small-Beer Chronicles'. While critical of inquiry office agents who stand on street corners as a breed (and Pollaky in particular), it is, nevertheless, a complex but amusing tale of relatives trying to win the favour of an elderly, wealthy aunt who keeps changing her will.

APPENDIX I

From: *All the Year Round*, 20 June 1863 by Charles Dickens

'Small-Beer Chronicles' [Extract]

In the second column of the Times advertisement-sheet appeared, the other day, these mysterious words, 'Audi, vidi, tace' – coupled with the announcement that a trustworthy personage was just about to start for the Continent with a view to certain 'private inquiries.' The advertisement was inserted by one Messrs Pollaky and Co.

Now, here is a new state of things. This organised spy system has sprung into existence quite recently. By the advertisements issued from this office of Mr Pollaky's, and from another similar establishment kept by retired Inspector Field, you are invited to place in the hands of these gentlemen any affair you want cleared up, entrusting the particulars to them, relying on their secrecy, and on the diligence they will show in serving you. But what sort of inquiries are those in which the ex-detectives are ready to engage? What sort of people are those who apply to Messrs Pollaky and Field for their secret services?

I wonder to what extent the establishments of these purveyors of useful information are patronised by the public? Of one thing I am quite sure – there are more men to be seen standing about at the corners of streets than there used to be. Are these men – they are generally seedy in their attire, and in the habit of sucking small pieces of straw or chewing the stalks of leaves to while away the time – are these men the agents of Pollaky and Co., and for what are they on the look-out? For more things, depend on it, than are dreamed of in our philosophy. When Mrs Drinkwater Dreggs gives two dinner-parties, one following the other, all the guests who are invited to one of those festivals are instantly seized with a firm conviction that the dinner to which they are not asked is the distinguished one, while the meal at which they are invited to figure is the second-rate affair. Now, it is not too much to suppose that these suspicious personages are in the habit of putting their difficulties in the hands of Messrs Pollaky and Co. Away goes the trustworthy emissary to Wilton-crescent. He plants himself under the lamp-post, he observes what proportion the cabs which drive up to Mrs Dreggs's door bear to the private carriages, he studies the appearance of the guests, and, being a shrewd individual, forms his own opinion as to their rank in the social scale; or, if unable to do this, perhaps he will get into conversation with the waiter, who comes to the door for a little air while the gentlemen are over their wine, and from him learns exactly what sort of company is being entertained within. With the information he has gained, the trustworthy one returns to his employer, and next morning the Seedymans, who were at the first party, and who had the pleasure of meeting a society of nobodies, who, for the most part, reached their destination in cabs and flies, learn that, on the occasion of the second festival, there was a 'regular swell turnout, with only one cab, and that a Hansom; and that the company comprised, among other distinguished persons, a baronet and his lady, a dowager-countess, a genius, two members of parliament, and consorts, and a cabinet minister'. This knowledge the Seedymans then take to their hearts, and batten thereon to their souls' hurt, but with a certain malignant pleasure, nevertheless.

Or, still keeping to this question of dinner-giving, what facilities are afforded to rival house-keepers, through the agency of Pollaky and Co., for observing the amount of aid which is given to each by the neighbouring pastrycook! When Mrs A. last dined with Mrs B., it struck her that the entrées had a professional look and flavour; so, the next time Mrs B. entertains her friend and neighbour, she – instructed by Pollaky – will remark, as the pastrycook's vol-au-vent circulates, 'My dear, what an excellent cook you have got; where *did* you find such a treasure?'

Probably, also, there is a certain amount of occupation furnished to the Pollaky fraternity by that cupidity and desire for gain which dwells in a few human bosoms. When the heirs apparent, presumptive, or expectant, of a wealthy gentleman clean past his youth, hear of his forming such and such new acquaintances, is it likely that Pollaky's Trustworthy one will be forgotten? Will he not be there, at the corner by the lamp-post, watching the frequency of the visits paid by the new friends? Or, suppose it is an aged and single aunt well represented in the British Funds, whose movements are viewed with suspicion. Suppose a host of cousins, with an enterprising mamma, come up from the country, and take a house a few doors from that of the interesting fundholder; is it likely that Pollaky will be forgotten then? Imagine the report which the Trustworthy one would send, in this case, and the consternation it would create. 'Sep.10, 186 – Took up position at corner at 11 a.m. – Position commanding a view of the premises occupied by both the parties whose movements I was directed to watch, namely, No.7, the residence of Miss Stocks, and No.13, occupied temporarily by Mrs Hunter and daughters.

'11.15. Servant-maid steps out from No.13 with plate of hothouse grapes and book, rings at No.7, holds long conference with servant – elderly female – leaves both book and grapes, and retires. Shortly afterwards, female servant emerges from No.7 with same book and grapes and rings at No.13, delivers grapes and book and message, which I was too far off to hear. Servant, however, of No.13 looks blank, and closes door. Servant from No.7 returns home.

'11.45. Bath-chair appears in street and draws up – empty – in front of No.7. A lady – middle-aged – is seen at window of 13; she observes the Bath-chair, and retires hurriedly. Presently door of No.13 is partially opened, and servant from time to time peeps out. In few minutes door of No.7 opens, and elderly man-servant appears with bundle of cloaks and wrappers on arm, which he arranges in Bath-chair, and at the same moment young lady comes hastily out of No.13, places small cushion, covered with red silk, embroidered, at back of chair and retires – door of 13 still a-jar. At twelve o'clock, door of No.7 opens again, and old lady descends steps very slowly, assisted by elderly man-servant. Chair opened, wrappers arranged. Old lady points fiercely to red silk cushion, and appears to be questioning elderly man-servant, who points towards No.13 as he replies. Old lady sends him off with cushion to 13, and gets into chair assisted by elderly female-servant of great respectability. Then young lady, same as observed before, comes out of No.13 apparently in tears, and holding cushion in hand. She approaches chair and addresses old lady, who pushes away cushion as often as offered, and gives directions for chair to move on. Young lady is retiring, when suddenly chair is brought to a stop again, and elderly female-servant is sent back. She hastens after young lady of No.13 and, overtaking her, the two return towards chair, young lady still carrying cushion. Old lady seems now to agree to receive cushion, for it is placed behind her head, and young lady again retires, smiling sweetly. Chair stopped again, and elderly female again sent back. Again overtakes young lady, and both return to chair. Short parley, and then chair moves on once more, young lady and respectable female, one on each side, arranging cushions and wrappers incessantly, till chair reaches corner of street and is lost to sight.

'12.50. Chair reappears at corner, and descends street. As it passes position occupied by self, young lady heard to say, 'Now, dear Aunt Stocks, you know it is just your luncheon-time, *do* let us send you in the grapes again.' Old lady replies, 'No; I don't want 'em.' Rest of speech, if any, lost in consequence of chair passing out of earshot. Servant hurries on to ring at No.7; door opens immediately; old lady enters, and young ditto is left standing outside. She retires to No.13, goes in, and all is quiet.

'2.5. Door of No.7 re-opens, female servant comes out bearing small note; takes it to No.13, and after short conversation with girl who opens door, leaves note and returns again to No. 7. Soon afterwards door of 13 again flies open, and young lady – same as observed before – passes from No.13 to No.7, and is admitted. In about five minutes, however, she appears again, and returns home. She would seem to be in tears.

'2.25. A young lady – not same observed before, but considerably younger – issues from No.13, rings at No.7, and goes in. Shortly afterwards, close carriage drawn by two fat horses, and driven by fat coachman, comes down street. It stops at No.7. It is empty. Door of No.7 opens, and middle-aged man-servant, standing on steps, conversed with coachman. Approaching as nearly as could judiciously, heard fragments of conversation. Both spoke low, and I was obliged to listen with all my ears. 'Well,' says Butler, 'she do seem to have took a fancy to t'other one to-day.' 'Ah!' replies coachman; ''taint long as she'll fancy e'er a one of the lot.' 'Yes, you're about right there, Simpson,' says Butler. And then there came a bit which I couldn't catch. Presently they talked a little louder, and then heard Butler say, 'Mr. Wyly, the lawyer, he was up here ever so long yesterday, and closeted with missus; and before he went Mrs Cookson and me, we was called in to witness the signature of one of these here codicils, or whatever they are; but lord! Simpson, she makes a new one 'most hevery month. Between you and me, Simpson, I shouldn't wonder if she was to leave every penny away from hall of 'em, and give it to the Fondling or the Indignant Blind.' 'And a good job too,' replied the other. They would have gone on longer, only old lady appeared at that moment at door, with same female servant, elderly and respectable, that I before noted, and young lady – not cushion, and Bath-chair one, but the other whom I had not seen before – and then they both got into the carriage, and after a deal of packing up in cloaks, and wrappers, and all the rest of it, the vehicle drove off, respectable serving-woman went back into house, and Butler was left standing on steps, and whistling softly to self. But soon after he went in too, slammed door after him, and all was again quiet.'

(Journal continued.) 'At this time retired to public-house at corner, and ordered chop. While partaking of same in parlour – window of which commanded No.7, house occupied by the old lady, who had just gone out for carriage-airing – observed middle-aged lady accompanied by a young ditto – not one of those whom I had previously seen – descend steps of No.13, and ascend steps of No.7. Door answered by respectable woman-servant, with whom both ladies shook hands cordially, then just standing inside door, opened a large light-looking whity-brown paper parcel which elder lady held, and taking out a very smart cap much bedizened with ribbons, presented same to respectable servant. Respectable servant made show of refusing cap, but ladies insisting, she yielded, and all shaking hands once again, ladies descended steps, smiling, and went away.

'5.15. Carriage returns, containing old lady of No.7 and young miss, who both go into No.7 together, and carriage drives away. About an hour afterwards, door being opened for servant to take in evening paper, and it being now dark, can see in lighted hall, plates and dishes, and other signs that dinner is going on. In about an hour, door re-opens, subordinate servant-maid leaving it on jar, takes small three-cornered note to No.13, and leaves same without waiting for answer. In very short space of time middle-aged lady, two daughters, and little girl, all emerge from 13, with wrappers over heads and smiling countenances, and knocking at No.7, are instantly admitted.

'9.50. The whole party from No.13 – middle-aged lady, three grown-up daughters, and little girl – come out of No.7. They take a polite leave of butler at hall door, and return home. Each of them carries small morocco-covered case in hand. SHOULD SAY THEY WERE PRESENTS.'

What would be the feelings of the individuals who had employed Messrs Pollaky's agent to watch those two houses, Nos 7 and 13, on perusing the above report! How they would foam with rage as they read that at last the embroidered cushion had been accepted; that one of those 'odious girls' had succeeded in forcing her company upon her aunt when the old lady took her Bath-chair exercise, while another was promoted to the honour of a seat in the carriage! Then, again, that present of the cap to the confidential servant, what depths of treachery would that act not suggest? Lastly, that hideous picture of the whole family retiring from the house of the opulent one, laden with presents – old family jewels, perhaps – and making night hideous with the exulting smiles which beamed upon their graceless countenances. Oh! surely here is something like an occasion for Mr Pollaky and his trustworthy young man, and surely the annals of that sinister office must contain such cases. If not, it soon will, to a dead certainty.

There is something almost terrible about this licensed spy system. That man at the corner of the street is a dreadful being. Suppose a Bishop should feel inclined to go to the Derby in plain clothes, what a wretched thing it is for him to reflect, as he puts on a pair of shepherd's plaid trousers and a paletot, in place of the usual apron and tights, that he will have to pass that man at the corner, who is possibly an emissary of a bishop of different principles, and who is there to watch the house. Suppose a family desirous of economising and prepared for a time to go through with a course of chop dinners, is it pleasant to have that man at the corner inspecting the butcher's tray, day after day, and making notes of its contents, to be written in the annals of the office, a copy being sent to our dearest enemies. Suppose that I get out of an invitation to dine with the Fingerglasses, giving the excuse that I shall be out of town on the day for which they are kind enough to ask me, is it pleasant on the evening of Fingerglass's festival to have Pollaky's young man scrutinising my appearance as I hand my consort into the cab in which we are conveyed to the theatre on the sly?

[The article continues with other matters.]

APPENDIX II

'The Agony Column'

One day not far from Regent Street,
Where cabs and buses whirl,
I saw beneath a horse's feet
A fascinating girl.
To save her life I risk'ed my own,
What mortal could do less,
She thank'd me warmly but refused
To give me her address.

[SPOKEN after first verse.]
I persuaded her but she would only consent to advertise in one of the papers making an appointment with me she said she would head it with her name Little Di_ I asked her whether she would put it in the Agony Column of –

The Standard or the Telegraph, the Echo or the Times,
Observer, Reynolds, Judy, Punch, or Bow Bells, or the Chimes,
The Hornet, Lloyds, or Figaro, or one of the Reviews,

Appendix 2

THE AGONY COLUMN

or

LITTLE DI.

Written by W. Burnot

Composed by T. Roberts

One day not far from Re - gent Street, Where cabs and bus - ses whirl,___ I

saw be - neath a hor - se's feet A fas - ci - na - ting girl.___ To

save her life I risked my own, What mor - tal could do less,___ She

thank'd me warm - ly but re - fused To give me her ad - dress___

*SPOKEN after first verse: I persuaded her but she would only consent to advertise in one of the papers
making an appointment with me she said she would head it with her name Little Di_
I asked her whether she would put it in the Agony Column of—*

The Stan - dard or the Tel - e - graph, the E - cho or the Times, Ob -

ser - ver, Rey - nolds, Ju - dy, Punch, or Bow Bells, or the Chimes, The

Hor - net, Lloyds, or Fig - a - ro, or one of the Re - views, The

Globe or Sun, Dis - patch or Fun, or Il - lus - tra - ted News.

The Globe or Sun, Dispatch or Fun, or Illustrated News.
She mentioned one in which she said,
She'd name a time and spot,
But which the paper was alas!
Somehow I've quite forgot.
In vain my memory I task,
It gives me no reply,
So every day as they come out,
I have to go and buy –

CHORUS

I have to read the whole lot through,
At least that part I mean,
Where column after column of
Sheer agony is seen;
How "Charlie is implored to come",
And "Jane is asked to call",
And if dear XY will return,
He'll be forgiven all.

[SPOKEN] And you'll find it in the Agony Column of –

CHORUS

I thought as I'd to sing tonight,
I'd ask if you had seen,
In any other paper,
The advertisement I mean;
If so pray kindly let me know,
It would be good indeed,
For you've no notion what it is,
Each day to have to read –

[SPOKEN] Yes! read the Agony Column of –

CHORUS

APPENDIX III

Of course, there is a famous song about Paddington Green, and to avoid disappointment, and for interest's sake, the music and lyrics follow here. The words have been taken from the copy published by Hopwood & Crew, London – there are other editions with slight variations, in particular later American versions, in which 'Paddington Green' becomes either 'Pemberton Green' or 'Abingdon Green'. The song dates from about 1863. The tempo direction 'Maestoso pomposo' (Majestic speed, pompously) should probably not be taken too seriously or the fun of the piece will be missed. 'Tempo Moderato, poco parlando' (Moderate speed in a conversational style) might be better.

There are many references to this song in connection with Pollaky. If Mortimer Collins's *The Ivory Gate* (1869) had become a successful novel, for example, perhaps Pollaky would be remembered differently – 'He had employed Scotland yard, and coquetted with "Pollaky Perkins of Paddington Green".'The song is also mentioned in 1870 in the *Cliftonian* magazine edited by members of Clifton College, Bristol:

> I have seen the mysterious name "Pollaky"; what is it? I'm told it is the name of a man who conducts secret enquiries. What can he be like? Stories are told me how he sits at a table with a brace of revolvers in front of him, and there conducts secret enquiries by means of "paid hirelings." Does he call his men "minions?" Do they walk about in large yellow boots, an enormous belt with pistols in it, and a brigand hat? Where does he reside? In Paddington. Then the mystery gets less, for I know Paddington; it is not a mysterious part of London. By the way, I've heard sung of "A broken-hearted milkman of Paddington Green". Did he consult Pollaky in the case in which this sad accident happened? I wonder!"

'Polly Perkins of Paddington Green'

I'm a broken-hearted Milkman, in grief I'm array'd
Through keeping of the company of a young servant maid;
Who lived on board wages, the house to keep clean,
In a gentleman's fam'ly near Paddington Green.
Oh! she was as

Beautiful as a Butterfly and proud as a Queen,
Was pretty little Polly Perkins of Paddington Green.

Polly Perkins of Paddington Green
or The Broken Hearted Milkman

Written and Composed by Harry Clifton

Maestoso pomposo

I'm a bro - ken-heart - ed Milk - man, in grief I'm ar - ray'd Through keep - ing of the com - pa - ny of a young ser - vant maid; Who__ liv - èd on board__ wa - ges, the__ house to keep clean, In a gen - tle - man's fam' - ly near Pad - ding - ton Green. Oh! she was as

(Last verse) In spite of all she was as

ad lib.

CHORUS

Beau - ti - ful as a But - ter - fly, and as proud as a Queen, Was__ pret - ty lit - tle Pol - ly Per - kins of Pad - ding - ton Green.

Her eyes were as black as the pips of a pear,
No rose in the garden with her cheeks could compare,
Her hair hung in 'ringerlets' so beautiful and long.
I thought that she loved me, but I found I was wrong.
Oh! she was as

CHORUS

When I'd rattle in the morning and cry "milk below"
At the sound of my milk cans her face she would show,
With a smile upon her countenance and a laugh in her eye,
If I thought she'd have loved me I'd have laid down to die.
For she was as

CHORUS

When I asked her to marry me, she said "Oh what stuff"
And told me to "drop it, for she'd had quite enough
Of my nonsense" At the same time I'd been very kind,
But to marry a milkman she didn't feel inclined.
Oh! she was as

CHORUS

"Oh the man that has me must have silver and gold,
A chariot to ride in, and be handsome and bold;
His hair must be curly as any watch-spring,
And his whiskers as big as a brush for clothing."
Oh! she was as

CHORUS

The words that she utter'd went straight thro' my heart,
I sobbed, I sighèd, and I straight did depart
With a tear on my eyelid as big as a bean,
Bidding goodbye to Polly and Paddington Green
Ah! she was as

CHORUS

In six months she married, this hard-hearted girl,
But it was not a 'Wicount', and it was not a 'Nearl',
It was not a 'Baronite' but a shade or two 'wus'
'Twas a bow-legg'd Conductor of a Twopenny 'Bus
In spite of all she was as

CHORUS

APPENDIX IV

Gilbert's mention of Pollaky's 'keen penetration' hardly seems complimentary
when placed in context; the suggested make-up of a soldier becomes more and
more absurd as the song progresses.

Colonel Calverley's Song from *Patience*
- Words by W.S. Gilbert
If you want a receipt for that popular mystery,
Known to the world as a Heavy Dragoon,
Take all the remarkable people in history,
Rattle them off to a popular tune.
The pluck of **Lord Nelson** on board of the Victory –
Genius of **Bismarck** devising a plan –
The humour of **Fielding** (which sounds contradictory –
Coolness of **Paget** about to trepan –
The science of **Jullien**, the eminent musico –
Wit of **Macaulay**, who wrote of **Queen Anne** –
The pathos of **Paddy**, as rendered by Boucicault –
Style of the **Bishop of Sodor and Man** –
The dash of a **D'Orsay**, divested of quackery –
Narrative powers of **Dickens** and **Thackeray** –
Victor Emmanuel – peak-haunting **Peveril** –
Thomas Aquinas, and **Doctor Sacheverell** –
Tupper and **Tennyson** – **Daniel Defoe** –
Anthony Trollope and **Mr Guizot**!
Take of these elements all that is fusible,
Melt them all down in a pipkin or crucible,
Set them to simmer and take off the scum,
And a Heavy Dragoon is the residuum !

If you want a receipt for this soldier-like paragon,
Get at the wealth of the **Czar** (if you can) –

PATIENCE
Song (Colonel Calverley and Chorus of Dragoons)
[2nd verse]

Words by W.S. Gilbert

Music by Arthur Sullivan

Allegro

2. If you want a re-ceipt for this sol-dier-like pa-ra-gon,

Get at the wealth of the Czar (if you can)— The fa-mi-ly pride of a

Span-iard from Ar-ra-gon— Force of Me-phis-to pro-nounc-ing a ban— A

smack of Lord Wa-ter-ford reck-less and rol-lick-y— Swag-ger of Ro-der-ick,

head-ing his clan— The keen pen-e-tra-tion of Pad-ding-ton Pol-la-ky—

Grace of an O-da-lisque on a di-van— The ge-nius stra-te-gic of

Cæ-sar or Han-i-bal— Skill of Sir Gar-net in thrash-ing a can-ni-bal—

Fla-vour of Ham-let— the Strang-er a touch of him— Lit-tle of Man-fred (but

not ve-ry much of him)— Bea-dle of Bur-ling-ton— Ri-chard-son's show—

Mis-ter Mi-caw-ber and Ma-dame Tus-saud!_____

The family pride of a Spaniard from Aragon –
Force of Mephisto pronouncing a ban –
A smack of Lord Waterford, reckless and rollicky –
Swagger of Roderick, heading his clan –
The keen penetration of Paddington Pollaky –
Grace of an Odalisque on a divan –
The genius strategic of Caesar or Hannibal –
Skill of Sir Garnet in thrashing a cannibal –
Flavour of Hamlet – the Stranger, a touch of him –
Little of Manfred (but not very much of him) –
Beadle of Burlington – Richardson's show –
Mr Micawber and Madame Tussaud!
Take of these elements all that is fusible,
Melt them all down in a pipkin or crucible,
Set them to simmer and take off the scum,
And a Heavy Dragoon is the residuum !

People listed
Horatio Nelson (1758–1805): English naval hero.
Otto von Bismarck (1815–98): First Chancellor of the German Empire.
Henry Fielding (1707–54): English playwright and novelist.
Sir James Paget (1814–99): British surgeon and pathologist.
Louis Antoine Jullien (1812–60): Flamboyant French conductor.
Thomas Babington Macaulay (1800–59): English writer and statesman.
Queen Anne (1665–1714): Queen of Great Britain from 1702.
Paddy: Irishmen as portrayed by **Dion Boucicault** (1820–90) in his plays.
Rowley Hill (1836–1887): Bishop of Sodor and Man.
Count Alfred Guillaume Gabriel D'Orsay (1801–52): French dandy.
Charles Dickens (1812–70): English novelist.
William Makepeace Thackeray (1811–63): English novelist.
Victor Emmanuel II (1820–78) King of Sardinia who united Italy in 1861.
Sir Geoffrey Peveril: Hero of Sir Walter Scott's novel *Peveril of the Peak*.
Thomas Aquinas (1225–74) Italian philosopher, theologian and writer.
Henry Sacheverell (*c*.1674–1724): Clergyman found guilty of libel.
Martin Farquhar Tupper (1810–89): English poet.
Alfred, Lord Tennyson (1809–92): English poet.
Daniel Defoe (*c*.1660–1731): English novelist and journalist.
Anthony Trollope (1815–82): English novelist.
François Pierre Guillaume Guizot (1787–1874): French statesman.
Czar: Emperor of Russia.
Spaniard from Aragon: A region in the north-east of Spain.

Mephisto: Mephistopheles (tempter of Faust).

Lord Waterford: Irish Marquis with a reputation for reckless behaviour.

Roderick: Roderick Dhu, Highland chieftain in Scott's *Lady of the Lake*.

Paddington Pollaky (1828–1918): Detective of 13 Paddington Green.

Odalisque: A concubine in a Turkish harem.

Julius Caesar (100–44 BCE): Emperor of Rome.

Hannibal (c.247–183 BCE): Carthaginian general.

Sir Garnet Wolseley (1833–1913): Anglo-Irish General.

Hamlet: From Shakespeare's play.

The Stranger: Protagonist of a play by August von Kotzebue (1761–1819).

Manfred: Gloomy hero of Lord Byron's poem of the same name.

Beadle of Burlington: Either the attendant who kept order in the Burlington Arcade, or, according to the G.E. Dunn (See Bibliography), Erastus F. Beadle of Burlington, New York, 'inventor of the "dime novel"'.

Richardson's show: A travelling theatrical troupe which staged melodramas. Described by Dickens in *Greenwich Fair (Sketches by Boz)*

Mr Micawber: From Dickens's novel *David Copperfield*.

Marie Tussaud (1760–1850): Founder of the famous London wax museum.

The first of Gilbert's earlier mentions of Pollaky

Patience was not the first time Gilbert had mentioned Pollaky in one of his pieces.

In 1869, twelve years earlier, Pollaky had found a place in Mr Churchmouse's song from Gilbert's musical piece *No Cards*. The original music was composed by German-Reed. That score is now lost. In 1895 a score was published with music by Lionel Elliott. The section beginning 'Mystic disguises' (see below) was not included in the new setting.

From *NO CARDS* a musical piece in one act for four characters Written by W.S. GILBERT Composed by THOMAS GERMAN-REED

First produced at the Royal Gallery of Illustration, Lower Regent Street, London under the management of Mr Thomas German-Reed, on 29 March 1869.

Mr Churchmouse (aside)
Annabella is the goal
I would fain arrive at,
But I dare not tell a soul
(This is strictly private!).
If my artful plans succeed
Then the girl I've wooed'll
Soon be mine, and mine indeed,
Given me by Coodle.

Ensemble Coodle–oodle–oodle, &c.

Churchmouse
Mystic disguises
Of various (sizes
Producing) surprises
I have close at hand –
In manner elective
Defying invective,
Like any detective
In Pollaky's band!
Pretty, pretty, pretty Pollaky!
Dee.
Pretty, pretty, pretty Pollaky!

Miss P
Pretty, pretty, pretty Pollaky!

All
Pretty, pretty, pretty Pollaky!

On Paddington Green!
He's a chrysalis or a butterfly,
As he changes his mien,
Is pretty, pretty, pretty Pollacky [*sic*]
On Paddington Green.
[Jane W. Stedman in her book *Gilbert Before Sullivan* suggests convincingly that
the final four lines were originally sung to the tune of *Polly Perkins of Paddington
Green*.]

Another mention of Pollaky by Gilbert

From *AN OLD SCORE*, an original comedy-drama in three acts
By W.S. Gilbert
First Performed at the New Gaiety Theatre, (under the management of Mr
Hollingshead) Monday, July 26 1869.
HAROLD. Yes. Perhaps I didn't feel it as acutely as I should. The right thing would
have been to have got him over to Calais – shot him – come back – married you,
and spent the remainder of my existence in dodging Mr Pollaky and the Scotland
Yard police authorities. The wrong thing was to grin and bear it. I chose the
wrong thing; I generally do. It gave less trouble; it generally does.

Bibliography and Sources

Anon. – Illustrated by 'Whew'. *Benjamin D_ His Little Dinner*. London: Weldon and Co., 1876

Ashton, John. *Social Life in the Reign of Queen Anne Volume 2*. London: Chatto & Windus, 1882

Assing, Ludmilla. *Vita di Piero Cironi*. Prato, Italy: FF Giachetti, 1865

Battles and Leaders of the Civil War Volume 4. New York: The Century Co., 1888

Bebel, August. *Assassinations and Socialism*. New York: Labor News Company, 1898

Bennett, John D. *The London Confederates*. Jefferson, North Carolina: McFarland & Co., 2008

Bulloch, James Dunwoody. *The Secret Service of the Confederate States in Europe or, How the Confederate Cruisers Were Equipped Volume 1*. New York: G.B. Puttnam's Sons, 1884

Burds, Jeffrey. *The Second Oldest Profession: A World History of Espionage Part 1 Lecture 12*. Maryland: Recorded Books, 2011

Burnand, F.C. and Sullivan, Arthur. *Cox and Box*. 1866 Vocal score. London: Boosey & Co., 1871

Byron, H.J. *Lucretia Borgia M.D.* London: Thomas Hailes Lacy, 1868

Campbell Law School, Vol. 7, Issue 2. Raleigh, North Carolina: Fall 1984

Clay, Alice. *The Agony Column of the Times 1800–1870 Vol. 1*. London: Chatto & Windus, 1881

Cobb, Belton. *The First Detectives and the Early Career of Richard Mayne*. London: Faber & Faber, 1957

Cohen, Morton M. *The Letters of Lewis Carroll Vol. 1*. London: Macmillan, 1979

Collins, M., *The Ivory Gate, Vol. 2*. London: Hurst and Blackett, 1869

Devonald, Erasmus Lloyd. 'Observations on the Pathology and Treatment of Cholera'. *London Medical and Surgical Journal*, 1833

Dickens, Charles. 'A Detective Police Party', *Household Words*, 27 July 1850
'Three Detective Anecdotes', *Household Words*, 14 September 1850
'On Duty with Inspector Field', *Household Words*, 14 June 1851

'Small–Beer Chronicles', *All the Year Round*, 20 June 1863

Discover the Royal Pavilion. Brighton: Royal Pavilion Museum, 2009

Drydon, Vaughan. Very Odd Fellows No.1: Pollaky: The Detective of Genius. *The Argus*: Melbourne, 1934

Dunn, George E. *A Gilbert & Sullivan Dictionary*. London: George Allen & Unwin Ltd, 1936

Fredeman, William E. (ed.). *The Correspondence of Dante Gabriel Rossetti 6: The Last Decade* Cambridge: D.S. Brewer, 2006

Gardner, Fitzroy. *Days and Ways of an Old Bohemian*. London: John Murray, 1921 *More Reminiscences of an Old Bohemian*. London: Hutchinson, 1926

Gilbert, W.S. *No Cards* 1869 – in *Gilbert Before Sullivan*. Ed. Jane W. Stedman. London: Routlege & Kegan Paul, 1969

An Old Score. London: Thomas Hailes Lacy, 1869

Gilbert, W.S., and Elliott, Lionel. *No Cards*. Vocal score. London: Joseph Williams Ltd, 1895

Gilbert, W.S., and Sullivan, Arthur. *Patience, or Bunthorne's Bride. A*. 1881. Vocal score. London: Chappell & Co., Ltd (1900 edition)

Goddard, Henry. *Memoirs of a Bow Street Runner*. London: Museum Press, 1956

Griffiths, Arthur. *Mysteries of Police and Crime Volume 1*. London: Cassell and Company Ltd, 1901

Haining, Peter (ed.). *A Sherlock Holmes Compendium*. Warner Books (revised edition), 1994

Hartley, Jenny (ed.). *The Selected Letters of Charles Dickens*. Oxford: Oxford University Press, 2012

Hoerr, Willmer A. 'The Case of the Archetypical Agent'. *The Baker Street Journal*, Vol. 18, No. 1, March 1968

Juxton, John. *Lewis and Lewis: The Life and Times of a Victorian Solicitor*. New York: Ticknor and Fields, 1984

Kellogg, John Harvey. *The Home Hand-Book of Domestic Hygiene and Rational Medicine*, Vol. 2. Battle Creek, Michigan: Health Publishing Co., 1880

Kenealy, Dr *The Trial at Bar of Sir Roger C.D. Tichborne*. London: Englishman Office, 1875

Kenealy, Maurice Edward. *The Tichborne Tragedy*. London: Francis Griffiths, 1913

Kuhns, Matt. *Brilliant Deduction*. Lakewood, Ohio: Lyon Hall, 2012

Labiche and Lefranc. 'Frisette 1846', *Théatre Complet de Eugène Labiche*, Vol. 3. Paris: Calmann Lévy 1883

Malcolm, James Peller. *Anecdotes of the Manners and Customs of London During the Eighteenth Century* Vol. 1. London: Longman, Hurst, Rees, and Orme 1810

Marx, Karl & Engels, Friedrich. *Werke*, Vol. 35. Berlin: Dietz Verlag 1967

Mayhew, Henry. *London Labour and the London Poor*, Vol 4. London: Griffin, Bohn & Co. 1862 (from *London: Griffin, B.* Quennell, Peter (ed.) London: Spring Books 1950)

Maynes, Mary Jo; Soland, Birgitte; Benninghaus, Christina, eds. *Secret Gardens, Satanic Mills: Placing Girls in European History, 1750–1960.* Chapter 14: Girls in Court. Bright Jones, Elizabeth (Author). Indiana University Press, 2004.

Moran, Benjamin. *The Journal of Benjamin Moran 1857–1865*, Vol. 2. Chicago: University of Chicago Press, 1948

Morton, J. Madison. *Box and Cox* (1847). London: Samuel French, 1920

Moss, Alan and Skinner, Keith. *The Victorian Detective*. Oxford: Shire Publications, 2013

Murray, David Christie. *A Novelist's Notebook*. London: Ward & Downey, 1887

Notes and Queries. Twelfth Series –Volume 4. January-December, 1918. London, 1919

Official Records of the Union and Confederate Navies in the War of the Rebellion, Series 1, Vol. 6. Washington. Government Printing Office, 1897

O'Shea, John Augustus. *An Iron-Bound City Volume 1*. London: Ward and Downey, 1886

Owsley, Harriet C. 'Henry Shelton Sanford and Federal Surveillance Abroad, 1861–1865'. *Mississippi Valley Historical Review*, Vol. 48, No. 2 (Sept.1961), pp. 211–28

Payne, Chris. *The Chieftain*. Stroud, Gloucestershire: The History Press, 2011

Physical and Moral Condition of the Children and Young Persons Employed in Mines and Manufactories, The. London: Her Majesty's Stationery Office/John W. Parker, 1843

Rumbelow, Donald. *The Houndsditch Murders and the Siege of Sidney Street*. Stroud, Gloucestershire. The History Press, 1973

Smith, Phillip Thurmond. *Policing Victorian London*. Westport, Connecticut: Greenwood Press, 1985

Stapleton, J. W. *The Great Crime of 1860*. London: E. Marlborough & Co., 1861

Summerscale, Kate. *The Suspicions of Mr Whicher*. London: Bloomsbury, 2008

Thompson, Guy and Gould, Malcolm. *Historic Building Recording of 11–13 Paddington Green, City of Westminster, London W2 1LG.* London: Pre-Construct Archaeology Ltd, 2010

Walbrook, H.M., *The Gilbert & Sullivan Opera: A History and a Comment, 1922.* L.V. White & Co., Ltd (p. 65)

Walsh, William S. *Handy-Book of Literary Curiosities*. Philadelphia: J.B. Lippincott Co. 1893

Ware, J. Redding. *Passing English of the Victorian Era*. London: George Routledge & Sons, 1909

Winkworth, Stephen. *Room Two More Guns*. London: Allen & Unwin, 1986

Other Sources

Ancestry: www.ancestry.co.uk

Archiv Hlavného Mesta SR Bratislavy (Bratislava City Archives), Markova 1, Bratislava: Rodný Index Nové Mesto Blumental 1770–1888

British Newspaper Archive: www.britishnewspaperarchive.co.uk

Cambridge University Library: Papers of George Airy
Mrs Pollaky inquiring about her brother RGO 6/43

City of London, London Metropolitan Archives
Minute Book of Proceedings of Committee commencing 4th January 1862 of St Saviour of Proceeding P87/SAV/44
Image of 11 to 13 Paddington Green SC PHL 01 280 56 4056

City of Westminster Archives: *Drainage Application 13 Paddington Green* WDP1/2/1639/811

Cliftonian, The, Eds Clifton College, March 1869, Vol. 1, p. 306

Family Search: www.familysearch.org

Hartley Library, University of Southampton – Palmerston Papers
PP/MPC/1575 and 1576 – *I. Pollaky to Palmerston 1859*
PP/GC/SM/47 – *Vernon Smith to Palmerston*
PP/GC/SM/47 enc. – *Mangles to Palmerston*

Hertfordshire Archives: DE/K/O26/159 (Pollaky's correspondence with Lord Lytton)

Leo Baeck Institute, New York
Toni and Gustav Stolper Collection 1866–1990
Photograph of Pollaky

London Gazette: www.london-gazette.co.uk

Metropolitan Police: content.met.police.uk/Site/historypolicing

National Library of Australia: trove.nla.gov.au (Australian newspapers)

Newspaper Archive: newspaperarchive.com

National Archives, London
Folios 86–7: *US civil war: French admiral ordered to salute flag of Confederate States* PRO 30/22/24/32
Blockade of the ports of the Confederate States. Papers. Part I. FO 414/20
Police correspondence MEPO 2/130
Naturalisation letters 1862 HO 45/7263
Naturalisation papers 1914 HO 144/1345/259618
Naturalisation certificate HO 334/64/25508
Papers relating to Edward Segers, prisoner PRIS 10/238/10

Ohio State University Billy Ireland Cartoon Library & Museum
Image of Pollaky from the London Figaro

Old Bailey Online: www.oldbaileyonline.org

Rush Rhees Library, University of Rochester
    William Henry Seward Papers, Rare Books, Special Collections and
    Preservation Department: *Sanford to Seward, Sanford to Pollaky, Pollaky to
    Seward, Moran to Pollaky*
Sanford Museum, Sanford, Florida
    HSS Box 139 Folder 12 *Morse's correspondence with Sandford*
    HSS Box 139 Folders 13 & 14 *Pollaky's correspondence with Sanford*
Somerset Heritage Centre Archives: *Letters of Lord Derby* DD\HY/18/4/7–9
University of North Carolina, Southern Historical Collection, Louis Round
    Wilson Special Collection: *Diary of Edward C. Anderson*
Thuringian State Archives, Gotha: Information on Ritterkreuz II. Klasse des
    Herzoglich Sachsen-Ernestinischen Hausordens
Times Digital Archive: gdc.gale.com (Gale Digital Collections)
Will of Ignatius Pollaky (London Probate Department)

Paddington Green Conservation Area Audit of 2003, published by the City of
    Westminster
Paddington: Report of the Vestry for the year ending 25th March 1871
Paddington Sanitary Report for the year 1870–71. Wm. Hardwicke, M.D.
Report on the Health of Paddington. Wm. Hardwicke, M.D. May 1870
Report on the Health of Paddington. Wm. Hardwicke, M.D. July 1870

Newspapers and Journals

(dates given in body of text)

    Cardiff Times
    Cheshire Observer
    County Observer and Monmouthshire Central Advertiser
    Der Deutsche Correspondent, Baltimore
    Der Vaterland, Vienna
    Dundee Courier and Argus
    Evening Courier and Republic, Buffalo, New York
    Figaro's London Sketch Book of Celebrities (*The London Figaro*)
    Fun
    Herald and Planter, Texas
    Le Palamède, Paris
    Lloyds Weekly London Newspaper
    London Daily News
    Monthly Times of London
    Morpeth Herald

Pall Mall Gazette
Public Ledger, Memphis
Shields Daily Gazette and Shipping Telegraph
Shields Gazette and Daily Telegraph
Western Daily Press
Worcester Journal
The Argus, Melbourne
The Berkshire Chronicle
The British Medical Journal
The Cliftonian
The Cork Examiner
The Cornwall Chronicle
The Courier, Brisbane
The Daily News, London
The Empire, Sydney
The Engineer
The Era
The Examiner
The Falkirk Herald
The Illustrated Photographer
The Isle of Wight Observer
The Jewish Chronicle
The Ladies
The Lancet
The Leeds Times
The Liverpool Mercury
The Manchester Evening News
The Morning Post
The Nambour Chronicle and North Coast Advertiser, Queensland
The Newsman
The Northern Echo
The Queensland Times
The South Eastern Gazette
The Southern Reporter
The Standard, London
The Sydney Morning Herald
The Taunton Courier
The Teesdale Mercury
The Times, London

The Tomahawk
The Wells Journal
The Western Mail
The Whitstable Times and Herne Bay Herald
The Worcestershire Chronicle

Acknowledgements

Alicia Clarke – Henry S. Sanford Papers, Sanford Museum

Rosemarie Barthel – Thuringian State Archives, Gotha

Letter written by C.L. Dodgson (Lewis Carroll) reprinted by permission
   of United Agents on behalf of Morton Cohen, The Trustees of the C.L.
   Dodgson Estate and Scirard Lancelyn Green
   Held by the Beinecke Rare Book and Manuscript Library, Yale University.
   GEN MSS 103, box 1, folder 53

Quotations from the Toni and Gustav Stolper Collection 1866–1990 and the
   photograph of Pollaky courtesy of the Leo Baeck Institute, New York

2010 Photograph of Paddington Green houses – Pre-Construct Archaeology –
   www.pre-construct.com

David Shore – image of Darrell Fancourt

Mark Beynon and Juanita Zoë Hall – The History Press

Gill Arnot – Hampshire Museum Services

Index

If you enjoyed this book, you may also be interested in …

The Sherlock Holmes Miscellany
ROGER JOHNSON & JEAN UPTON

Facts, trivia and quotes from Sir Arthur Conan Doyle's legendary stories, the reader can also explore the often weird and wonderful characters who graced Conan Doyle's pages. Do you know the difference between a Penang Lawyer and a Tide-Waiter? And if you think a 'life preserver' is a cork-filled flotation device, how does Wilson Kemp fit one into the sleeve of his jacket?

978 0 7524 7152 5

The Chieftain
CHRIS PAYNE

George Clarke joined the Metropolitan Police in 1841. His career took off when he was transferred to the small team of detectives at Scotland Yard in 1862, where he became known as 'The Chieftain'. This book paints a detailed picture of detective work in mid-Victorian Britain, covering 'murders most foul', 'slums and society' and Victorian frauds. One particular fraudster, Harry Benson, was to contribute to the end of Clarke's career and lead to the first major Metropolitan Police corruption trial in 1877.

978 0 7524 7152 5

Visit our website and discover thousands of other History Press books.

www.thehistorypress.co.uk